AMBROS

THE EARLY CHURCH FATHERS
Edited by Carol Harrison
University of Durham

The Greek and Latin fathers of the Church are central to the creation of Christian doctrine, yet often unapproachable because of the sheer volume of their writings and the relative paucity of accessible translations. This series makes available translations of key selected texts by the major Fathers to all students of the early church.

Already published:

MAXIMUS THE CONFESSOR
Andrew Louth

IRENAEUS OF LYONS
Robert M. Grant

Further books in this series will be on
Gregory of Nyssa and Origen.

AMBROSE

Boniface Ramsey O.P.

London and New York

First published 1997
by Routledge
11 New Fetter Lane, London EC4P 4EE

Simultaneously published in the USA and Canada
by Routledge
29 West 35th Street, New York, NY 10001

© 1997 Boniface Ramsey O.P.

Typeset in Garamond by
RefineCatch Limited, Bungay, Suffolk
Printed and bound in Great Britain by
TJ International (Padstow) Ltd, Padstow, Cornwall

British Library Cataloguing in Publication Data
A catalogue record for this book is available from the British Library

Library of Congress Cataloging in Publication Data
A catalogue record for this book has been requested

ISBN 0–415–11–8417
0–415–11–8425 (pbk)

For
Brian Shanley, O.P.

CONTENTS

PREFACE

Ambrose of Milan was one of the most influential persons of his time, and his influence endures to this day, but he seems somehow to be more remote to us than his two great contemporaries of Latin Christianity, Jerome and Augustine. The personalities of these two men spill onto the pages that they wrote – Jerome irritable and spontaneous, Augustine searching and reflective. Ambrose produced nothing approaching the famous self-revelations of Jerome's Letter 22 or Augustine's *Confessions*, and so it is that much harder for us to grasp hold of him as a man and to understand him as we would wish to.

But the relative obscurity of Ambrose's personality has not prevented biographers, historians and patrologists from exercising their craft. The twentieth century has seen the publication of several important works on the Bishop of Milan by scholars like Hans Von Campenhausen, F. Homes Dudden and Michele Pellegrino. Recently two important books have appeared – Neil B. McLynn's *Ambrose of Milan: Church and Court in a Christian Capital* (1994) and Daniel H. Williams' *Ambrose of Milan and the End of the Arian–Nicene Conflicts* (1995). It was inevitable that the Ambrose of the legends that were already abroad when Paulinus penned his biography shortly after the bishop's death would eventually be subjected to an extensive scrutiny in which the most iconoclastic questions would be posed, and such has been the case. But recent works sometimes convey the impression that there was little more to Ambrose than his political side. Each generation writes history and draws its characterizations from the perspective that is most congenial to it, as is well known, so it is hardly surprising that Ambrose's theology and spirituality would be viewed today within the context of his politics rather than the other way around. Future studies of Ambrose will undoubtedly reflect other preoccupations, and in each of them there will be truth, even if not truth in all its unattainable fullness.

The present book too manifests its author's own concerns and beliefs. Chief among them, if not always directly expressed, is the conviction that Ambrose was above all a man of the spirit, whose activities in the public forum were guided overwhelmingly by spiritual considerations, however ill conceived they occasionally were. It is impossible, at least for me, not to posit a deep spirituality in a man in whose writings the mystical meaning of the Song of Songs plays so prominent a role, and who was capable of composing such extraordinary hymns. Bernard of Clairvaux comes to mind as an analogous figure – a redoubtable personage in the political affairs of twelfth-century Europe who was also, and more importantly, an interpreter of the Song of Songs and an accomplished hymnodist.

The purpose of this book, in any event, is quite simply to make Ambrose better known to the reader, and to show as many aspects of him as can be fitted into a limited number of pages. The opening chapter on Ambrose and his times is followed by a series of new translations of some of his own writings, which it is hoped will display the versatility of Ambrose's interests and allow the reader the opportunity of more or less direct exposure to him. Paulinus of Milan's classic account of his hero's life concludes the book; it is so crucial to our image of Ambrose that it did not seem right to omit it.

My thanks go in a special way to Dr Carol Harrison, the editor of this series, whose encouragement made my efforts less onerous. I also want to express my gratitude to my friend Father George Lawless, O.S.A., whose kindly hand is present here on several levels. Of course any errors or infelicities are mine alone.

B.R.
4 April, 1997

LIST OF
ABBREVIATIONS

CCSL	*Corpus Christianorum*, Series Latina, Turnhout, 1953ff.
CSEL	*Corpus Scriptorum Ecclesiasticorum Latinorum*, Vienna, 1866ff.
De Romestin	H. De Romestin, trans., *Some of the Principal Works of St Ambrose*, in *A Select Library of Nicene and Post-Nicene Fathers of the Church*, 2nd series, vol. 10, repr. Grand Rapids, Eerdmans, 1979.
ET	English translation.
FC	Fathers of the Church, Washington, DC, The Catholic University of America Press, 1947ff.
LT	Latin text.
PL	J.-P. Migne (ed.), *Patrologia Latina*, Paris, 1841ff.
SC	*Sources chrétiennes*, Paris, Editions du Cerf, 1941 ff.

1

INTRODUCTION

I

The period of time that concerns us in this book, at least to the degree that it provided the setting for the life and work of Ambrose of Milan, is the final quarter of the fourth century, when, as Bishop of Milan, Ambrose played a dominant role in Western Christianity. Thanks in large part to Ambrose and how he approached the issues that he faced, it was a time of decisive importance for the West. But it was, quite apart from Ambrose, a time with its own characteristics, and if we are to make any sense of Ambrose we must first try to appreciate some of those characteristics. They helped to shape him, and he reflected them.

Those who have read Ambrose in our own day and have had the opportunity to contrast him with his contemporaries might well agree that he is one of the Fathers of the Church – as the earliest non-scriptural Christian writers and preachers are conventionally known – who are the most approachable by us, due to his generally straightforward manner and to the practical rather than speculative bent of his thinking. Still, he is very different from us, and he is so very much because his times were different.

Until perhaps a few years ago we might have said that the chief difference between Ambrose's times and ours consisted in the fact that religion was taken seriously then and is taken less so now. But we have learned from recent experience what we should have known all along, namely, that in most places religion is almost always taken quite seriously indeed and that its powers for good and for ill should never be underestimated. The difference, then, really lies more in the *way* religion was expressed in Christian antiquity.

For example, whether practiced or not, religious toleration, or respect for the other person's religious point of view, whatever it might be, within certain commonly accepted limits, is a much endorsed value today. But it was not so in Christian antiquity, where passionate rejection of an opposing opinion was expected and was the norm. This was certainly true in Ambrose's case, and we can see it full-blown in the letters that he wrote concerning the possible re-establishment of the Altar of Victory in the Roman Senate. We are at some remove here from the pleas for toleration and fair treatment made by Christians on their own behalf in the second century, when they were a persecuted minority. Toleration and respect, we might say, were desirable if one were powerless; otherwise, not.

This intolerance, or passionate rejection of an opposing point of view, on the part of Christians (to say nothing here of Jews and pagans), can almost certainly be related to the immense self-confidence of the early Christian community. A reading of ancient Christian literature, starting with the New Testament, reveals very little if any self-doubt (which of course must be distinguished sharply from an awareness of sinfulness), even in time of persecution. This may be linked to the dearth of self-analysis that seems to be typical of early Christianity's first three centuries; active introspection is not strongly evident until roughly the time with which this book deals, although there are passages from Origen in the first half of the third century that suggest otherwise. It was Augustine above all, many would say, who introduced self-reflection to the Church in the West, while the monastic movement would do somewhat the same for the East. Such self-confidence as we have spoken of is perhaps hardly surprising in a religion that was still in its beginnings. How would it have survived the trials of hostility and suspicion had it not been sure of itself? Of this self-assured attitude one could not find a more apt representative than Ambrose. The decisions that he made and the positions that he took – some of them founded on reasoning that thoughtful persons today might consider rather dubious – were embraced with the firmness that is the evident sign of a clear conscience. And in many of the most famous of these decisions, with a fearlessness born of self-confidence rather than of any certitude that he would not suffer on account of them, he set himself against no less a rival than the imperial authorities. The age of self-assurance may have been in its evening in Ambrose's day, but the quality itself demarcates that day from our own at least as radically as anything else does.

Another difference worth mentioning in the area of religion has to do with the world of the invisible. To be religious almost necessarily means believing in an invisible realm, the realm of God and also of spirits and various 'influences.' In Christian (as in Jewish and pagan) antiquity, the invisible realm, rather than being a pallid and abstract reality, as it is for many moderns, was always just beneath the surfaces and appearances of things. It was intensely and even throbbingly present in the unseen form of angels and demons and the divine power itself. The monastic literature of the Egyptian desert is full to the point of extravagance of this intangible but potent world. We are also made somewhat aware of it, in a more restrained and theological fashion, in passages like the following from the treatise *On the Mysteries*. 'You saw there the levite [i.e., the deacon],' Ambrose tells those who have just been baptized, as he gives a brief account of the ministers of baptism:

> You saw the priest, you saw the high priest [i.e., the bishop]. Consider not their bodily forms but the grace of their ministries. . . . You must think of him [i.e., the bishop] in terms not of his outward appearance but of his office.
>
> (2.6)

And again, as he explains the grace of the water of baptism:

> You ought not, then, to believe solely with the eyes of your body. What is invisible is more completely seen, because the other is temporal, whereas this is eternal. What is not grasped by the eyes but perceived by the spirit and the mind is more completely viewed.
>
> (3.15)

Christians today would doubtless acknowledge the truth of what Ambrose says here, but they would probably not express it in precisely the same manner or give it the same emphasis.

The heightened awareness of the presence of spiritual beings and forces that we have alluded to contributed to facilitating a more ready belief in the ability and indeed the willingness of those beings and forces to cross over the very slender boundary between their world and ours in ways that would go beyond the normal workings of grace and sacramental dispensation of which Ambrose speaks in *On the Mysteries*. It would facilitate, in other words, a belief in miracles and divine and demonic interventions. A belief in miracles and supernatural interventions is, to be sure, part and parcel of modern Christianity as well. The difference between modern and ancient

Christianity in this matter, however, lies in the openness to accepting such things. In antiquity that openness seems to have been far wider and far more evident among all classes, including the intelligentsia, than it is today. Along these lines one may cite the remarkable happenings that Paulinus of Milan sees fit to recount in his life of Ambrose. It is true that Paulinus is conscious that his work may be met with some disbelief, and hence he insists on his veracity (cf. 2). But the very fact that he narrates so many strange occurrences at all is a testimony to what he presumes that his readership is capable of ingesting.

Yet another difference between our age and that of Ambrose has to do with the treatment of Scripture. Modern biblical scholarship has helped us to place the Scriptures in the settings in which they were produced and to have a more accurate understanding of these settings. Antiquity had its own kind of biblical scholarship, with as much right to be called scientific, according to the norms that it established for itself and the seriousness with which they were applied, as does its modern and far-removed descendant. Ancient exegetes were interested in the original biblical contexts as well, and in the human authors' conscious intentions – what those authors meant to say when they said such and such a thing. But they were generally more interested in what they considered to be the deeper or spiritual meaning of a given text, the meaning that lay below the surface and that might have been hidden from the human author himself. This deeper, spiritual meaning may usually be referred to as allegory, and the stress that the ancients laid upon it is complementary to the stress that they laid upon the invisible, spiritual world. Ambrose was an accomplished practitioner of allegory, and the manner in which he deals with the Song of Songs in his treatises *On Virgins* and *On the Mysteries* is illustrative of this. For him this book of the Bible is not about what it seems to be about – namely, the intimacy between two human lovers – but, rather, concerns the relationship between Christ and a particular human soul or between Christ and the Church, which many modern exegetes might allow to be merely a secondary meaning.

The contrast between the seen and the unseen, between the manifest and the concealed, brings to mind yet another duality – that between what contemporary thinkers have been accustomed to refer to as the secular and the sacred. Although in ancient times religion and other aspects of human life may have been conceptually distinct, in practice they were rarely separable. Some ancient Greeks and Romans may have been sceptical about their pagan gods, and some may have even ceased to believe in them, but the majority could not have imagined public or private life without them and the monuments and ceremonies associated with them. The presence of the Altar of Victory in the Roman Senate, and the official acts connected with it, were but a small example of the omnipresence of the sacred and of, from a modern perspective, its virtual indistinguishability from what we think of as secular life. The task that lay before the Christian leadership was not to drive a wedge between these two elements, since separating them would have been as unheard of to the Christians as to the pagans, but instead to replace one form of the sacred with another. The fourth century was above all the moment when this replacement was being orchestrated, and the role that Ambrose played in the process was crucial.

Under the heading of the religious character of the late fourth century and its difference from modern times a few words ought to be said about the function of the bishop. In antiquity the bishop was supreme in his see; although he was in communion with other bishops world-wide, he was accountable, except in fairly unusual circumstances, to no one else, including the Bishop of Rome. He was elected by the clergy of the see that he would govern (we are told in Ambrose's case that the laity also took a significant part, which was not uncommon; the laity's acceptance of the clergy's candidate was at any rate an important factor), and his overwhelmingly primary responsibility was to care for the well-being of his flock. It is true that Ambrose himself was occasionally absent from Milan and was sometimes occupied with imperial affairs, but none of that would have caused a substantial shift in his focus. The bishops of the Constantinian and post-Constantinian era, from 312 on, may have suffered under heavy administrative burdens laid upon them by imperial legislation, but the literature of the time emphasizes that they considered their pastoral duties to be of overriding importance. They preached and celebrated the eucharist several times a week, if not on a daily basis. They also busied themselves with the needs of the poor, of widows and orphans, of virgins, of their own clergy (of whom they seem to have had relatively few in comparison to many modern bishops). But the ancient texts suggest that, despite their numerous responsibilities and the fact that they enjoyed an exalted social status, at least if they exercised their functions in important cities, most bishops were remarkably accessible to the people: they replied to letters personally, practiced hospitality and generally made themselves available. A bishop like Ambrose, then, may have had a far-reaching reputation even in his own lifetime, but at bottom he was, as were his confrères in the episcopate, primarily a local personage.

This local quality is accentuated by the fact that local customs rather than universal rules were observed with regard to different religious activities. In a letter to a certain Januarius, Augustine mentions several such variations based on custom: in some places there is a fast on Saturday, in others not; in some places communion is received every day, in others not; in some places the eucharist is offered every day, in others only on Saturday and Sunday, and in still others on Sunday alone (cf. Letter 54.2). We know that even within the celebration of the liturgy there were variations from place to place. Ambrose provides us with a notable example of one when he tells us in his treatise *On the Sacraments* (3.1.4; cf. *On the Mysteries* 6.31–33) that the Milanese baptismal ceremony included a footwashing; this unusual custom seems not to have existed outside Milan. Ambrose was well aware of such differences and evidently quite untroubled by them, for in the same letter to Januarius, Augustine cites Ambrose's own words to his mother Monica, in which he explained to her that he adapted himself to whatever customs prevailed wherever he happened to be, and encouraged her to do the same.

Were we not familiar with the history of the early Church we might somehow be under the impression that it was a golden age of religious orthodoxy. It was, rather, a golden age of religious ferment and controversy such as – it could well be argued – would not be seen again until the Reformation, more than a millennium later. Religious issues, particularly in the fourth century, were of consuming interest, or at least of engrossing curiosity, to much of the population. Orthodoxy had its best-known representatives among the Fathers, although they themselves often had to grope in the dark and even, in some cases, embraced positions that the Church of later times would reject.

When Ambrose was ordained to the episcopacy in Milan, he succeeded an Arian bishop. Arianism – a term that applies to a wide range of sometimes mutually contradictory teachings – denied the full divinity of the second person of the Trinity and had convulsed the Church for much of the fourth century. By Ambrose's day it was in slow decline but far from having breathed its last: Ambrose's struggles with it occupied his energies for more than half of his term as bishop. He was also acquainted with and wrote against the views of Apollinaris of Laodicea, who negated the full humanity of Christ by refusing to accept his human soul and mind for the reason that these would have made him susceptible to sin. The Donatists, who claimed exclusive legitimacy for their church by insisting that it alone was morally pure, had divided a North Africa only too drawn to moral extremism of this sort; they were at the height of their success during Ambrose's episcopate. From the harsh imperial legislation enacted against it and from the treatises of Augustine we have an idea how influential the dualistic tenets of Manicheanism were and what a threat they were seen to be. Not long after Ambrose's death Pelagianism would burst upon the scene, with its doctrine of human perfectibility; it would even cite Ambrose in its own defense, which Augustine, Pelagius' chief adversary, pointed out as an absurdity (cf. *On the Grace of Christ and on Original Sin* 1.43.47–50.55). Meanwhile various ascetical movements of suspect leanings – Priscillianism is one of them whose name has come down to us – enjoyed a vogue in certain circles. On the other side of the spectrum the monk Jovinian, against whom Jerome directed an especially excessive treatise, questioned the value of ascetical practices, particularly virginity. The writings of the great Alexandrian theologian Origen, who had died *c.* 253, had long proven to be a two-edged sword: they contained countless brilliant insights, but several of them were exceedingly problematic as well. The struggle over Origen's legacy would disrupt the Church more than ever before in the waning years of the fourth century.

Nor, when speaking of religious controversy during this period, must one forget Judaism and paganism. Judaism, it appears now, was probably more attractive to many early Christians than scholars had previously realized, which helps to explain some of the virulence of the attacks on it by the Fathers. Paganism, for its part, may have become less appealing for various reasons, but it was not in the nature of things, or of human beings, that it would ever disappear entirely. In Symmachus, who fought unsuccessfully against Ambrose to restore the Altar of Victory to the Roman Senate, it found one of its most talented spokesmen. Finally, as aspects of paganism, there were astrology, magic and simple superstition, beneath which lay the powerful ancient inclination to fatalism.

In the face of all these rivals orthodox Christianity was not an impassive object. In reacting to them it defined itself and assumed more and more of the contours that we recognize today. Against the Arians it spelled out its teaching not only on the second but also on the third person of the Trinity. (Ambrose's treatise *On the Holy Spirit* bears witness to this concern.) Donatism was the occasion for developing a theology of the Church and the sacraments. The reaction to Apollinarianism was responsible for further understanding Christ's human nature. Paganism helped the Church to elaborate its relationship with the state.

Contributing to the ferment characteristic of the time was monasticism. Still a very young phenomenon in the last quarter of the fourth century, it was introducing to the Christian world a new way of living the gospel message on the fringes of society, and it contained within itself the seeds of both religious renewal and, less happily, religious élitism. At this time, too, the function of the Virgin Mary, of the saints and of relics (Ambrose himself was a notable promoter of the cult of the Virgin as well as a discoverer of the relics of long-dead martyrs) was becoming an issue. The role of the priest in the Church was gradually changing: the priesthood was now, after three centuries, starting to emerge from under the long shadow of the episcopate. The Bishop of Rome, on the other hand, was just beginning to claim for himself the privileges and powers that a later age would spontaneously and unquestioningly associate with the papacy. Clearly this was a time of intense and complex religious activity rather than merely of sedate religious orthodoxy.

One place where this activity was particularly evident was in the sphere of the ascetical life, which has just been alluded to under the rubric of monasticism. By the last quarter of the fourth century monasticism, whose origins in the shape that we know can be traced to Egypt in the first quarter of the same century, had made a profound impression on the East in general and on a number of influential eastern bishops in particular, among them Athanasius and Basil the Great. It was in the process of taking root in the West, with Martin of Tours as its best-known exponent. Among its Latin-speaking advocates, although he lived mostly in Greek-speaking Palestine, was Jerome, whose romantic portrayals of the monastic vocation made it highly attractive to many. One of monasticism's greatest discoveries was the desert, the huge unpopulated wilderness, whether of the sands of Egypt or the forests of Gaul, and the vast majority of monks lived in the desert. Still, despite their distance from society, they had a powerful effect upon it that would be hard to recapture today. The monks held up the possibility of a more immediate contact with God and the invisible world and of an evangelical life that exerted a fascination upon a religiously susceptible age. The mystique of voluntary poverty was in the air as well. The second half of the fourth century and the beginning of the fifth are replete with stories of wealthy men and women who experienced a religious conversion that resulted in the embracing of poverty and the leading of a life that was close to being monastic, without perhaps being fully so. A letter of Ambrose (58) is partly devoted to the praise of two of the most spectacular of such converts, Paulinus and his wife Therasia, who gave up vast properties in Aquitania and settled in Nola in Campania, where they led a quasi-monastic existence. Given this atmosphere, it is hardly surprising to learn that Ambrose himself, according to Paulinus' biography (38), gave away all his property on becoming a bishop, so that he might be able to 'follow the Lord Christ.'

And there was also virginity. There had been virgins, both men and women, since the time of the gospels, but the late fourth century saw what seems to have been a fresh interest in the practice of virginity. Athanasius published several treatises on the subject, Gregory of Nyssa wrote on it, and so did John Chrysostom, Jerome (whose ardent defense of it was sometimes embarrassingly one-sided) and Ambrose himself, while Augustine's work *On Holy Virginity* would appear at the very outset of the fifth century.

The popularity of monasticism, voluntary poverty and virginity, or in any event the acclaim that they received, testifies to a deeper phenomenon that separates early Christianity from its present-day counterpart, namely, a strong emphasis on the eschatological, on the next world conceived of as the goal of existence in this world. Of course an eschatological emphasis belongs to the essence of Christianity, but in antiquity it was so pronounced as to suggest a significant disinterest on the part of very many in the world around them. Monasticism, voluntary poverty and virginity were embodiments of this disinterest, inasmuch as the ideal of those who embraced any of these ways of life was to detach themselves as much as possible from this-worldly concerns, whether in the form of human society or wealth or sex or family or all of these (and more) together. And regularly monks and virgins in particular were compared to angels and their lives characterized as paradisal and heavenly (cf. Ambrose, *On Virgins* 1.3.11).

A final word, in the context of discussing the religious spirit of

9

Christian antiquity, about devotion. Early Christianity distinguished itself from the paganism of the time by its firm belief in the possibility of a tender intimacy with the divine – an intimacy that went not only from man to God but that was believed to go as well from God to man. It expressed itself in prayers and hymns, in the manner in which God and Christ were spoken of even in more narrowly theological writings, as well as in treatises on monasticism and more especially on virginity. By Ambrose's time, if not before, the circle of intimacy had begun to include, at least in a more overt and intense way, the Virgin Mary. The saints of one's own locality, and some others of more universal appeal (like Peter and Paul, whose graves in Rome were the object of pilgrimage, or the now little-known martyr Menas, the ruins of whose huge shrine may still be seen in the sands of the Egyptian desert to the west of Alexandria), were also part of it.

It is instructive to view the mosaics and wall paintings that date approximately from this period and to see how these venerable personages – Christ, Mary and the saints – are depicted. They have an austerity that precludes an easy familiarity with them, and clearly they inhabit another world. Yet they do not in any way repulse the possibility of contact between themselves and the viewer, so long as the viewer is disposed to enter into their world.

After this brief sketch of the religious temper of Ambrose's time something should be said about some aspects of society and the state, bearing in mind that what has already been observed about religion is obviously also related to what will follow here.

Ambrose lived in an era of relative class immobility. Movement among the different strata of society was not impossible, but it was difficult. The two great classes were the rich and the poor, within each of which, as might be expected, there was a certain spread. There was also a middle class, but it was not comparable to the middle class of contemporary North America and Western Europe: a late fourth-century middle-class household might possess several slaves, and the family itself would be able to enjoy a degree of cultured leisure. Augustine's family, as he describes it in various places in the *Confessions*, belonged to this grouping. We know that the middle class was hard-pressed by the civil obligations which were draining it of its resources and to which Ambrose makes brief reference in Letter 18.13–14. The disastrous condition of the majority of the poor, depicted with high rhetoric in the treatise *On Naboth*, and the precarious situation of the middle class may help to explain the attractiveness both of monasticism as an alternative way of life and of the eschatological emphasis that monasticism so well incorporated.

The Roman Empire that Ambrose knew was increasingly a rural society and less and less urban-centered. The great days of the major cities of the western Mediterranean basin were over, not to return in most cases for centuries. This was particularly and poignantly true of Rome: although it maintained the unparalleled prestige of its name and its history, its former political power hardly existed any more; the emperor's headquarters were elsewhere, and the Senate's influence was severely limited. Carthage, at one time the second city in the West, was now of little consequence. The upstart Constantinople, dedicated as recently as the year 330, was by Ambrose's day the dominant political city of the East. The much older Antioch and Alexandria continued to be important, but they had started on the long road to being regional cities. In the West new centers were emerging. Trier and Milan, both associated with Ambrose and both housing imperial residences, are good examples in this respect. The ascendency of each, however, was brief. Milan's lasted from the early 290s until 452, when it was destroyed by Attila. Trier rose about the same time as Milan but fell even more rapidly: it was sacked four times by the Franks between 410 and 428.

The fate of Milan and Trier hung over numberless other cities of Roman Europe. In the last quarter of the fourth century the Germanic peoples were a hovering presence that could not be adequately dealt with and whose movements were unpredictable and often violent. Some of the Germans, to be sure, had found their way into the Empire and even been accepted into the imperial service, thereby becoming at least partially Romanized. But even Romanized barbarians often evoked suspicion and fear, and of course most were outside the frontiers of the Empire, un-Romanized and that much more fearsome. Any attempt to understand late antiquity must take into account the menacing atmosphere of imminent pillage and destruction in which the inhabitants of Roman Europe lived, and from which they experienced only intermittent relief. The defeat at Adrianople in 378 and the sack of Rome in 410 were only moments of particularly grievous disaster, not solitary incidents.

In a letter to a fellow bishop, Severus (probably of Naples), written in 392 on the occasion of a barbarian outbreak, Ambrose offers a glimpse of his preoccupation with the German threat. He compares the peaceful coast of Campania, Severus' homeland in southern Italy, with Milan and its surroundings, which were much closer to the frontier. Ambrose's yearning for peace, stylized as it may be in its expression, is utterly genuine.

Your coastal region, removed not only from dangers but from any turmoil, fills the emotions with tranquility and transports the soul from the fearful and surging waves of anxiety to a solid sense of calm, so that what David says of the holy Church in a general way seems to fit and be appropriate to you in a particular way: 'He established it upon the seas, and he made it firm upon the rivers' (Ps. 24:2). For the mind that is undisturbed by the invasions of the barbarians and by the afflictions of war is free to pray, is attentive to God, occupies itself with the things of the Lord, and promotes what is peaceful and tranquil. We, however, are exposed to barbaric disturbances and to the storms of war. We are tossed about in the midst of a sea of all kinds of troubles, and from these toils and perils we infer the still graver perils of the life to come.

(Letter 59.2–3)

In time, though, peaceful Campania would itself suffer the same troubles.

The difficult position of the middle class and the intolerable situation of the poor, the decline of many of the great traditional urban centers and the threat of the barbarians, and their actual incursions, were all significant factors in the slow dying process of the Empire in the West. In fact it is perhaps surprising that the Empire survived as long as it did. It was also too far-flung for adequate central administration, and Diocletian's solution to this problem, dating from 283, of dividing the Empire in two and having two emperors was not overwhelmingly successful: it only incited rivalry between the two supreme authorities and contributed to the breaking apart of East and West. There was, moreover, no universally acknowledged and, more important, universally respected way of providing for the imperial succession or for guaranteeing the legitimacy of an emperor. There were those who would be designated as usurpers of the imperial title. (Ambrose had dealings with two such: Maximus, who ruled Gaul from 383 to 388, and Eugenius, who held uneasy sway in Italy from 392 to 394.) But the designation of usurper only applied to those who, after having grasped power, had foundered; had they endured in power and died peacefully in

their beds they would almost certainly have been regarded as legitimate. As for the legitimate emperors themselves, an indication of
the unsure futures that they faced is given by the fact that during
Ambrose's episcopacy three of them died violently – Valens in 378,
at the battle of Adrianople, Gratian in 383, at the hands of one of
his officials, and Valentinian II in 392, by either murder or suicide
(more likely the former).

One of the few vital forces remaining in the Empire – indeed, the
most important in terms of lasting consequence – was Christianity.
The proof of its vigor could be seen in its ability to provide the
impulse for the monasticism, voluntary poverty and virginity that
have been mentioned earlier.

Christianity was not so constantly the object of persecution as it
is often presented as having been in the first centuries of its existence. On the contrary, it sometimes enjoyed peace for decades at a
stretch, and by the third century its periods of peace were marked by
notable material prosperity. But at the very beginning of the fourth
century it underwent its fiercest attack under the Emperor Diocletian. The Great Persecution, as this attack was known, lasted about a
decade and was most savage in the East. It had already run its course
when the Emperor Constantine, who had risen to power in 306,
granted toleration to Christianity with the so-called Edict of Milan
in 313. Toleration, on Constantine's part, moved almost immediately
to out-and-out promotion of the Church over paganism. The
emperor's legislation and his other acts demonstrate how favorable
he was to the Church, and his reign, in terms of the opportunities,
both good and bad, that it offered to the Church was without any
doubt one of the great watershed events in the history of
Christianity.

But Constantine's interest in the Church was not balanced by an
unwavering commitment to what would later be defined as religious
orthodoxy. When around 318 the Alexandrian priest Arius publicly
proposed a new way of understanding the Word, the second person
of the Trinity, which degraded his divinity, and when he succeeded
in stirring up unwanted discussion on the nature of the Word, it was
evident that Constantine did not wholly grasp the theological prin-
ciples that were at issue and that he was more concerned with the
threat to the Empire's unity that religious dissension was occasion-
ing than with theological niceties. But Constantine not only did not
comprehend some refined theological notions; he eventually

13

showed himself, or seemed to show himself, sympathetic to Arianism, even allowing himself to be baptized on his deathbed, in 337, by a prominent Arian bishop. All of this despite the fact that it was he who had convoked the Council of Nicaea in 325, which had anathematized Arianism and published a creed declaring that the Word was fully divine.

Constantius II, the longest reigning and most powerful of Constantine's three surviving sons, all of whom succeeded him at his death, was openly hostile to Nicene orthodoxy and promoted Arianism. Julian, who is known to history as 'the Apostate' and who followed Constantius in 361, after the latter had been sole ruler for eleven years, played orthodoxy and Arianism off against one another, at the expense of orthodoxy. His great project, in which he was ultimately unsuccessful, was to revive paganism. Jovian, emperor from 363 to 364, was orthodox but did little on behalf of the Church during his brief reign. After him came Valentinian and his brother Valens. The two divided the Empire again after it had been treated as a single unit from Constantine to Jovian (with the exception of the years from 337 to 350, when Constantius ruled with at least one of his brothers), and Valentinian served in the West until 375, while Valens ruled in the East until 378. Valentinian, although personally orthodox, maintained a careful neutrality towards orthodoxy and Arianism while Valens, on the other hand, favored Arianism. During all this time there were numerous synods in both East and West in which, particularly in the East, Nicene orthodoxy suffered one setback after another. Arianism, moreover, which had denied the full divinity of the second person of the Trinity, had led as a logical consequence to Pneumatomachianism, as it was called, which denied the full divinity of the third person, the Holy Spirit. The tide, none the less, was gradually turning to orthodoxy thanks in large part to the dogged determination and political and theological skills of its great champion, Athanasius of Alexandria, who died in 373. (That the Nicene cause could produce such men as Athanasius, Hilary of Poitiers, Basil of Caesarea and Gregory Nazianzen, all brilliant theologians and all active in the struggle against Arianism at this period, often at considerable personal cost, is further proof of Christianity's vigor.) When Ambrose was elected Bishop of Milan in 374, then, the religious situation was still unsettled, and before him lay the task of contributing to its resolution. In Milan, the capital of the West, the new bishop was strategically positioned to address not only the problem of Arianism but also that of the appropriate relationship between the Church and the state, in which he would make what was perhaps his most striking contribution, but by no means his only lasting one, to the history of the West.

II

How Ambrose became Bishop of Milan is one of the most familiar stories to have been transmitted to us from Christian antiquity. We owe the detailed account to Paulinus, who recorded it in his biography (Rufinus of Aquileia had produced an earlier but far briefer report). There is little reason to doubt the overall shape of Paulinus' narrative, although not everyone agrees as to the authenticity of particular aspects.

Ambrose, we are told (cf. Paulinus, *Life* 6–9), had recently come to Milan as the governor of the provinces of Liguria and Aemilia, which consisted of much of northwestern Italy. Shortly after his arrival – but perhaps not so shortly that he would have been unable to establish an attractive reputation as a fair administrator and judge – the Bishop of Milan died. His name was Auxentius and he had been an Arian. As were most of the Arians in the West at the time, it would seem, Auxentius had been a member of the Homoian wing of Arianism, which held that the Son, the second person of the Trinity, was 'like' (*homoios* in Greek) the Father. To orthodox Catholics, whose faith was defined by the Nicene Council of 325, which had proclaimed that the Father and the Son were of the same essence (*homoousios* in Greek), this was true as far as it went, but it did not go far enough. Hence the Homoian refusal to affirm anything beyond the Son's likeness to the Father – their refusal, in other words, to confess that he was of the same essence as the Father – made the Homoians heretics.

Auxentius' episcopate had been a tumultuous one: it began in 355 with the deposition and exile of his orthodox predecessor Dionysius, and in the course of his nearly twenty years as bishop he survived at least two attempts to remove him from office. At his death Milan was divided, as it must have been for several decades, between Arians (who may have constituted the majority) and Catholic Christians, and whatever tensions might understandably have existed between the two groups now broke out into the open. Paulinus describes an unruly crowd gathered at the cathedral, with each of the two factions demanding a bishop of its own religious convictions. As governor of the area, it was Ambrose's responsibility to maintain order in such a situation, and he himself appeared on the scene with his troops in order to pacify the mob. Suddenly the voice of a child was heard crying *Ambrosius episcopus* – 'Ambrose for bishop!' The crowd at once took up the cry, and the unexpected agreement on a single candidate introduced an unhoped-for harmony between the factions. It is quite possible that the throng found their governor acceptable for the episcopate because they believed that he would be as neutral in matters of religion as was his master, the Emperor Valentinian.[1] In any case Ambrose, according to Paulinus' account, was dismayed at the turn of events and tried in different ways to extricate himself from his nomination, but with no success. He was at the time not even baptized, although he was a catechumen. The people, however, were not put off by the resistance that he manifested or by his unbaptized state, and they insisted upon him all the more. At last, then, he was baptized and, a week later, ordained bishop. The ordination occurred on either 1 or 7 December, 373, or on 7 December, 374, with the last date currently receiving the most acceptance on the part of scholars.[2]

Ambrose was born in Trier, on the banks of the Mosel River in present-day Germany, probably in 339. The date, which is disputed, is suggested by a reference in Letter 59.4, in which Ambrose speaks of being 53 years old at the time of some barbarian unrest that several scholars claim can be situated in 392.[3] Ambrose's father bore the same name. According to Paulinus, he was prefect, or governor, of the Gauls and hence responsible for a vast territory, which he administered from Trier.[4] We know little of him apart from the office that he is said to have held and the fact that he died while his son was relatively young, leaving behind a wife, who is unnamed, an older daughter called Marcellina, an older son called Satyrus, and Ambrose himself.

Paulinus tells of a marvelous incident involving the infant Ambrose: as he lay in a cradle in the courtyard of the prefect's residence, a swarm of bees was seen to settle on his face and to go in and out of his mouth. To the child's father this was a sign that his son was destined for greatness. Paulinus finds in the incident a prophetic reference to Ambrose's writings, which he likens to honeycombs (cf. 3). Whether the event ever really happened or not, bees are a propitious symbol, suggesting community, virginity (they were believed to reproduce asexually), diligence, selflessness and, of course, sweetness, and Ambrose himself praised them at length in his treatise, *The Six Days of Creation* (5.21.67–72).

At some point in Ambrose's youth, either before or after his father's death, his family moved to Rome. The move was in fact probably a return to the family home, located in Rome. While there, Ambrose's sister Marcellina formally embraced the virginal life and resided most likely in semi-seclusion at home with her family (Jerome describes such domestic virginity in his famous Letter 22), with another virgin as her companion. Ambrose's treatise *On Virgins* (3.1.1) indicates that she made public profession of her virginity one Christmas Day in the Basilica of Saint Peter, in the presence of Bishop Liberius. This event undoubtedly took place in the period from 352 to 354, since Liberius was elected bishop in May 352 and was forcibly removed from Rome by the Arian Emperor Constantius II not long before Christmas 355. Liberius did not return to his see until 358; at that time Ambrose would have been 19, according to most calculations, and almost certainly too old for his mother and his sister, by then already a virgin, to declare, as Paulinus says, that he was 'a young man who did not know what he was talking about,' when he would joke with them that he was going to become a bishop (cf. 4).

The fact of Marcellina's virginity throws into relief the piety of the household in which Ambrose was raised. Indeed, his family could claim a heritage of unusual holiness: the very end of the treatise *On Virgins* tells us that it could count the virgin martyr Soteris, who had died at the beginning of the century in the Great Persecution of Diocletian, among its members. It is initially somewhat surprising, then, that Ambrose was not baptized as a child. Paulinus does not expatiate on this, although, when the time comes for him to narrate the story of Ambrose's episcopal election, his lack of baptism makes the account all the more remarkable (albeit not unprecedented, as will be shown). Ambrose himself draws no attention to this situation in his writings. But his brother Satyrus was not baptized as a child either, as certain passages in the funeral oration that Ambrose pronounced over him indicate (cf. 43–48), and Ambrose in no way suggests that it was regrettable that Satyrus should have submitted to baptism only in his thirties or even forties, as an act of gratitude to God after having survived shipwreck. However, we recall that, for better or for worse, it was not necessarily the custom at this time for children even of a devout household to be baptized directly after birth. The cases of Basil the Great, his brother Gregory of Nyssa, and Gregory Nazianzen, whose parents all enjoyed a reputation for sanctity, come to mind, along with that of Augustine, the son of the ultra-pious Monica.

The fact of Marcellina's virginity, or at the very least the fact of a domestic environment in which virginity would be cherished, helps significantly to explain Ambrose's own fascination with the virginal life. It must be remembered that he pursued the slightly unusual (for those times) course of bachelorhood until his mid-thirties, when he became a bishop, although we do not know why. After his ordination he wrote no fewer than four treatises on the topic of virginity, and he referred to it frequently elsewhere. Satyrus too remained unmarried, and in his funeral oration Ambrose praises his brother's chastity, even describing his face as 'suffused with a certain virginal modesty' (52). There is surely something remarkable in that all three offspring of a widowed mother would elect to live as celibates.

In Rome Ambrose took up the liberal arts, which were the regular course of studies for a youth at that time. They would have consisted primarily, if not exclusively, in the development of oratorical skills and in the appreciation of a limited number of classics written by the great Latin authors, Virgil being chief among them. There was normally no training in science or history or philosophy or art apart from what the authors in question might themselves have said about such topics. Ambrose's education also included law and Greek – the former with a view to his following his deceased father in a career of civil service, the latter perhaps because his family, as is argued by some scholars,[5] was of Greek descent. Whereas Augustine, who was a brilliant student, informs us that he disdained his own education (which, with the exception of law, was in its main thrust probably not so very different from Ambrose's) as vacuous (cf. *Confessions* 1.12.19–18.30), we have little idea what Ambrose might have thought about the matter; we may assume, however, from the perspective of his success in civil affairs, which he never demeaned, that his views were somewhat more pragmatic than Augustine's.

His schooling over, Ambrose left Rome to practice law under the praetorian prefect Sextus Anicius Petronius Probus, who was a monumental figure in the life of the Western Empire in the second half of the fourth century. Probus had been prefect of Italy and Illyricum since 368, and his usual residence was in Sirmium – modern Sremska Mitrovica in northwestern Serbia, on the Sava River, not far west of Belgrade. He was impressed with Ambrose, whom he might have known earlier in Rome, and he appointed him his counsel, or legal adviser. Sometime after that he was instrumental in having Ambrose, now not much older than 30, raised to the rank of consularis, which brought with it the honorific *clarissimus*, and made governor of Liguria and Aemilia. Paulinus notes that, as Probus was dismissing his protégé, he told him prophetically: 'Go, and act not as a judge but as a bishop' (8).

By modern standards Ambrose's ordination to the episcopate was a dubious affair: the unremitting pressure exerted upon an unwilling candidate would be sufficient to call its legality seriously into question today. But such standards were not operative in Christian antiquity, and ordinations like Ambrose's were not so uncommon at the time. Somewhat the same thing, for example, happened to Augustine, who relates how he wept and protested during his forced ordination to the priesthood in Hippo, nearly two decades after Ambrose became Bishop of Milan. A letter of Bishop Epiphanius of Salamis, dating to 394, recounts unblushingly how he ordained a monk named Paulinian to both the diaconate and the priesthood while he was bound and gagged, so that he could not adjure Epiphanius to desist. The purpose of the letter was to defend Epiphanius' right to perform an ordination in Palestine, outside his own territory, rather than to justify his use of force, which he must have presumed would not have troubled his addressee. The accent in antiquity was clearly more on the discernment and the will of the local church, clergy and laity, than on the desires and wishes of the person under consideration for ecclesiastical promotion. In Ambrose's case the people had determined, for whatever reason, that he was capable of the episcopate. Even if their clamor for him was not so spontaneous as Paulinus would have us believe but was somehow stage-managed, it was clear that the crowd had to be part of the decision. The laity did not always have such a strong voice in the election of their bishop, but there were certainly times when their views prevailed. Paulinus informs us that the Emperor Valentinian – himself of course a layman – played a role as well: a report of the popular choice was sent to him, and his approving response was decisive in persuading Ambrose to abandon his reluctance and submit to what seemed to be God's will. We know from a letter of Ambrose, written in 386 to Valentinian's son, the young Valentinian II, that Valentinian had communicated to the reluctant candidate that, if he accepted the office, he, the emperor, would guarantee religious peace in Milan (cf. Letter. 21.7). It appears unlikely that the emperor was consulted in every episcopal election, but he almost surely was when it was a question of the more important sees, and Milan was at the moment the most important in the West. As for choosing an unbaptized person, neither was that unheard of in the ancient Church. The neoplatonist philosopher Synesius of Cyrene, for instance, was prevailed upon to become the bishop of Ptolemais in Libya in 410, where he ruled the local church successfully until his death a few years later. There is good reason for believing that Synesius was not only unbaptized at the time but that, in addition, he knew relatively little about Christian doctrine. Ambrose, at least, had been brought up in a devoutly Christian family.

Part of Ambrose's hesitation to accept ordination may have stemmed from a real interest in pursuing a life of philosophy.[6] Paulinus mentions such motivation when he discusses the events surrounding the election and ordination: 'Returning to his house in distress, [Ambrose] determined to become a philosopher. But he was to be Christ's true philosopher' (7). Here, though, we probably have to understand a life of calm, study and reflection of the sort that was possible for and desirable to a wealthy and leisured gentleman of that era. Certainly Ambrose was drawn to study, and a passage in Augustine's *Confessions* (6.3.3) is memorable for telling how he would snatch moments to read in the midst of his busy schedule and how, while he was engaged in reading, he would be oblivious to the people around him. Perhaps, in fact, he had taken celibacy upon himself in accordance with the common notion that marriage was incompatible with a life of study.

And so Ambrose was baptized and, eight days later, ordained bishop. While it is true that there was hardly an alternative for him as a Catholic catechumen, the form that his baptism took none the less sounds a programmatic note: 'He asked to be baptized by no one but a Catholic bishop, for he was anxiously on guard against the perfidy of the Arians' (Paulinus, *Life* 9). He would find himself fighting against the Arians throughout much of his episcopal career, although now, as he was about to embark upon it, they were evidently willing to put differences aside in the expectation that the new bishop would be fair in his dealings with them.

The words with which Paulinus describes the week between Ambrose's baptism and his ordination read: *Baptizatus itaque fertur omnia ecclesiastica officia implesse atque octavo die ordinatus est* (9) The phrase may be translated: 'Once he was baptized he is said to have fulfilled all the ecclesiastical offices, and on the eighth day . . . he was ordained bishop'. The Latin is usually taken to mean that Ambrose passed through all the ecclesiastical grades, from porter to priest, before receiving episcopal ordination. It has been argued, however, both that Paulinus misrepresented what actually happened in order to spare Ambrose the charge of having contravened a canonical rule that a newly baptized person might not be raised immediately to the episcopate, and that to understand that Ambrose had thus to pass through all the ecclesiastical ranks is anachronistic. Instead, the argument runs, Ambrose went simply from baptism to episcopal ordination after a week's interval. He himself suggests that this may well have been the case when he writes in Letter 63.65 that the Western bishops approved his ordination explicitly and the Eastern bishops did so implicitly, despite the canonical rule.[7]

Milan, Ambrose's seat first as governor and now as bishop, was ranked by Ausonius, some ten years after Ambrose's election, as the seventh city of the Roman world. In the brief poetic sketch of Milan contained in his *Order of Famous Cities* he writes:

> At Milan there are all sorts of wonderful things – an abundance of goods, innumerable elegant homes, men of marvelous eloquence and pleasing manners. Moreover, the beauty of the place is accentuated by a double wall. And there are a circus, which is the people's delight, the wedge-shaped bulk of the theater, the temples, the bulwarks of the palace, the splendid mint, the district that is celebrated because of the Baths of Herculeus, all the colonnades adorned with marble statues, the encircling defenses that are banked up at the city's edge. All these things, which rival each other, so to speak, by their massive workmanship, are of surpassing excellence, and the proximity of Rome does not detract from them.

Milan was obviously a city to be reckoned with.

Ausonius mentions no churches in any of the twenty sites that he describes in his work. Had he done so for Milan, though, he would without a doubt have spoken of the cathedral. Built sometime before 355 and located in the center of the city, it had five aisles and could hold a congregation of 3,000. This immense structure, known as the New Basilica and later called Santa Tecla, had replaced a smaller and slightly earlier one, still standing and still used, that was referred to as the Old Basilica.

About the very time that Ausonius was limning his portrait of Milan, three other major churches had just been or were in the process of being put up outside the city walls. One of these was the Portian Basilica, later dedicated to Saint Lawrence and hence known now as San Lorenzo. It was situated to the south of the city and seems to have been an imperial foundation; as such it was to play an important role in the orthodox–Arian wrangling that marked the mid-380s.

The other two were foundations of Ambrose himself. These were the Ambrosian Basilica, now known as Sant' Ambrogio, to the west of the city, and the Basilica of the Apostles, now known as San Nazaro, lying slightly southeast. Ambrose would eventually be buried in the Ambrosian Basilica, along with the martyrs Gervasius and Protasius, whose bones he had discovered. That Ambrose would have arranged to have his body placed beneath the altar of his own basilica (the first bishop that we know of to have done so) has been seen as an intentional rebuke of the Emperor Constantine, by then dead for nearly fifty years, who was originally buried either beneath or near the altar of the Church of the Holy Apostles in Constantinople. It makes sense that Ambrose, who distinguished sharply between clergy and laity, would have objected to Constantine's arrogation of sanctuary space to himself. (Theodoret of Cyrus reports in his *Ecclesiastical History* [1.18] that Ambrose had once forbidden the Emperor Theodosius to remain in the sanctuary after he had brought his offering to the altar – and that Theodosius admired him for it.) Finally, a third church was planned by Ambrose, although he did not live to see it constructed. This was the Basilica of the Virgins, now called San Simpliciano, and it was situated north of the city wall.

It has been suggested that Ambrose had these three churches built with the cities of Rome and Constantinople in mind. All three were intended to recall the great churches of Rome that were located outside the city walls – the churches of Saints Peter, Paul, Lawrence and Agnes. Christian Milan, in other words, was to be like the ancient capital and perhaps even to rival it. One of the three, the Basilica of the Apostles, appears to have been modeled on the Church of the Holy Apostles in Constantinople, thus establishing a link with the new capital as well. Moreover, since the Council of Constantinople in 381, the new capital of the Roman world had been purged of Arianism and had become a symbol of Catholic orthodoxy. The erection of the Basilica of the Apostles, then, might have been intended to indicate Ambrose's plan for Milan – that it too would be rid of Arianism and become a symbol of orthodoxy.[8]

There is some dispute over what is alleged to have been one of Ambrose's first acts as bishop. Part of a letter attributed to Basil of Caesarea (197.2) seems to show that Ambrose requested and obtained Basil's help in getting back the body of his predecessor Bishop Dionysius, who for his orthodoxy had been exiled to Armenia, where he died at an unknown date. The return to Milan of the relics of the city's last orthodox bishop would have been, in Ambrose's eyes, the anticipation of the return of orthodoxy itself to Milan. But at least two problems have been raised here. In the first place, there is serious doubt as to the authenticity of the part of the letter in question. Second, we have no knowledge whatsoever from any source either of the reception of Dionysius' remains in Milan or of the existence of a monument to Dionysius in Milan in Ambrose's lifetime. What the undoubtedly authentic part of Basil's letter (197.1) shows, however, is that the strongly anti-Arian Bishop of Caesarea believed that he had discovered a kindred spirit in Ambrose, which implies that Ambrose's own letter, now unfortunately lost, must have expressed anti-Arian sentiments.[9] The new Bishop of Milan, in any event, whatever his plans for re-establishing orthodoxy may or may not have been, did not gratuitously attack either Arianism or the Arians themselves in Milan. Instead he appears initially to have pursued reconciliation by accepting Auxentius' Arian clergy as his own – although, practically speaking, he may have had little choice in the matter if the vast majority of the city's priests and deacons were Arian, which would have been very likely after nearly twenty years of Auxentius' rule.

But Ambrose was at work against Arianism outside of Milan. At a synod in Sirmium in either 375 or 378 he was largely responsible for the condemnation of six local Arian clerics. At another time during the same period, it would seem, he was in Sirmium to secure the election of the orthodox Anemius as bishop of the city and to ordain him. As we learn from Paulinus (11), this did not happen without incident. The Arian population was vociferous in its demand for an Arian bishop, and it was encouraged by the Empress Justina, about whom more will soon be said. While Ambrose was in the cathedral facing the throng, an Arian virgin suddenly rushed upon him in a bizarre attempt to drag him to the section of the church reserved for women, where he would be beaten and driven from the building. Ambrose, it turned out, was master of the situation, and the worst did not occur. But he must then have been made aware – had he not adverted to the possibility before – that the struggle between Arianism and orthodoxy might involve violence for himself.

Not long after Ambrose's election, on 17 November 375, the Emperor Valentinian, personally orthodox but politically neutral in matters of religion, died suddenly of a stroke. His son Gratian, at the time only 16 years old, succeeded him to the throne in the West, and the new emperor's still younger half-brother, Valentinian II, became co-ruler.

Gratian was at first not inclined to discontinue his father's hands-off policy regarding religion, but sometime early in the year 378 the young emperor requested of Ambrose an exposition of orthodox belief, presumably for his own instruction (even though the bishop begins the work by stating that it was written not for his education but for his approbation), and by the summer of the same year Ambrose had completed the first two books of his lengthy treatise *On the Faith* in response to that request. Then, on 9 August 378, occurred the devastating defeat of the Roman army by the Goths at Adrianople (now Edirne in European Turkey) and with it the battle-field death of Gratian's uncle, the Emperor Valens. Valens had embraced Arianism, and it is possible that the debacle of Adrianople, which was one of the most fateful encounters in military history, seemed to Gratian to be a divine judgement leveled against Arianism and its sympathizers. Yet, if it is true that the emperor was being drawn gradually to abandon his neutrality and to turn towards orthodoxy, the turn was marked by fits and starts, for in late 378 he issued an edict from Sirmium in which he granted toleration to all religious groups with the exception of Manicheans and extreme Arians, who denied any similarity between the Father and the Son. By the summer of 379, however, the edict had been withdrawn, thanks probably to pressure exerted by Ambrose. Again, at a date that cannot be accurately determined and for reasons that remain tantalizingly obscure to us, Gratian seized an orthodox basilica. It is very conceivable that he was making it available for worship to the Arian members of the imperial court – among them the Empress Justina, the widow of Valens and the mother of Valentinian II – who had fled to Milan after Adrianople.[10] Gratian kept the basilica for perhaps longer than two years, returning it to Ambrose shortly before the latter composed his treatise *On the Holy Spirit* in 381;

there, in 1.1.19–21, we may read virtually all that is to be known of the affair.

The year 381 seems to mark Gratian's definitive acceptance of a role actively favorable to orthodoxy. On 27 February 380 the pro-orthodox Theodosius, whom Gratian had named emperor in the East in January 379 to replace Valens, had issued an edict in which he declared that all inhabitants of the Empire should conform to Catholic belief. It is reasonable to believe that Gratian was consulted on this. Then, in September 381, a council of bishops from northern Italy assembled in Aquileia at Gratian's behest. The details of the convocation are not entirely clear. It appears, however, that the Arian Bishop Palladius of Ratiaria (now Arcar in present-day Bulgaria) had hoped for and expected a council to which pro-Arian eastern bishops would be invited, but that Ambrose had persuaded the emperor, unbeknownst to Palladius, to restrict the gathering to northern Italians, upon whose orthodoxy Ambrose could count. This was but one of several maneuvers, none of them entirely praiseworthy, engineered by Ambrose in order to achieve his objective. As a result the council easily obtained the condemnation of Palladius and also of Secundianus of Singidunum (modern Belgrade). In his reports on the council to Gratian, Valentinian and Theodosius, Ambrose then urged the emperors to act decisively against all deviations from Catholic orthodoxy. The final lines of the first of these reports are indicative of what he expected from them, and they demonstrate nicely the kind of relationship between the Church and the Empire that he had in mind:

> We beseech Your Clemency . . . to order that respect be given first to the Catholic Church, and then as well to your laws. Thus, with God as your protector, you shall triumph, once you have provided for the peace and tranquility of the churches.
>
> (Letter 10.12)

From this time on, until his assassination in 383, Gratian seems to have been firmly in the camp of orthodoxy under the tutelage of Ambrose, who saw himself as the young emperor's guardian and guide.

Ambrose's most celebrated confrontation with the partisans of Arianism occurred in Milan in 385 and 386. When the struggle broke out Gratian had been dead for two years. Had he been alive, the situation would have been entirely different, for now Ambrose was contending with the imperial court itself. We can reconstruct the course of events in 385 from Letter 20, one of Ambrose's letters to his sister Marcellina, to whom he seems to have been in the habit of providing detailed information concerning crucial moments in his career.

In late March of 385, Valentinian, doubtless urged on by his mother Justina, expressed the wish to have a church in which the imperial court, now heavily Arian in composition, could celebrate its own liturgy, inasmuch as at this point all the churches of Milan were orthodox and hence in the hands of Ambrose. Specifically, Valentinian wanted to have the Portian Basilica at his disposal. As has been noted, this church may have been an imperial foundation, which would have made the young emperor feel that he could reasonably lay claim to it for his own purposes. One scholar argues that, even were the basilica not an imperial foundation, the emperor had certain rights over local churches that could not easily be dismissed.[11] Ambrose, in any case, refused him. A demand was then made to give up the New Basilica, the cathedral, although pressure continued to be exerted on the bishop to comply with the former request and to part with the smaller Portian Basilica. Nothing, however, seems to have come of this second demand regarding the New Basilica.

On Palm Sunday, very soon after Valentinian had made his wish known, Ambrose was preaching in the cathedral when word came to him that imperial functionaries had entered the Portian Basilica and were putting up hangings in it, in order either simply to decorate it with the imperial colors or to designate it as imperial property. Ambrose went on with the celebration of the eucharist, but meanwhile an orthodox mob was threatening the life of an Arian priest whom they had somehow laid hold of. Ambrose sent a small contingent of his clergy to rescue the hapless man, which they succeeded in doing, but the emperor responded to the tumult by imposing heavy fines on certain citizens. The next day both the Portian Basilica and the New Basilica were filled with people, and the former, if not also the latter, was surrounded by imperial troops. The situation throughout the city was tense, and Ambrose confesses to his sister that he was frightened at the possibility of such wholesale anarchy breaking out that Milan would be destroyed, although he declares that he himself would have been willing to die if necessary. Still he refused to give in. Finally Ambrose was commanded outright to surrender the Portian Basilica. His letter recounts how he responded, evidently via intermediaries, to Valentinian. Sketching out a principle that had previously been unknown and that was to have historic consequences, he recorded for his sister's benefit:

> It is neither lawful for me to hand [the basilica] over nor proper for you, O Emperor, to accept it. Under no law may you violate the house of a private person. Do you think that you may seize the house of God? It is alleged that everything is permitted to the emperor and that all things are his. I reply: Do not so burden yourself, O Emperor, as to believe that you have any imperial right to those things that are divine. Do not so exalt yourself. Rather, if you wish to rule longer, be subject to God. It is written: 'What is God's is for God, what is Caesar's is for Caesar' (Mark 12:17). The palaces belong to the emperor, the churches to the bishop. To you has been committed jurisdiction over public buildings, not over sacred ones. Once more the emperor is said to have commanded: I too must have a basilica. I responded: You are not allowed to have one. What are you doing with an adulteress [i.e., the Arian heresy]? For she is an adulteress who is not joined to Christ by lawful wedlock.
>
> (Letter 20.19)

There were more words exchanged and there was further jockeying for advantage, but by the end of the week the emperor had backed down – not, however, without having uttered threats against Ambrose. All the churches of Milan were once again indisputably in the hands of the orthodox, and the fines that had been imposed a few days before were lifted. The emperor had retreated both because Ambrose was by far the more unyielding in his position and because the people seem to have supported their bishop.

The second phase of this confrontation took place a year later, in the winter and early spring of 386. Toward the end of January of that year Valentinian – once again almost surely at the urging of Justina – issued an edict allowing Arians to hold church services and promising to retaliate against those who in any way might seek to obstruct this new law, which of course flew in the face of Theodosius' edict of 380. The Bishop of Milan was the implicit object of this menacing vow.

In the latter half of March Ambrose convoked a synod of the bishops of the locality who apparently offered him the support that he needed to continue to resist the court. Very soon after, an imperial official named Dalmatius approached Ambrose with an order from Valentinian to appear at court in order to debate with Auxentius, an Arian bishop (not to be confused with the Arian bishop of the same name whom Ambrose had succeeded in Milan) who had recently taken up residence in the imperial household. The debate would, according to plan, be judged by laymen chosen by both Auxentius and Ambrose. Auxentius had already agreed to the proposal and had selected his judges. As for Ambrose, his reply to the emperor can be found in Letter 21, addressed to Valentinian. He refused to accede to the order, stating as his chief reason his conviction that clerics should not be judged by the laity. Were his beliefs and those of Auxentius to be submitted to a synod of bishops, he would, he said, willingly appear before it. He also pointed out to Valentinian that, given the court's pro-Arian stance, any of the lay judges who might show themselves partial to orthodoxy would be subject to the wrath of the court.

Valentinian's reaction to Ambrose's letter, which (as it has come down to us) had been phrased in such a way as to be both courteous and firm, was immediate. An Arian mob attacked the Portian Basilica and soldiers were stationed outside it in order to prevent the orthodox from entering. But the soldiers were evidently not convinced of the justice of their cause, and in fact they permitted Catholics to go into the church and demonstrated in other ways that their sympathies did not necessarily lie with the Arians. Meanwhile, within the basilica, the people encouraged one another with praying and singing. There was little else for Valentinian to do on seeing the response to his unpopular action than to perform an about-face. Ambrose had won a second time against the imperial court, and this time the victory appears to have been decisive. Valentinian's pro-Arian legislation of the previous January was a dead letter. Never again did the court offer serious opposition to Ambrose in the matter of religion, and never again did Arianism itself threaten Catholic orthodoxy in Milan as it once had.

Should this victory have needed reinforcement, it received it three months later, on 17 June, in the form of the discovery of the bodies of two hitherto unknown martyrs, Protasius and Gervasius. Letter 22, written by Ambrose to his sister, supplements the information supplied by Paulinus in this regard. It tells us that Ambrose was persuaded by the people to consecrate the newly built Ambrosian Basilica on the condition that he would find the relics of some martyrs to place in it. With that, and under the inspiration of 'a kind of prophetic ardor,' he ordered the ground to be excavated near the graves of the martyrs Felix and Nabor, and in a short while the still bloody bones of two men of extraordinary size were exhumed. They were identified – we are not told exactly how – as the remains of Protasius and Gervasius, two martyrs who had died in an early persecution. The two skeletons, accompanied by an enthusiastic crowd, were brought first to the so-called Basilica of Fausta and then, on the following day, to the Ambrosian Basilica. As they were being transported to their final resting place, to the spot beneath the altar that Ambrose had originally reserved for himself alone, numerous miraculous cures were effected, most notably that of a blind man named Severus. It has been argued that all of these events were somehow staged by Ambrose in order to promote the cause of orthodoxy.[12] Be that as it may, the discovery of the bones of the two men and the cures of the sick, especially the restoration of Severus' eyesight, were widely accepted as proof that God was on the side of Ambrose and the orthodox.

While Ambrose faced Arianism on one front, on another he was pitted against paganism. It is true that the pagan religion had for the most part experienced a steady and surprisingly unresisting decline since the first third of the fourth century, when Constantine had adopted Christianity and indicated his disfavor toward the ancient gods. Even the reign of Julian, from 361 to 363, hardly represented a triumph for paganism: Julian himself did not have the commanding personality that might have given his program of pagan revival greater plausibility, and he was unable to persuade the people that a resurgent paganism was the wave of the future. He was, in any event, succeeded in the imperial office by convinced Christians. Still, the old religion was far from moribund, and many pagan customs survived until Ambrose's day, and beyond.

Among the customs that continued into the final quarter of the fourth century was the maintenance of an altar to the goddess Victory, along with a statue of the goddess herself, near the entrance to the Senate in Rome. The deliberations of the Senate were understood by the pagans to occur under the influence of the goddess, and at certain times the senators were expected to sprinkle incense on the altar in honor of the goddess and to swear upon it. Toward the end of his reign the Emperor Constantius II removed the altar as being incompatible with the Christian tone that he was seeking to promote. (To what extent the statue of Victory was involved in the controversy over the altar is uncertain; it too seems to have been removed at some point or points, but the same opprobrium does not appear to have been attached to it as to the altar.) There was little adverse reaction to this change. It was, anyhow, not long-lasting, since Julian restored the altar at the beginning of his reign. There it stayed in the Senate house until 382, when Gratian removed it once again as part of a wider campaign that both he and his co-emperor in the east, Theodosius, were waging against paganism and in which we may be sure that Ambrose played a significant role, although in fact there is no direct evidence of such on his part. The campaign included the elimination of the state subsidies enjoyed by the temples and the pagan priesthoods along with several other measures designed to weaken the pagan cult.

In the spring of 383 Magnus Maximus, who was commanding Roman troops in Britain, was proclaimed emperor by his rebellious soldiers. On 25 August of the same year Gratian was assassinated at Lyons by one of his own officials and the usurper Maximus soon after gained control of Gaul. The West was in turmoil. In an attempt not to alienate a large part of the population, Gratian's successor, Valentinian II, ceased to enforce his half-brother's anti-pagan legislation. Sensing that the troubled situation was to their advantage, in August of the following year the pagan senators – apparently the minority in a now mostly Christian Senate – commissioned one of their own, Quintus Aurelius Symmachus, the prefect of Rome and a man of considerable standing, to ask Valentinian for the restoration of the Altar of Victory. The result was Symmachus' celebrated *relatio*, or appeal, addressed to the young emperor and translated on pp. 179–84 of the present volume. The relatively brief document is a masterful plea for the toleration of the pagan cult that, Symmachus asserts, had brought Rome to greatness. The pagans did not demand a return to the exclusive privileges of former times; they were willing to live with Christianity on an equal basis, as Symmachus implies in the most memorable lines of the appeal:

> It is equitable that whatever all worship be considered one. We gaze upon the same stars, the sky is common to all, the same world envelops us. What difference does it make by what judgement a person searches out the truth? So great a mystery cannot be arrived at by one path.
>
> (10)

Combined with the pleas for the acceptance of the pagan cult, and particularly for the reinstatement of the Altar of Victory, was a request for the restoration of the public subsidies that had been abolished by Gratian and that were deemed necessary for the maintenance of the cult.

Ambrose was somehow apprised of the existence of the *relatio*, in a letter of his own to Valentinian, translated on pp. 174–79, he demanded a copy of it so that he could see it for himself and compose a suitable response. Anticipating that Valentinian could easily yield to Symmachus' powers of persuasion or be moved by his nobility and prestige, Ambrose threatened him, should he give in, with episcopal resistance and with the reproaches of his dead brother and father. He even cut out from under the 13-year-old emperor the excuse of his youth:

> What will you reply [to the bishop who refuses your offerings]? That you are a boy who made a mistake? Every age is perfect as far as Christ is concerned ... Even children have with fearless words confessed Christ before their persecutors.
>
> (Letter 17.15)

This letter seems to have been sufficient to convince Valentinian that he must not countenance the pagan demands. Ambrose's actual reply to the *relatio*, translated on pp. 184–94, indicates that, by the time he had written it, Valentinian had already made up his mind (cf. Letter 18.1). Now Ambrose's tone is blandishing, and he compliments the emperor on the strength of his faith. But the bulk of this second letter, which seems to have been composed as a kind of formal statement of the bishop's position, probably with a view to posterity, is a detailed refutation of Symmachus' arguments.

Some years later, in 389 or 390, the pagan senators approached the Emperor Theodosius to ask him to restore the public subsidies for the cult. This time there seems to have been no mention made of the Altar of Victory. Theodosius (who was by now the most important of the three emperors, including not only Valentinian but also Theodosius' own son Arcadius) hesitated, but Ambrose managed to convince him to turn down the request. None the less, upset with the fact that the bishop was being informed of some of the confidential decisions of the imperial consistory, and annoyed with him for what he considered to be his interference in state affairs, Theodosius forbade Ambrose from being thus informed and prohibited him, at least for a time, from coming near him. Ambrose respected the emperor's desire to be undisturbed almost surely with the realization that he must not press Theodosius lest he lose any advantage that he had gained.

There next occurred the tragic event that, from the political perspective, gave Ambrose a clear ascendency over the emperor. In 390, perhaps toward the middle of the year, the people of the Greek city of Thessalonika rioted over the imprisonment of one of their favorite charioteers on a charge of immorality, and in the course of the uproar the commander of the garrison, Botheric, was slain, along with several other officials. Theodosius, enraged by this act, allowed his fury to overcome him, and he devised a punishment that stunned even a world habituated to imperial excesses: he ordered his soldiers to lure the citizens of Thessalonika into a public theater and to massacre them there. Ambrose, as in the past, was somehow informed of the emperor's decision. Although Theodosius' prohibition on the bishop's access to him was still in force, Ambrose approached him several times to plead with him to rescind his order. When at last he did so, it was too late. Theodoret reports in his *Ecclesiastical History* (5.17) that as many as 7,000 died in the carnage.

Ambrose now wrote privately to the emperor (Letter 51), expressing his affection for Theodosius but demanding that he do penance. Paulinus gives the impression, which has been seized upon by the popular imagination, that Ambrose turned Theodosius away at the door of his cathedral when he came to participate in the eucharist shortly after word of the massacre had reached Milan (cf. 24). What took place, however, aside from the fact that the emperor was not permitted to receive the sacraments and that he performed public penance, is the subject of speculation. The excommunication and penance considered appropriate for the crime were, at any rate, short by the standards of the ancient Church: by Christmastime they were lifted, and the extraordinary drama of an emperor's ecclesiastical humiliation was over.

Not long after Theodosius' rehabilitation, in late February of 391, the emperor, joined by his co-emperors, issued the most stringent edict against paganism that had yet come from the imperial hand. It forbade not only sacrifice but even approaching or wandering through the pagan shrines, and it imposed heavy fines in gold on certain public officials who ignored the law. Since Theodosius was in Milan when the edict was issued, it is perfectly reasonable to assume that Ambrose had influenced the recently shriven emperor. Another law directed specifically against the pagan cult in Egypt followed in June of that year. In 392 the pagan senators addressed themselves to

Valentinian to ask for the restoration of the cult subsidies, only to be
rebuffed by him for a final time. On 15 May the young emperor died
in Vienne, whether by suicide or murder it is uncertain.

A final important encounter with the forces of paganism still
awaited Ambrose. Arbogast, a pagan Frank who had seized high
office in 388 and who in that same year had defeated the usurper
Magnus Maximus in battle, was soon after designated by Theodosius
as a kind of guardian for Valentinian, who was only 7 years old at the
time. The appointment turned out to be a tragic mistake, for the
relationship between the young emperor and his mentor was
strained at best, and several ancient historians accused Arbogast of
having murdered Valentinian. In August of 392, a few months after
Valentinian's death, Arbogast found himself well enough positioned
to raise a rhetorician named Eugenius to the imperial throne – his
own intention being to act as the power behind the throne. Eugenius, who had initially been reluctant, now sought recognition from
Theodosius as legitimate emperor, and to that end he wrote to
Ambrose, knowing that the bishop's opinion carried weight with
Theodosius. Ambrose, however, did not reply. Meanwhile, a delegation of pagan senators went to Gaul to see Eugenius and to make
the familiar request concerning the restoration of the cult subsidies.
They might well have thought that this time they would receive a
positive hearing since, although Eugenius was a Christian, his
religion seems to have been for the most part a nominal affair. But
Eugenius turned down not only this delegation but also a second
one: despite his lackluster commitment to Christianity and his political debt to the pagan Arbogast, he was determined to have good
relations with the Church.

Before the coming of the second delegation Eugenius wrote once
more to Ambrose. When at last the bishop replied in a letter that has
not survived, he appears to have done so without endorsing the
usurper's claim to legitimacy. It is evident that Ambrose was waiting
to see whether Theodosius would recognize Eugenius, and that he
would follow Theodosius' lead. Then, in early 393, Theodosius
decided against Eugenius, whereupon the usurper sent the subsidies
for the cult that had been requested to the pagan senators: politically
speaking, there was no place for him to turn now but to his pagan
supporters. With that, Ambrose himself broke definitively with
Eugenius, explaining to him in a letter (57.11) what had been his
thoughts all along – that he had never trusted Eugenius, and that he
was sure that he would eventually accede to the pagan demands.

Indeed, when Eugenius left Gaul to confront Theodosius militarily in Italy in the spring of 393, Ambrose refused to see the usurper, fleeing instead to Bologna, then to Faenza and Florence. He only returned to Milan the following year, when Eugenius and his troops had left the city. Toward the beginning of September 394 Eugenius and Arbogast and their forces were defeated by Theodosius in a battle at the River Frigidus, not far from Aquileia. Arbogast's boast, recorded by Paulinus (cf. 31), that he would turn the cathedral of Milan into a stable once he had returned victorious to the city, had come to naught. Theodosius was now the undisputed emperor, and Ambrose praised him fulsomely in a letter (61) as the restorer of peace to both the Empire and the Church. Paganism had ceased to be a threat.

Between the conflict with Valentinian and Justina in 385–86 over the imperial court's demand for a basilica and the events of 389–90 that culminated in the Thessalonikan massacre and Theodosius' public penance, there was yet another incident involving Ambrose on the one hand and the emperor on the other. Sometime in the summer of 388, the Bishop of Callinicum, a relatively insignificant frontier town on the banks of the Euphrates, was accused of having instigated the burning of a local synagogue in reaction to an unspecified offense supposedly committed by the Jews against the Christians. About the same time, a group of monks burned down a temple of the Valentinian gnostics, situated in a village probably located not far from Antioch, when the Valentinians interfered with a procession of theirs. Theodosius was told of these two occurrences by one of his officials in the east, and he decided that those who had set fire to the synagogue should be punished, that the bishop (whose name we are not told) would have to pay to rebuild it, and that the monks who had destroyed the Valentinian temple must be penalized.

When Ambrose was alerted to Theodosius' decision he sent him a long letter urging him to change his mind. He warned the emperor that if the Bishop of Callinicum submitted to rebuilding the synagogue it would be an act of apostasy, whereas if he resisted the imperial order he might become a martyr. Much of the letter is a kind of defense of the burning of the synagogue (the loss of the Valentinians' temple seemed to be of considerably less consequence), and Ambrose went so far as to declare that he was willing to take responsibility for the arson himself:

34

This is what I myself ask, O emperor – that you punish me instead, and, if you think this a crime, that you ascribe it to me. Why pronounce judgement on the absent? Here you have someone at hand, here you have someone who is confessing his guilt. I declare that I burned down the synagogue. In any event I ordered them to do it lest there be some place where Christ was denied.

(Letter 40.8)

These words and many more of the same tone, which put Ambrose in the worst possible light, apparently persuaded Theodosius to back down at least on his insistence that the bishop rebuild the synagogue. More persuasion was to follow.

A further letter to Marcellina, some of the details of which are taken up by Paulinus in his biography (cf. 23), describes Ambrose's first encounter with Theodosius after he had written to him. The bishop was preaching a long homily in the cathedral of Milan, in which he was comparing the Jews unfavorably with the Christians, when suddenly and unexpectedly he began to address himself to the emperor, who was part of the congregation. Boldly he told him that he owed his lofty position to God and that he must not allow God's enemies – the Jews – to gain the upper hand over his servants; rather, he must forgive those of God's servants who had erred and restore peace to the Church. With that he came down from the pulpit, and a brief exchange took place between him and the emperor, interrupted once by an officer of Theodosius, whom the bishop instantly rebuked for interfering in a matter that was none of his concern. Unless Theodosius promised to lift every sanction against all the Christians involved in the damage done to the synagogue and the Valentinian temple, Ambrose threatened not to go on with the liturgy. The emperor, faced with a bishop whose determination he had no reason to doubt, and surrounded by a congregation that almost surely shared their bishop's harsh sentiments about the Jews, had little alternative but to surrender, and he did. The eucharist was then celebrated and, as Ambrose stated at the very conclusion of his letter to his sister,

so great was the grace of the offering that I myself sensed that that grace was all the more pleasing to our God, and that the divine presence was not lacking. And so everything was done in accordance with my wish.

(Letter 41.28)

Much of what has been recounted thus far of Ambrose's public activity may give the impression that his stance *vis-à-vis* the imperial authorities, and particularly the emperor himself, was overwhelmingly adversarial. But this was by no means the case. Mention has already been made of the close relationship that the bishop enjoyed with Gratian, at least in the final years of his life. Ambrose was Gratian's mentor, and he remarks in his funeral oration on Valentinian (80) that Gratian often spoke his name shortly before he was murdered in Gaul. As for Valentinian, the same funeral oration suggests a different relationship with Ambrose than one might infer just from the story of the confrontation between the bishop and the imperial court that occurred in 385 and 386. Sometime after this crisis the young emperor, undoubtedly following the death of his domineering mother Justina in 388, had a change of heart and expressed a desire to be baptized by Ambrose. Valentinian in fact never received baptism; he was a catechumen at the time of his death, but, if we are to believe Ambrose's eulogy of him (52-53), his desire to be baptized was strong and persistent. Ambrose refers obliquely to the crisis of·385–86, but that was a thing of the past, and the bishop's praise of the deceased emperor is unstinting. In the course of his eulogy (28) he also reminds the grieving congregation that twice he had undertaken a mission to Gaul (in late 383 and again probably in 386) on Valentinian's behalf to plead with the usurper Maximus for the return of Gratian's body and, if possible, to secure peace between the two. Ambrose, in other words, was a person of nuance and hardly a spontaneous and unreflecting adversary of the imperial house or its aims, even under Valentinian.

Of the three emperors with whom Ambrose was particularly associated, Theodosius is the one whose name is perhaps mentioned most frequently in tandem with that of the bishop. Whereas Gratian and Valentinian were youths, Theodosius was no more than seven or eight years younger than Ambrose, and unlike them he was not almost constantly in Ambrose's shadow: he was a great personage in his own right, with a long list of achievements to his credit. Despite their occasional disagreements, despite Ambrose's insistence that the emperor perform a humiliating public penance, the bond between the two men seems to have been deep and sincere. And when the time came for him to preach Theodosius' eulogy, as it did on 25 February 395, the fortieth day after the emperor's death, Ambrose's words made it clear that he saw in Theodosius the ideal of the Christian ruler.[13]

Ambrose is best known for his activity in the area of Church–state relations, but there were other sides to him that must not be overlooked. As Bishop of Milan his chief task was to lead the Christian community in that city, and his leadership did not confine itself to dramatic events like facing down the imperial court over the issue of Church property or obliging an emperor to perform public penance. Chances are that Ambrose's flock would have experienced their shepherd primarily as a liturgical presence. He tells us himself in one of his letters to Marcellina (20.15) that he celebrated the eucharist every day, which was not a universal practice at the time. We do not know exactly to what extent Ambrose was a liturgical innovator. The Ambrosian Rite, which takes its name from him and which is to this day followed in Milan, cannot be traced directly back to him. He was, however, the author of hymns that were intended to be sung congregationally (the four undoubtedly authentic ones have been translated in this volume: Cf. pp. 167–73), and he introduced antiphons into the Western Church. Moreover, he was a frequent, if not daily, preacher. He would certainly have agreed with Gregory Nazianzen (cf. Oration 2.35), although he did not say it quite so directly, that preaching was a bishop's foremost responsibility. Letter 2, written by Ambrose in early 379 to a certain Constantius, shortly after its recipient had been ordained to the episcopacy, is by and large an instruction in the sort of preaching that a bishop should engage in. We know from the *Confessions* (6.3.4) that Ambrose's sermons were instrumental in convincing Augustine of the plausibility of the Christian faith. The quality of these sermons we can judge for ourselves, since many of them have survived in the form of treatises.

As has been said earlier in this essay, accessibility was an important episcopal virtue in antiquity. Another passage from Augustine's *Confessions* (6.3.3) gives us an insight into the public character of Ambrose's life: his residence, we are told, was open to whoever wanted to come in, and none of his visitors was announced beforehand. Sometimes, as visitors arrived, they might even have found him absorbed in his reading, trying to snatch a few moments of quiet from a busy schedule. Augustine relates that at such occasions he would not interrupt him, but most likely not everyone was so sensitive. As a kind of unintentional testimony to his approachability, Paulinus recounts an incident that occurred when Ambrose was a guest at the home of a distinguished Roman matron (cf. 10). A female bathkeeper – in other words, a woman of very low social standing – sought him out because she had heard that he was nearby and she believed that he could cure the paralysis that had disabled her. She had herself transported directly to him at the matron's home, and she clung to him as he prayed for her and placed his hands on her. A further aspect of Ambrose's accessibility which was shared, it would appear, by all his great contemporaries, and notably by Augustine, was his readiness to correspond with those who wrote to him, whether to answer serious theological questions or just to be friendly. Indeed, his correspondence was usually written in his own hand (cf. Letter 47.1–3).

Concern for the poor was yet another value that was central to the ancient understanding of the episcopacy, and Ambrose was exemplary in this regard. His writings, of which the treatise *On Naboth* is particularly striking, indicate a passionate commitment to alleviating the misery of the poor. And Ambrose practiced what he preached: at the time of his ordination, Paulinus notes, he gave away all his property to the Church and to the poor, after seeing to it that his sister Marcellina was provided for (cf. 38). Some years later, as we know from his own account in the treatise *On the Duties of Ministers* (2.28.136–43), he melted down the sacred vessels of the Church at Milan in order to ransom captives. For this he was blamed by the Arians, who were only too happy to find something to accuse him of, but he defended himself by asserting that 'the Church has gold not for keeping but for disbursing and for aiding those in need.'

Letter 5, written to Bishop Syagrius of Verona, gives us an insight into Ambrose's handling of one of the tasks that particularly occupied the bishops of the post-Constantinian Church – namely, that of hearing and deciding cases involving both civil and ecclesiastical matters. The letter in question deals with the case of a Veronese virgin named Indicia, who had been accused of impurity. On flimsy evidence Syagrius had ordered her to be inspected by a midwife, but the outcome of the inspection was unclear, due to the midwife's supposed lack of expertise. The case eventually made its way to Ambrose. The letter to Syagrius shows that Ambrose felt that the Bishop of Verona had acted poorly throughout the affair, both by accepting the admissibility of evidence that was really no more than rumor and by subjecting Indicia to the humiliation of having her virginity examined. On the day appointed by Ambrose for the trial in Milan, no one came forward to accuse her. So Ambrose then questioned three women whose judgement he trusted, including his sister, who had known the defendant in Rome, and, when they had testified to Indicia's probity, he declared her innocent. He also excommunicated three men who had spread calumnious rumors about her. The case, which must have been one of hundreds that Ambrose would have heard, demonstrates the bishop's decisiveness and the anger of which he was capable when faced with a likely injustice. We may also look to Letter 82, which has to do with a civil suit regarding property rights within a single family (and hence no less potentially volatile than a case of possibly squandered virginity). Here Ambrose decided that the best course was to effect a compromise between the parties, while acknowledging that not everyone would be completely satisfied.

Finally, it fell to bishops in antiquity to reconcile sinners to the Church. Ambrose did this not only in the famous instance of Theodosius but, if we are to trust his biographer, in numerous others also. Paulinus speaks movingly of Ambrose's sympathy for the sinners who confessed their offenses to him: 'he so wept as to compel the other person to weep as well, for he seemed to himself to be cast down along with anyone else who was cast down' (39). In his treatise *On Repentance* (2.8.73) Ambrose himself drew a connection between his having been raised from unworthiness to the episcopate and how he must deal with sinners:

> I knew that I was not worthy to be called a bishop since I had given myself to this world, but by your grace I am what I am. Indeed, I am the least of all the bishops and the lowest in terms of merit. Yet, inasmuch as I too have taken up some labor on behalf of your Church, protect this fruit, so as not to allow to perish as a bishop him whom you called to the office of bishop when he was lost. And grant first that I may know how to console sinners with profound sensitivity, for this is the highest virtue ... Whenever the offense of some sinner is laid bare, let me be compassionate. Let me not rebuke him proudly but mourn and weep, so that as I shed tears over someone else I may weep for myself.

Any bishop, but especially the bishop of a city as influential as Milan, would eventually be called upon to involve himself in matters further afield and in the larger affairs of the Church. This meant, for example, ordaining bishops for other cities. Ambrose tells us that he was responsible for at least two such ordinations – that of Anemius in Sirmium in the late 370s and that of an unnamed bishop for Pavia in 397, shortly before his death – but there were certainly many more, including the famous Gaudentius of Brescia, who refers to his having been ordained by Ambrose.

It also meant arranging for and attending synods and councils. Ambrose participated in at least six of these, and possibly more (in addition to the local synods that he probably held once a year around Eastertime in Milan). The first of these took place at Sirmium in the second half of the 370s. Although Ambrose had only recently been elected bishop, he was the natural leader of the gathering both because of the importance of Milan and because of his connections with the highest circles in Sirmium. The result of the synod, which has already been mentioned, was a strengthening of the orthodox Christian position through the deposing of several Arian clerics. A second synod in which Ambrose participated was held in Rome in 378, under the presidency of Damasus, who was Bishop of Rome at the time. This synod regulated some affairs of the Roman see and determined that bishops should be judged by their peers and not by civil authorities. Possibly a year later a synod was convened at an unknown location in northern Italy, presided over by Ambrose, at which Bishop Leontius of Salona was deposed for his Arian tendencies. In 381 the Bishop of Milan played a major role at the council of Aquileia, which has previously been alluded to and which struck an important blow against Arianism.

Ambrose was present at a council that met in 382 in Rome, which he had helped to organize and which he had originally intended to be a kind of western counterpart to the great Council of Constantinople, held the previous year. Although eastern bishops were invited to attend, only two of them responded positively to the invitation – Paulinus (not Ambrose's biographer), whose claim to the see of Antioch was hotly disputed, and Epiphanius of Salamis. Since they brought with them the priest Jerome as their interpreter and adviser, Ambrose and the soon-to-be translator of the Vulgate would have met during the course of the gathering for their first and only time. The council made provisions for those who were converting from the Apollinarian heresy to orthodox Christianity. It also tried, with less success, to solve the knotty problem of the Antiochene episcopate, which had caused ecclesiastical disarray since 362 and which is known to history as the Meletian Schism, by recognizing Paulinus as the legitimate Bishop of Antioch, whereas the eastern hierarchy overwhelmingly favored his rival Flavian. The Roman council only added to the already rampant confusion.

The next and last synod which we know that Ambrose attended was convened in Capua about ten years later, in either late 391 or early 392, and its sole purpose seems to have been to resolve the Meletian Schism. This time the bishops acted with greater circumspection. Evagrius had succeeded Paulinus, who had died in the interim, and both he and Flavian had been requested to attend the synod. While only Evagrius appeared, the assembled bishops refrained from endorsing him, while simultaneously faulting Flavian for his absence. On behalf of the synod, Ambrose, who seems to have set the tone of balance that marked the gathering, wrote to Bishop Theophilus of Alexandria, asking him to call both Flavian and Evagrius to Alexandria to make a judgement in the matter. In his letter he reported:

> We do not grant that our brother Evagrius has what looks to be a good case when he believes that he occupies the more defensible position because Flavian shuns him, or when he thinks that his opponent is in the same situation that he is, with each of them focusing more on the defects of the other's ordination than on the validity of his own.

> (Letter 56.5)

The synod of Capua did not put an end to the Meletian Schism, which continued until 413, but at least it showed a greater sensitivity to the complexities of the matter than had the council of Rome some ten years previously, and that greater sensitivity appears to have been Ambrose's contribution and the fruit of his considerable diplomatic skills.

It would not be an exaggeration to say that, during his more than two decades as Bishop of Milan, Ambrose was the most important ecclesiastical figure in Italy and even in the West. The two Bishops of Rome (the only see in Italy or the West that could rival his) in those years, Damasus (366–84) and Siricius (384–99), were not inconsequential persons, to be sure. Far from it: both were intelligent and active men, and both promoted the claims of the papacy with success. Ambrose, for his part, was not embarrassed to defer to the Roman Church, which he describes in a document sent to the emperors after the council of Aquileia as 'the head of the whole Roman world, and that sacred trust of the apostles ... from which the rights of a venerable communion flow out upon the people' (Letter 11.4). When he wrote to Theophilus of Alexandria, asking him to hear the case of Flavian and Evagrius, he advised him to inform Damasus of the outcome and declared that he would accept his verdict himself once he had learned of Damasus' approval (cf. Letter 56.7). In his treatise *On the Sacraments* (3.1.5–7) he defended a baptismal footwashing ceremony that was part of the Milanese liturgy but unknown in Rome. It is clear that Rome set some kind of standard that should not lightly be deviated from, for Ambrose writes: 'I desire to follow the Roman Church in all things.' But he adds: 'Yet we too have human intelligence,' and he goes on to say that Peter himself, 'a bishop of the Roman Church,' had had his feet washed by Christ. In other words, Ambrose justified the ritual of baptismal footwashing at Milan in the face of Roman criticism (or at least criticism favorable to Roman liturgical practices) by a clever appeal to Peter, the ultimate Roman authority.

For all his deference to Rome, however, Ambrose had a moral stature with which Damasus, for one, could not compete. The latter's rise to the Roman episcopate had been a scandalous affair that shocked the Church. A deacon named Ursinus had been elected first by one faction, followed a few days later by Damasus' election by another. The two groups battled it out, leaving more than a hundred dead, before Damasus was securely in office. About five years later Ursinus' partisans lodged a charge, apparently of adultery, against Damasus, which must not at all have seemed absurd in view of the luxurious lifestyle that he was known to lead. He was acquitted by the emperor, but his moral authority had suffered a severe blow. As for Siricius, although he was not universally respected, his character was relatively blameless.

But Ambrose overshadowed them both. Not only was he the bishop of what had become the capital of the West, with access to the imperial court; he was also a man of unquestioned integrity in the sense that, even when he acted unjustly, as was the case more than once, he did so not for private gain of any kind but in the service of a greater cause. With all his redoubtable skills he had embraced the Church's good, for better or for worse, as his own. It is not surprising that he enjoyed a vast reputation. In the winter of 381–82 he was visited by the ill-fated and rather mysterious Spanish bishop, Priscillian of Avila, who was seeking support with regard to the accusations of Manicheanism and immorality that had been made against him. Ambrose offered him no help, nor did Damasus, whom he also saw, but both men recoiled with disgust when he was executed on the charge of magic in 385 under Maximus. Paulinus mentions two sages who traveled from Persia to Milan in order to form an estimation of Ambrose's wisdom (cf. 25). When they left Milan, it was in amazement and admiration. Their next stop was Rome, and it is somewhat telling that their goal there was not the bishop (whether Damasus or Siricius we do not know, since no date is hinted at) but rather the illustrious Probus, Ambrose's erstwhile patron. And another visitor from afar who appears in the pages of Ambrose's biography is the otherwise unknown Queen Frigitil of the Marcomanni, a Germanic tribe that inhabited the region of present-day Bohemia. She had corresponded with Ambrose and sent him gifts, but by the time she came to Milan to see him he was already dead (cf. 36).

It would probably not be inaccurate to say that, after the death of the towering Basil of Caesarea ('the Great') in 379, Ambrose was the most important ecclesiastical figure in the entire Christian world. Augustine's career only began as Ambrose's was drawing to a close, and, although Augustine was the more brilliant thinker of the two, he was not the mighty public personage that Ambrose was. Theophilus, Bishop of Alexandria from 385 to 412, was perhaps the only such personage who could compare to Ambrose, but too much unscrupulousness, ambition and violence are linked to his name, and too little love for the Church outside of Alexandria and Egypt.

Ambrose was also, of course, a man with a more private side to his life. His funeral oration for his brother Satyrus, who died a few years after Ambrose's ordination, and the contact that he maintained with his sister Marcellina imply bonds of deep affection among the three siblings. About his feelings for his father and mother he says nothing, but there is no reason whatsoever to imagine that they were less than pious. His parents, certainly his father and most likely his mother too, had died by the time of his ordination. Hence Ambrose's immediate family was small, since his brother and sister never married.

But his friends and connections must have been many. Among the former particular mention should be made of Simplicianus, the man who was to succeed him as Bishop of Milan, although he was older than Ambrose. Ambrose refers to him as both a friend and a father (cf. Letter 37.2), and Simplicianus may have served as a kind of mentor to him. It is even possible that he counted the pagan Symmachus among his friends (eight of Symmachus' surviving letters, in any event, are addressed to the bishop), although he strenuously opposed him in the matter of the Altar of Victory. Yet Ambrose does not bare his soul about friendship and about his friends as do Augustine, for instance, or Gregory Nazianzen. When he concludes his lengthy treatise *On the Duties of Ministers* with several pages on the virtue of friendship (3.22.125–38) he does so without ever betraying anything necessarily personal. And his letters to his friends have a standard formality to them, even when they are playful (like Letter 3 to a certain Bishop Felix, thanking him for a gift of truffles), which suggests the fundamental reserve typical of *Romanitas*.

The early fifth-century mosaic of Ambrose in the Chapel of San Vittore in Ciel d'Oro in the Basilica of Saint Ambrose in Milan portrays a rather gaunt and even haggard figure. Allowing for a certain desire on the part of the unknown artist to emphasize the ascetical, 'the holy,' the particularity of the depiction forbids us from dismissing it as false. We may infer from it that, physically, Ambrose was not a robust man. From Augustine's *Confessions* we learn something about Ambrose's health that must have preoccupied him, given the amount of public speaking that he was obliged to do. In the well-known passage (6.3.3) that relates the bishop's habit of reading silently to himself rather than aloud, as seems to have been customary in antiquity, Augustine ventures that perhaps his reason for doing this was to spare his voice, which easily grew hoarse. In other words, Ambrose evidently suffered from some chronic malady of the throat, which he himself appears to hint at toward the end of one of his sermons (cf. *On the Sacraments* 1.6.24).

As for Ambrose's character, his soul, some of its qualities have already at least been alluded to, or can easily be gleaned from his behavior at various moments – determination, decisiveness, fearlessness, zeal, compassion, hospitality, the identification of the Church's good (and hence, as he saw it, Christ's good) as his own, political astuteness, reserve, and also intolerance. To this catalogue Paulinus adds another trait or traits indispensable to the holy man of Christian antiquity – a love of fasting, of vigils and of prayer. His willingness to part with his property upon ordination points not only to a concern for the poor but also to an attraction to poverty itself, which Paulinus underlines when he describes Ambrose as Christ's 'stripped and unencumbered soldier,' desirous of following his Lord, who had himself embraced poverty when he embraced the human condition (38).

Ambrose's letters reveal a willingness to endure martyrdom. Twice, in writing to Marcellina (Letter 20.5, 28), he expressed a readiness to shed his own blood in the context of the confrontation with the imperial court in 386. Two months later he wrote to her of what he had told the people of Milan after having discovered the bones of the martyrs Gervasius and Protasius – that he had found them because (and here one senses a thwarted yearning) he was unworthy to be a martyr himself (cf. Letter 22.12). And a year after that, in a letter to the priest Horantianus, he declares:

> I plead for a martyr's suffering, and the Holy Spirit is disposed [to grant it], but when he sees the weakness of my flesh, lest in desiring greater things I let slip smaller ones, he says: 'This you cannot accept.' What sorts of opportunities I have had, and almost at the very brink I have been called back!
>
> (Letter 36.4)

These words seem to be more than mere bravado or lip service paid to the ideal of martyrdom that so fascinated the early Christians.

From Ambrose's attraction to poverty and, even more, his longing for martyrdom it is not too far a distance to go to his devotion to Christ. Occasionally dropping his natural reserve, he displays to his readers the testimony of a deeply affective relationship with Christ. Thus, in his early treatise *On the Faith*, while discussing Christ's human nature and the sufferings that he took upon himself on behalf of humankind, Ambrose suddenly ceases speaking of the Savior in the third person and begins to address him directly and with touching warmth:

> You are afflicted, Lord Jesus, not because of your wounds but because of mine, not because of your death but because of my frailty. As the prophet says: 'For he is afflicted on our account' (Is 53:4). And we, Lord, thought that you were in affliction when you were afflicted not on your own account but for me.
>
> (2.7.54)

The later treatise *On Repentance* contains a series of such direct addresses, all in the context of the theme of repentance, for example:

> Would that you might reserve for me, O Jesus, the washing of your feet, which you sullied by walking in me!
>
> (2.8.67)

Would that you might deign to come to this tomb of mine,
Lord Jesus, and that you might wash me with your tears! For
my eyes are hard and I do not have such tears as to be able to
wash away my sins. If you weep for me, I shall be saved.

(2.8.71)

Ambrose's absorption with Christ is further evidenced by the great
number of times that he mentions him in his treatises on the Old
Testament, where he finds the Savior prefigured everywhere. This,
however, is not so very unusual in the writings of the Fathers.

What is noteworthy in Ambrose's approach to Christ is his extensive application of the Song of Songs to him. The treatises *On
Virgins* and *On the Mysteries*, both translated in the present volume, see
Christ as the bridegroom of the Song of Songs in reference to
virgins and to the Church, particularly the newly baptized. Elsewhere, as in Letter 29.9–10, for instance, the bridegroom of the
Song of Songs is the bridegroom of the soul. A few lines from that
letter are illustrative:

Let us hasten, then, to him, in whom is the highest goodness,
for he himself is goodness ... If the soul, in its desire and
delight, should taste of this true and highest good and drink it
up by means of these two affections, casting out sadness and
fear, it will glow in an unbelievable way. For when it has kissed
the Word of God (cf. S. of S. 1:2) it does not hold him in his
entirety, nor is it sated, as it says: 'You are sweet, Lord and in
your joy teach me your justifications' (Ps. 119:68). When it has
kissed the Word of God, it yearns for him more than for
anything else beautiful, it loves him more than any other joy; it
desires to see him frequently, to listen to him often; it desires
to be drawn to him so that it may follow him. 'Your name,' it
says, 'is ointment poured out' (S. of S. 1:3). Therefore we
maidens love you (cf. ibid.), therefore we contend over you,
but we are unable to lay hold of you. Draw us, so that we may
be able to run, so that by the fragrance of your perfumes (cf.
ibid.) we may receive the strength to follow you.

It is highly improbable that, when Ambrose writes here of the
Christian soul in general, he is excluding his own in particular.
Although in passages like these he lets himself be inspired by the
great Alexandrian theologian Origen, the fact that he saw Origen's
language as congenial and attractive indicates that, *mutatis mutandis,*

the Alexandrian's relationship to Christ was Ambrose's too. It is a relationship that, with Origen, he finds perfectly appropriate to express in the erotic vocabulary of the Song of Songs. Beneath his Roman reserve, Ambrose's passion had an outlet in his highly expressive love for Christ.

The same Ambrose to whom Paulinus attributes several miracles, including the resurrection of a little boy from the dead (cf. 28), also possessed the gift, according to his biographer, of prophesying the day of his death: it was to be Easter in the year 397 (cf. 40). As the day approached there was a premonition of sorts, which Paulinus himself, who was by then the bishop's secretary, claimed to have seen. While Ambrose was dictating to Paulinus his commentary on a psalm, a small flame descended upon him and entered his mouth. The bishop's face briefly turned snowy white, but then regained its usual color. From that moment on he ceased his writing and dictating (cf. 42).[14] Not very long thereafter Ambrose fell sick, and it was clear that this was to be his final illness. The realization was an alarming one for many people. What would become of Milan and Italy itself after his passing? But even on his deathbed Ambrose had a role of no small importance to play in view of the future, for in effect he named his elderly friend Simplicianus his successor as he lay dying. Then, shortly before the dawn of Easter Sunday, 4 April, with his arms outstretched in the form of a cross (the ancient gesture of prayer) and just after having received Holy Communion, he breathed his last. He was 57 or 58 years old.

Ambrose was laid to rest, as he desired, in the Ambrosian Basilica, at the side of the martyrs Protasius and Gervasius. Miracles surrounded the event. Moreover, as if reluctant to diminish his hero's influence one whit by his death, Paulinus presents him as appearing in visions at strategic moments, offering sorely needed help with vast consequences (cf. 49–52). And those who dared to detract from the great man's reputation were meted out a terrible end. But with or without such occurrences, Ambrose had left his mark on Milan and on the Christian world.

III

As has already been observed, Ambrose is probably best known today as a churchman who exerted an extraordinary influence in the political sphere. He himself, had he been asked about the matter, would undoubtedly have said that he had no alternative but to seek to shape events as he did, as the occasion presented itself. The western world to this day experiences, whether consciously or not, the force of Ambrose's views regarding the relationship between Church and state, articulated over the course of numerous clashes between the Bishop of Milan and the imperial authorities. What Ambrose ended up doing, although there is no clear indication that he set out to do it, was to establish a sphere in which the Church could act independently of the state and as an entity completely responsible for governing itself. His position is encapsulated in his famous response to Valentinian II after he had been commanded to hand over the Portian Basilica for Arian worship:

> It is alleged that everything is permitted to the emperor and that all things are his. I reply: Do not so burden yourself, O Emperor, as to believe that you have any imperial right to those things that are divine ... The palaces belong to the emperor, the churches to the bishop.

> (Letter 20.19)

We may even say that Ambrose contributed to defining a distinction between Church and state where one had hardly existed before. It was a distinction that needed to be made because, as the history of the fourth century demonstrated, the orthodoxy and moral probity of the Empire could not always be taken for granted. In articulating this distinction Ambrose helped to break in the West the pattern that had existed there for half a century, since Constantine, and that would continue for better or for worse in the East.

Not that this distinction meant that the Church and the state were unrelated to one another and had no responsibilities toward one another. At certain times the distinction might even come close to disappearing. Ideally, the Church's responsibility, as borne out by the manner in which Ambrose dealt with the emperors, was to instruct and judge the state, to set the moral and doctrinal perimeters within which the state might legitimately act. And, ideally, the state's responsibility was to foster and protect the true religion proclaimed by the Church in such a way as not to infringe upon its independence. Ambrose treated Gratian and Theodosius in particular as if they were to some extent co-workers with him in caring for the Church. These mutual responsibilities, as Ambrose understood them, may have been neglected or disregarded in recent years, but in much of the world the framework in which they were embedded still flourishes – namely, the distinction between Church and state that allows for the independence of the former.

The moral and doctrinal authority that Ambrose exercised over the emperors in his role as instructor and judge of the state was almost always exercised with courage and even daring; often it was fully justified by the circumstances; but sometimes it was injurious. It says a great deal for Ambrose's self-confidence that he was able to browbeat emperors, but it makes his courage and daring somehow less appealing to his modern readers. When he intimidated Theodosius in the affair of the synagogue at Callinicum, his threats, as we know from the perspective of 1600 years later, were not in the service of a justifiable cause. Ambrose's confrontation with Theodosius over what had occurred at Callinicum is an example of the wrongheaded use of religious authority *vis-à-vis* the state. One might even characterize it, and other such incidents, as mean-spirited were it not for the fact that Ambrose was without a doubt absolutely convinced that Christianity demanded these tactics of him.

Ambrose's inner-Church activity was as significant as his involvement with the Empire, and preaching and the celebration of the liturgy were, on a daily basis, its most important components. Many of his surviving works that were originally sermons are, from our point of view, long-winded and repetitive, but they may not have been seen that way by Ambrose's contemporaries. Thus Augustine, a sophisticated speaker himself, refers only to Ambrose's attractive style and gives his preaching much of the credit for his own conversion (cf. *Confessions* 5.13.23–14.24, 6.3.4). Like a number of the other great preachers of Christian antiquity, Ambrose was not shy about making at least minimal intellectual demands on his congregation. His very appeal to the allegorical meaning of the scriptural text suggests this, and his treatises that were originally sermons are scattered with difficult passages, or in any event with passages that would have required close attention on the part of his listeners. He also, of course, made moral and spiritual demands. The treatise *On Naboth*, originally a sermon or sermons, is an excellent example of the former, with its excoriation of avarice and its call to heed the plight of the poor. Ambrose's willingness to tackle a sensitive issue, the blunt language that he used and the vivid picture that he painted of the condition of both rich and poor (sometimes in borrowed

INTRODUCTION

words) must have captured his hearers' attention completely. His promotion of virginity in the treatise *On Virgins*, also originally sermonic, is an obvious example of the latter. Although his audience in this case may actually have been composed of virgins, we know that he often preached to the general public on the subject of virginity (cf. *On Virgins* 1.11.57–58).

The contributions that Ambrose made in the two areas just mentioned, in his reflections on wealth and virginity, are notable. Like most of the other Fathers of the Church who expressed their views on the subject, Ambrose felt a certain ambivalence toward wealth and property: he could both acknowledge that wealth was not evil (cf. Letter 63.92) and claim that it was unnatural (cf. *Commentary on Luke* 7.246). His sympathies were clearly for the poor, as the treatise *On Naboth* shows, and he believed that poverty was closer to God than wealth was (cf. *Commentary on Psalm 118* 3.37), but he was also, on the other hand, realistically aware of the vices of the poor (cf. *The Six Days of Creation* 5.17.57). Probably Ambrose's most familiar idea with respect to wealth is that private property was a usurpation of what was intended by God in the beginning to be held in common. As he writes in his *Commentary on Psalm 118* (8.22): 'The Lord our God wished this earth to be the common property of all and its fruits to be at the disposal of all, but avarice divided the rights of possession.' This notion, frequently repeated by Ambrose, was one that he shared with a number of other early theologians. But he laid more emphasis on it than almost any of the others, and as a result he is often cited favorably by modern proponents of socialism. He was not, however, entirely consistent, as his refusal elsewhere to categorize wealth as evil demonstrates.

Emphasis as well characterizes much of Ambrose's contribution to the theology of virginity. The second half of the fourth century was a crucial period in the Church's reflection on virginity, and the stress that as respected a person as the Bishop of Milan placed on it served, quite by itself, to add to its already considerable prestige. Also important was his interpretation of the virginal life in terms of the Song of Songs, which he developed at length and which became part of the heritage of Western Christianity. Finally, although Ambrose followed the ancient Christian tradition in seeing virginity as superior to marriage, he did not fall into the temptation of deprecating marriage, which his contemporary Jerome so egregiously did.

Ambrose's views on virginity lead us quite naturally to the related issue of his Marian theology. In this regard, too, sheer emphasis played a role: Ambrose spoke of the Virgin Mary with a frequency and to a degree that were unusual up until then. He insisted upon Mary's perpetual virginity and, in particular, upon her virginity *in partu,* i.c., in the very act of giving birth. Here, in opposing the monk Jovinian, whom he condemned at a Milanese council around the year 390 for holding, among other opinions, that the birth of Jesus had occurred in a natural way (cf. Letter 42.6–7), Ambrose carried with him other Western theologians, especially Jerome. He saw in Mary a model for both virgins (cf. *On Virgins* 2.2.6–18) and mothers (cf. Letter 63.109–11). She was, in addition, thanks to her being at once virginal and married, a symbol of the Church, which was likewise virginal and espoused to Christ (cf. *Commentary on Luke* 2.7). We do not yet find the doctrines of Mary's immaculate conception and her assumption in Ambrose, but his was the most comprehensive teaching on Mary produced up to that point, and it would help create an atmosphere conducive to further developments.

Ambrose tells us that he celebrated the eucharist daily (cf. Letter 20.15; in *On the Sacraments* 5.25 he encourages the daily reception of communion), and there are fragments of the eucharistic prayer that he used in *On the Sacraments* 4. But we can only imagine how he carried out the liturgy. We do, however, know something of Ambrose's theology of the eucharist. It is realistic in the sense that he believed that the eucharist was truly the flesh (or body) and blood of Christ rather than a mere symbol of that flesh and blood; it was the same flesh, in other words, that was crucified and buried (cf. *On the Mysteries* 9.53). Ambrose's witness to this is the first in the West to be so clear and unambiguous. He was also the first of the Latin Fathers to attempt an explanation of the change of the bread and wine into the flesh and blood of Christ, in which he was perhaps inspired by Greek theology. 'Through the mystery of the sacred prayer,' he writes in *On the Faith* 4.10.124, the elements of bread and wine 'are transfigured into the flesh and blood' of the Lord. This transfiguration or consecration, effected by Christ's own words ('This is my body . . . This is my blood') alters the very nature of the elements just as, for example, Moses' prayer altered the nature of the Nile and changed its waters into blood (cf. *On the Mysteries* 9.50–51).

If a human blessing was so powerful that it could alter nature, what shall we say of that divine consecration in which the very words of the Lord, the Savior, are at work? . . . [If] the word of

Christ ... was able to make out of nothing what had not existed, can it not change what already exists into what it had not been?

(Ibid. 9.5.2)

While Ambrose's language indicates that he did not believe in the coexistence of the bread and the wine with the flesh and blood of Christ, he did not address the knotty problem of what would later be called the 'appearances' of bread and wine. We cannot fault him for this, though, inasmuch as his contemporaries did not discuss this issue either. Ambrose's understanding of the effects of the eucharist would be somewhat pedestrian in contrast to that of the Greek Fathers, who spoke in terms of deification (cf., e.g., Gregory of Nyssa, *The Great Catechism* 37), were it not for the fact that, in add- ition to referring to such consequences as the remission of sins (cf. *On the Sacraments* 4.28) and the strengthening of the soul (cf. *On the Mysteries* 9.55), he also used the bridal imagery of the Song of Songs to describe the relationship of the communicant with Christ (cf. ibid., 9.55–58).

Considering the extent to which Ambrose had to contend with Arianism and also, to a lesser degree, with Apollinarianism, it is somewhat surprising that his christology does not represent a sig- nificant advance over that of his predecessors. He was, as a modern christologist has written, 'completely unconcerned to make any speculative examination of the christological question.'[15] Instead he attempted political solutions to unorthodox opinions of Christ (which were themselves of course to some extent politically based) and contented himself with repeating the christological formulas that he had inherited.

The same can largely be said of Ambrose's theology of the Holy Spirit. His work *On the Holy Spirit* was the first Latin treatise on the subject, but it represents a considerable amount of borrowing from other sources. The easily incensed Jerome was so outraged by the derivative character of the text that, in his own preface to Didymus the Blind's treatise on the Holy Spirit, from which Ambrose had drawn, he compared Ambrose, without mentioning him by name, to 'an ugly crow ... adorned with others' plumage.' And he went on:

A short while ago I read a certain person's books on the Holy Spirit and, in the words of the comic writer [Terence], I saw bad things in Latin taken from good things in Greek. Nothing there was closely argued, nothing was manly or firm so as to convince the reader even involuntarily, but everything was flaccid, soft, glistening and cute, painted here and there in exquisite colors.

(Jerome's entry on Ambrose in his book *On Illustrious Men* [124] is famous for a scorn that he did not intend to conceal: 'Ambrose, Bishop of Milan, continues to write. Since he is still alive I shall withhold my judgment lest, should I express any opinion, I be blamed for either flattery or truthfulness.') Rufinus of Aquileia, Jerome's sometime friend, defended Ambrose stoutly and met the charge of plagiarism head on in his *Apology against Jerome* (2.25), composed about three years after Ambrose's death. He addresses himself directly to Jerome:

The holy Ambrose wrote about the Holy Spirit not only with words but also with his blood. For he offered his blood to his persecutors, having poured it out within himself, but God spared him for yet other labors. What if he followed Greek Catholic writers who belong to our camp and took something from their writings? Should it have been your chief concern ... to make his 'thefts' known, when perhaps he was under pressure to write in response to the raving heretics of the time?

There is a certain degree of irony in Jerome's accusation of 'thievery', since he himself borrowed heavily from Origen when writing his scriptural commentaries. There is a certain irony too in the fact that Ambrose would in turn be 'plagiarized' by someone like Maximus of Turin, who made very extensive use of his *Commentary on Luke* when composing his sermons at the beginning of the fifth century without ever acknowledging his source. Rufinus' defense, in any event, suggests that Ambrose was 'under pressure' (*necessitatem ... passus est*). By way of explanation it can also be said that he approached his sources with discretion and exercised a measure of creativity by rearranging the material that he had at hand. In the case, moreover, of the treatise *On the Duties of Ministers*, he gave Cicero an entirely Christian thrust. The fact remains, though, that Ambrose's writings are overwhelmingly derivative. His real originality (which is a concept that the ancients would have vigorously rejected: they were interested not in being original but in handing on unblemished the tradition that they had inherited) consisted less in the development of doctrine than in what he chose to emphasize of the doctrine that he had himself received.

But thanks precisely to Ambrose's 'thievery' of Greek theologians (not only Christians like Didymus the Blind and Basil the Great but also the Jew Philo) and to the prestige that he enjoyed as a pillar of orthodoxy, he served as a major conduit of Greek theological thought to the Latin West. Hilary of Poitiers had already acted before him in this capacity, and Jerome and Rufinus would follow not long after, especially through their translations of Origen. Thus Ambrose belonged to that crucial group of thinkers and writers who, by making Greek ideas accessible to Westerners who knew nothing or relatively little of the Greek language, opened the way to a florescence of Latin theology that began with Augustine and continued sporadically all the way to the High Middle Ages. It could even be argued that, of the various mediators of Greek thought, Ambrose was the greatest simply because he exercised a direct influence on Augustine, who was by far the most important of all Latin Christian thinkers. Indeed, it is impossible to imagine Augustine apart from Ambrose.

But Ambrose was much more than the person who, so to speak, made Augustine possible. He was a figure in his own right – a public figure of immense if sometimes flawed moral and political proportions who, as the pastor of the Catholic church of Milan, also preached and wrote. When we think of Augustine it is theological depth and power of expression which come to mind, and that is appropriate. When we think of Ambrose it is the decisiveness and courage of the Christian public figure that should come to mind, in tandem with an unexpected and remarkable mystical streak, revealed in his attachment to the Song of Songs, and a wonderful poetic sense that is at work in his hymns. It is hoped that the writings which have been translated in this volume will disclose something of all these qualities at first hand and provide a hint to the reader of their author's grandeur of spirit.

2

WORKS

It is remarkable that a man as busy as Ambrose was with the affairs of the Church and the Empire should have left behind as large an accumulation of writings as he did. He had, it is true, the help of a secretary, but he did not always rely on him. On the other hand, he did not write to the extent that (or on the same level as) his great contemporary Augustine did, who was almost a writer by profession. Ambrose was by profession a man of the law and an administrator, whose intelligence and whose acquaintance with the classics of Greek and Roman literature and with Scripture and the theology of the Fathers made him at minimum a passable writer and occasionally a great one.

One may analyze an author's *œuvre* under any of several rubrics, for example, sources, style, chronology, length, influence. For Ambrose a useful rubric to add to these others would be that of original form. Much if not most of Ambrose's writing was, in its original form, sermonic material, which was later either recast into or simply published as treatises. (This might help to explain his productivity, assuming that it is less time-consuming to convert sermons into treatises than it is to compose sermons and treatises as separate entities.) Of the works translated in this volume, at least three – *On Virgins*, *On Naboth* and *On the Mysteries* – began as sermons, and a fourth, the prologue to the *Commentary on the Gospel according to Luke*, while perhaps never a sermon itself, introduces what had started out as a series of sermons on Luke. Despite what must have been a large sermonic output on Ambrose's part, however, a surprisingly small number of his sermons have survived as such, apparently no more than four or five.

In addition to the two categories just mentioned – sermons made over into treatises and sermons as such – there are three others of significance in this context. First there are the treatises that were not originally sermonic, which are few in number. Second there are letters, and third there are hymns. And finally, as a fourth and minor category, there are a few epigrams and titles that seem attributable to Ambrose.

The following is a list of Ambrose's writings, arranged according to genre, with some indications as to where both the original Latin text (LT) and an accessible English translation (ET) may be found, and a brief description of each work.[1]

I EXEGESIS/WRITINGS ON SCRIPTURE

1 *The Six Days of Creation (Exameron)* (LT: PL 14.133–288; CSEL 32.1.3–261. ET: FC 42.3–283.) Of Ambrose's exegetical writings, this has been by far the most popular. In six books, it is based on nine sermons that Ambrose preached, sometimes two in one day, during an undetermined Holy Week between 386 and 390. Ambrose used Basil the Great's treatise of the same name as a model, without following it slavishly, and he quotes frequently from a number of classical authors. The text of Gen. 1:1–2:2, upon which he was commenting, gave him sufficient scope to touch upon a vast array of the natural sciences, from astronomy to zoology, with the intention of using the natural world to point out moral lessons. The result, however, is that *The Six Days of Creation* is also a compendium of the popular science of the day.

2 *On Paradise (De paradiso)* (LT: PL 14.291–332; CSEL 32.1.265–336. ET: FC 42.287–356.) In this commentary on Gen. 2:8–3:19, the author relies heavily on the great Alexandrian Jewish exegete Philo. It is possibly the first of all of Ambrose's writings, and he refers (with a slight tone of dismissal) to his having produced it when he was 'not yet an experienced bishop' (Letter 45.1). Ambrose begins this work by identifying the Garden of Eden with the paradise of which Paul speaks in 2 Cor. 12:4, and he then proceeds to allegorize the scriptural account of the former.

3 *On Cain and Abel (De Cain et Abel)* (LT: PL 14.333–80; CSEL 32.1.339–409. ET: FC 42.359–437.) This treatise in two books, which discusses Gen 4:1–16, was planned as a sequel to *On Paradise* and was probably composed soon after. Ambrose makes extensive use of Philo's *On the Sacrifices of Cain and Abel*. The work seems to be based on sermonic material.

4 *On Noah (De Noe)* (LT: PL 14.381–438; CSEL 32.1.413–97). Probably written between 378 and 384, and owing a considerable

amount to Philo, this work offers an allegorical interpretation of Gen 5:28–9:29.

5 *On Abraham* (*De Abraham*) (LT: PL 14.441–524; CSEL 32.1.501–638.) The two books of this treatise, which differ widely from one another, seem to have been composed sometime in the 380s. The first of them covers the entire life of Abraham, as recorded in Gen. 12:1–25:8, from a moral perspective; 4.23 indicates that this book was originally in the form of sermons delivered to catechumens. The second deals only with about the first half of the account of Abraham's life, approaching it allegorically; there is no hint of whether it began as sermons and, if so, to whom they were directed. This arrangement of two books – one moral and one allegorical, both interpreting the same scriptural text – anticipates Gregory of Nyssa's better-known *Life of Moses*.

6 *On Isaac and the Soul* (*De Isaac et anima*) (LT: PL 14.527–60; CSEL 32.1.641–700. ET: FC 65.9–65.) Dates between 387 and 391 have been mentioned in connection with the production of this treatise, which discusses the relationship between Christ and the soul in terms of the love of Isaac and Rebekah (Gen. 24–26) and the love of the bridegroom and the bride (S. of S.)

7 *On the Good of Death* (*De bono mortis*) (LT: PL 14.567–96; CSEL 32.1.707–53. ET: FC 65.70–113.) This work, written perhaps in 390, seems to have been put together from two sermons. Ambrose begins by linking it to *On Isaac and the Soul*, of which it should be considered a continuation. Evidencing the influence of Plotinus, he speaks of three different kinds of death (of sin, mystical, and natural) and also of resurrection and judgement.

8 *On Flight from the World* (*De fuga saeculi*) (LT: PL 14.597–624; CSEL 32.2.163–207. ET: FC 65.281–323.) This appears to be a revision of some sermons on the ascetical theme indicated by the title, and scholars date it to between 391 and 394. Ambrose manifests particular dependence on Philo's *On Flight and Discovery* and illustrates his point by extended reference to Num. 35:11–14.

9 *On Iacob and the Happy Life* (*De Iacob et vita beata*) (LT: PL 14.627–70; CSEL 32.2.3–70. ET: FC 65.119–84.) Published sometime between 386 and 388, this work is in two books and was originally in the form of sermons. The plan of the work is made clear in 2.1.1: the first book is something like a theological treatise on the acquisition of happiness by way of virtue and discipline, whereas the second, more practical in nature, offers examples of

Old Testament figures (especially Jacob and the Maccabees) who maintained their happiness despite suffering.

10 *On Joseph* (*De Ioseph*) (LT PL 14.673–704; CSEL 32.2.73–122. ET: FC 65.187–237.) This commentary on Gen. 37:2–46:27 represents a single sermon, probably preached in 387 or 388. Ambrose exalts Joseph as a model of purity and also as one who foreshadows Christ (cf. 9.47: Christ 'is the true Joseph').

11 *On the Patriarchs* (*De patriarchis*) (LT: PL 14.707–28; CSEL 32.2.125–60. ET: FC 65.243–75.) Probably written not long after *On Joseph*, and revised from a sermon or set of sermons, this work comments on Jacob's blessings of his sons in Gen. 49:3–27. According to Ambrose, the words of the blessings all have reference ultimately to Christ and the Church.

12 *On Elijah and Fasting* (*De Helia et ieiunio*) (LT: PL 14.731–64; CSEL 32.2.411–65. ET: M.J.A. Buck [1929].) This was either one or several sermons in its original form, preached during Lent either as early as 377 or as late as 391. Its purpose is to recommend the practice of fasting, and chief among the scriptural testimonies that it marshals in defense of the value of fasting are those bearing on the prophet Elijah. Ambrose also devotes considerable attention to the vice of drunkenness. The treatise is dependent on three sermons of Basil the Great.

13 *On Naboth* (*De Nabuthae*). Cf. pp. 117–44.

14 *On Tobias* (*De Tobia*) (LT: PL 14.797–832; CSEL 32.2.519–573. ET: L.M. Zucker [1933].) Scholars date this work as early as 376 or as late as 390. Originally in sermonic form, it is directed against the vices of usury and avarice. Ambrose, who follows here both a genuine sermon of Basil the Great and one falsely attributed to him, cites Tobias with approval because he has been told by his father Tobit to be generous with the poor (cf. Tobit 4:7–11).

15 *The Prayer of Job and David* (*De interpellatione Iob et David*) (LT: PL 14.835–90; CSEL 32.2.211–96. ET: FC 65.329–420.) This treatise consists in four books and was once a series of sermons. Among the problems that the work poses are those of dating (383, 387–89 and 394 have all been offered as possibilities) and of the original order of the books. Job and Pss. 42, 43 and 73 provide the basis for a reflection on suffering in general and on the suffering of the faithful in particular, contrasted with the apparently untroubled state of the impious.

16 *A Defense of the Prophet David* (*Apologia prophetae David*) (LT: PL 14.891–926; CSEL 32.2.299–355; SC 239.) David is presented in this

writing, which may once have been a sermon, as the model of the repentant sinner and the ideal king. The topic seems to be related to some misdeed on the part of an emperor, which Ambrose is addressing; the dating depends on the misdeed that one finds fitting the text with the most plausibility. Two of the many manuscripts of the *Defense* bear the dedication 'To the Emperor Theodosius,' raising the possibility that it has some connection with the massacre at Thessalonika in 390, which was followed by Theodosius' public penance.

17 *Explanations of Twelve Psalms of David (Enarrationes in xii psalmos davidicos)* (LT: PL 14.963–1238; CSEL 64.) The twelve psalms that Ambrose interprets here, and originally preached on, are (in the Greek enumeration) 1, 35–40, 43, 45, 47–48 and 61. Paulinus notes in his biography (42) that Ambrose was dictating his commentary on Ps. 43 when he had the mystical experience that preluded his death; as a result, that commentary is incomplete. The dating of the individual explanations, apart from that of Ps. 43, is difficult to determine, although the work as a whole must have been compiled after the author's death. Ambrose gives both a moral and a christological meaning to the psalms and relies on Origen and Basil the Great for some of his insights.

18 *A Commentary on Psalm 118 (Expositio in Psalmum cxviii)* (LT: PL 15.1197–1526; CSEL 62.) This commentary on the longest of the psalms (119 in the Hebrew enumeration) was probably written between 386 and 390 and may at least partly be taken from sermonic material. The commentary is divided into twenty-two sections, corresponding to the twenty-two sections, each one eight verses long, into which the psalm itself is divided. Ambrose looks to Origen for much of his exegesis, which has both a moral and an allegorical thrust.

19 *A Commentary on the Prophet Isaiah (Expositio Esaiae prophetae)* (LT: CCSL 14.405–8.) Only six fragments of this commentary survive, all of them quoted in various works of Augustine. Since it is referred to by Ambrose in his *Commentary on Luke* (2.56), it was clearly written before that.

20 *A Commentary on the Gospel according to Luke (Expositio evangelii secundum Lucam)* (LT: PL 15.1527–1850; CSEL 32.4; SC 45, 52; CCSL 14.1–400.) This is the only work on the New Testament by Ambrose of which we are aware. Of its ten books (with a prologue, translated in the present volume), all but the third are undoubtedly based on sermons. The influence of Origen, Eusebius of Caesarea

and Hilary of Poitiers, among others, is evident. The commentary does not pretend to cover the gospel in its entirety, and there are some surprising omissions (e.g., the Magnificat and the Benedictus in Luke 1, the Lord's Prayer in Luke 11). Ambrose discusses the literal sense of Luke and, as often as possible, then passes on to its moral and mystical senses, which he refers to respectively in the prologue under the terms 'natural,' 'moral' and 'rational.' The work seems to have been composed between 377 and 389, but most likely toward the end of that period. Cf. also pp. 161–5.

II WRITINGS ON MORAL AND ASCETICAL THEMES

1 *On the Duties of Ministers* (*De officiis ministrorum*) (LT: PL 16.25–194. ET: De Romestin 1–89.) Probably the best known of all Ambrose's writings, there is no general agreement as to when it was composed (perhaps as early as 377 or as late as 391) or whether or not it was constructed out of sermons. The ministers of the title are the Milanese clergy, and the treatise is an instruction on moral virtue addressed to them. Ambrose uses Cicero's *De officiis* as his model, following it closely but Christianizing it by, among other things, regular references to Scripture. Like Cicero's treatise, Ambrose's is in three books: the first deals with the good and the appropriate (*honestum ac decorum*), particularly the cardinal virtues of prudence, justice, fortitude and temperance; the second with the useful or the utilitarian (*utile*); and the third with a comparison between the two in which it is shown that the good must always be chosen over what is merely useful (cf. 2.6.22, 3.2.8).

2 *On Virgins* (*De virginibus*.) Cf. pp. 71–116.

3 *On Widows* (*De viduis*) (LT: PL 16.247–76. ET: De Romestin 391–407.) The first words of this treatise give the impression that it was published soon after *On Virgins* and was a kind of sequel to it, but whether or not it was originally sermonic material is unknown. Ambrose praises widowhood and, in terms of chastity, locates it between virginity and marriage. He strongly recommends against second marriages but does not forbid them. In addition to exalting widowhood, the treatise exposes the virtues that Ambrose believes to be essential to the life of a widow.

4 *On Virginity* (*De virginitate*) (LT: PL 16.279–316. ET: St Ambrose [1963:77–125.]) This treatise was initially in the form of a sermon or series of sermons, at least one of which was delivered

on the Feast of Saints Peter and Paul (29 June), as is clear from 19.24, possibly in 378. Ambrose defends his promotion of virginity and speaks of the virgin largely as the disciple of Christ.

5 *An Instruction for a Virgin* (*De institutione virginis*) (LT: PL 16.319–43.) Published in either 391 or 392, this treatise is addressed to a certain Eusebius of Bologna, a friend of Ambrose and the recipient of Letters 54 and 55; he may have been the Bishop of Bologna. The work is a sermon given by Ambrose on the occasion of the virginal consecration of Ambrosia, the granddaughter of Eusebius. As such it offers Ambrose the opportunity to expatiate briefly on the virginal state. But in fact much of the sermon is devoted to an attack on the notion that Mary the mother of Jesus was not perpetually a virgin – an opinion that was being voiced at the time by Bonosus of Sardica and a certain Helvidius. Ambrosia is mentioned elsewhere with affection in Letter 55.1

6 *In Praise of Virginity* (*Exhortatio virginitatis*) (LT: 16.351–80.) This was a sermon given sometime between 393 and 395 at the dedication of the Basilica of Saint Lawrence in Florence, which had been built by the wealthy widow Juliana (cf. 2.10). In it Ambrose encourages Juliana's children to embrace a life of virginity, and in so doing he sets forth the advantages of virginity.

III DOGMATIC WRITINGS

1 *On the Faith* (*De fide*) (LT: PL 16.549–726; CSEL 78. ET: De Romestin 201–314.) This work was published in two stages in response to two requests from Gratian. In five books, Books 1–2 were completed by the summer of 378, and they were supplemented by Books 3–5 by the end of 380; the latter set of books may have been constructed from sermons. Although the title of the treatise suggests a general exposition of Christian belief, in reality it is devoted to a refutation of Arianism and hence focuses on the doctrine of Christ, whom Ambrose shows to be equal to the Father in his divinity albeit inferior to him in his humanity. Williams (1995:128–53) advances the opinion that Ambrose produced the first two books of *On the Faith* at Gratian's request not in order to provide the emperor with a compendium of orthodox christology but so as to defend the orthodox in general and himself in particular against Arian accusations that Catholic Christianity was tritheistic, i.e., that it held for three gods.

2 *On the Holy Spirit* (*De Spiritu Sancto*) (LT: PL 16.731–850; CSEL

79.15–222. ET: De Romestin 93–158; FC 44.35–214.) Published in 381, this treatise in three books is a sequel to *On the Faith* and, like it, was destined to be read by Gratian. Relying heavily on Didymus, Athanasius and Basil the Great, Ambrose seeks to prove the divinity of the Spirit against the Macedonians and Pneumatomachians, who denied it. He applies four marks of the divinity to the Spirit – sinlessness, the ability to forgive sin, creativity rather than createdness, and the receiving rather than the giving of worship (cf. 3.18.132). Of particular interest is the fact that at least one passage of the treatise (1.15.152) and perhaps two others (1.11.119, 1.11.120), can be understood as asserting the procession of the Spirit from the Son as well as from the Father. Ambrose thus anticipates Augustine (cf. *On the Trinity* 15.17.29, 15.26.47) and goes counter to the common Greek view, which was that the Spirit proceeded from the Father through the Son. The difference between the two theologies of the Spirit, Augustinian and Greek, is for various reasons a serious point of contention between western and eastern Christians to this day.

3   *On the Sacrament of the Lord's Incarnation (De incarnationis dominicae sacramento)* (LT: PL 16.853–84; CSEL 79.223–81. ET: FC 44.219–62.) Scholars seem agreed that this work was produced in 381 or 382. Thanks to Paulinus (18), we know that the heart of this treatise (3.14–7.78), which deals with Christ's human nature in the context of the Arian controversy, was originally a statement prepared by Ambrose in response to a question on the subject posed by two Arians, who were to have debated with him in the Portian Basilica but never made an appearance. The statement is preceded by a few words on one of the readings of the day, Gen. 4:1–16 (1.2–2.13), and followed by a kind of appendix (8.79–10.116) devoted to answering the question of 'how the unbegotten [Father] and the begotten [Son] could be of one nature and substance,' which had been asked by the Arian bishop Palladius.

4   *An Explanation of the Creed for Those about to be Baptized (Explanatio symboli ad initiandos)* (LT: PL 17.1193–96; CSEL 73.1–12; SC 25bis, 46–59. ET: R.H. Connolly [1952].) This brief sermon, which cannot be dated, accompanied the ceremony of the *traditio symboli*, when the catechumens heard the creed for the first time. In this case the creed that is used is the ancient Roman one, and Ambrose explains it article by article. Only recently has the sermon been established as a genuine work of Ambrose.

5   *On the Sacraments (De sacramentis)* (LT: PL 16.435–82; CSEL

73.13–116; SC 25bis, 60–155. ET: FC 44.269–328.) This is a series of six short sermons, now in the form of six books, that were delivered to the newly baptized during Easter week and probably published around 390. They deal with much the same material that the treatise *On the Mysteries* does, but in a somewhat less cohesive manner. This has led to a questioning of its authenticity, but recent scholarship tends to favor Ambrose's authorship.

6 *On the Mysteries* (*De mysteriis*). Cf. pp. 145–60.

7 *On Repentance* (*De paenitentia*) (LT: PL 16.485–546; CSEL 73.117–206; SC 179. ET: De Romestin 329–59.) Written between 384 and 394, this treatise is a refutation of the Novatianist position, which was that the Church did not have the power to forgive all sins. (Novatianism traced itself to Novatian, a Roman priest of the mid-third century.) Ambrose argues in favor of the divine mercy while also counseling the practice of penance. The work, which is in two books, shows the influence of Tertullian and Cyprian.

8 *An Explanation of the Faith* (*Expositio fidei*) (LT: PL 16.847–50.) In his treatise entitled *Eranistes*, composed about 447, Theodoret of Cyrus cites this christological confession, which he attributes to Ambrose. Theodoret uses it, among numerous other quotations from the Fathers, as evidence against Monophysitism, which held that Christ had only one (divine) nature. Whether Ambrose actually wrote the confession is a disputed question.

9 *On the Sacrament of Regeneration, or On Philosophy* (*De sacramento regenerationis sive de philosophia*) (LT: CSEL 11.131.) This is a lost work, except for some fragments preserved in Augustine.

IV SERMONS

1 *On the Death of his Brother* (*De excessu fratris*) (LT: PL 16.1345–1414; CSEL 73.207–325. ET: De Romestin 161–97; FC 22.161–259.) Ambrose's brother Satyrus died in either 375 or 378, according to most calculations. It was then that this set of two sermons was delivered – the first on the day of his funeral, the second a week later at the grave. The first is far more personal and contains much useful information about both Satyrus and Ambrose, while the second is a theological reflection on the resurrection from the dead (cf. 2.1–2). The sermons, which were reworked for publication, display intimate knowledge of the classical consolatory style.

2 *On the Death of Valentinian* (*De obitu Valentiniani*) (LT: PL 16.1417–44; CSEL 73.327–67. ET: FC 22.265–99.) Although

Valentinian died in Vienne on 15 May, 392, his body was not returned to Milan for burial until some months later. The exact date of the burial, when this sermon was preached, is unknown, but it was probably in August. The sermon, somewhat surprisingly, makes considerable use of the Song of Songs; it also includes details about Valentinian and his relationship with Ambrose that cannot be found elsewhere.

3 *On the Death of Theodosius* (*De obitu Theodosii*) (LT: PL 16.1447–88; CSEL 73.369–401. ET: FC 22.307–32.) This sermon was delivered on 25 February 395, forty days after Theodosius' death and just before his remains were to be brought from Milan to Constantinople for interment. In view of the political uncertainty resulting from the emperor's death, Ambrose's aims were to present Theodosius as a model Christian ruler and to solidify the position of his son Honorius. The Empress Helena and the tradition of her finding of the cross are recalled in 40–51.

4 *Against Auxentius on Handing over the Basilicas* (*Contra Auxentium de basilicis tradendis*) (LT: PL 16.1049–53. ET: De Romestin 430–36.) Auxentius was the Arian court bishop of Milan, and this sermon was given during the second phase of the crisis of the basilicas, on Palm Sunday 386. In it Ambrose offers firm and occasionally even pugnacious resistance to the pro-Arian policies of the imperial court.

V LETTERS

(LT: PL 16.913–1342; CSEL 82 [3 vols.]. ET: De Romestin 411–73 [selections]; FC 26; S.L. Greenslade [1956: 182–278; selections.] The ninety-one letters of Ambrose that have survived can only be a fraction of what must have been a far vaster correspondence, the rest of which has disappeared. They include, *inter alia*, admonitions to emperors, friendly exchanges with a variety of people, treatments of exegetical points handled at the request of correspondents, conciliar missives and letters to his sister, and together they constitute one of the most important epistolary collections of Christian antiquity. It would almost certainly be false to view these letters as private documents, since Ambrose himself evidently kept transcripts of them and quite likely arranged for the majority of them to be put into publishable form. In the process of being prepared for publication they may have lost some of their original freshness. Of course, not unexpectedly, they always recount events from

Ambrose's own perspective, and perhaps sometimes as he may have wished them to be viewed by his readers. There are two enumerations of the letters: the first is that of Ambrose's Benedictine editors, which is the more popular and which is followed in the present volume; the second is that established more recently by Otto Faller in his critical edition in CSEL 82.

VI HYMNS

(LT: August Steier [1903: 651–60]; Jacques Fontaine *et al.* [1992].) Although Ambrose may well have composed hymns – not only words but also music – before the crisis of the basilicas in 386, it was then that his hymnody became famous as both a consolation and a kind of rallying cry for the faithful of Milan. (Paulinus provides us with background material in a few words of his *Life* [13].) In his sermon *Against Auxentius* (34) Ambrose recognizes the power of song in the context of religious controversy, as Arius had before him and as Augustine would after him. But, even though Ambrose's hymns may be rich in doctrinal content, they were not necessarily all produced in the heat of doctrinal strife. It is hard to know how many hymns Ambrose may have written, but his reputation was such that a fairly large number were ascribed to him, including the *Exsultet* and the *Te Deum*. Certainly the hymns that are genuine are of a very high quality, and as an ensemble they have been characterized as 'one of the most original and perfect poetic creations of Latin Christianity' (Fontaine, 1992: 11). The four that are unanimously considered to be his are translated in this volume (pp. 166–73). To these four many scholars add another four, while others add eight or fourteen or even more. It is probably the case that the bulk of Ambrose's hymnody has been lost.

VII EPIGRAMS AND TITLES

1 Epigrams (LT: PL Suppl. 1.585–87.) Four epigrams are ascribed to Ambrose, although of these at least one is doubtful. They are brief inscriptions composed for public places. The three with the most claim to genuineness were written for the Basilica of the Apostles in Milan, for the Baptistry of Saint Thecla in Milan, and as an epitaph for Ambrose's brother Satyrus.

2 Titles (LT: PL Suppl. 1.587–89.) These titles, or verses, of

which there are twenty-one, each two lines long, were supposedly used as descriptions of various scenes from the Old and New Testaments, perhaps depicted in the Ambrosian Basilica in Milan. The second, for example, reads:

See John reclining upon the breast of Christ,
whence out of love he learned to profess God the Word.

Scholars do not unanimously attribute these verses to Ambrose.

VIII DOUBTFUL AND SPURIOUS WRITINGS

Over the centuries Ambrose was credited with certain writings that he probably did not compose. In this he was not unlike many other Fathers. These works include the *Te Deum*, a hymn of praise sung on solemn occasions, and the great Easter proclamation known as the *Exsultet*. His name has also been attached to writings of considerably less renown, such as *Hegesippus, or On the Jewish War* (*Hegesippus sive de bello iudaico*); *The Law of God, or A Collation of Mosaic and Roman Laws* (*Lex Dei, sive mosaicarum et romanarum legum collatio*); *A Second Defense of David* (*Apologia David altera*), which was intended to serve as a companion piece to the *Defense of the Prophet David*; and *On the Fall of a Virgin* (*De lapsu virginis*). An early twentieth century scholar attributed the famous Athanasian Creed to Ambrose; subsequent scholarship, however, has shown that it is of neither Athanasian nor Ambrosian origin. Finally, in this connection some mention should be made of the so-called Ambrosiaster, the name given by Erasmus in the sixteenth century to the anonymous author of a set of commentaries on the Epistles of Paul, dating to the end of the fourth century. Previous to Erasmus this highly important work had been almost universally assigned to Ambrose, but the great Dutch humanist cast doubt on this attribution, and later research demonstrated that his doubt was justified. The identity of Ambrosiaster has never been satisfactorily established, but he may also be the author of *The Law of God, or A Collation of Mosaic and Roman Laws*.

A glance at the list of Ambrose's surviving works shows a pre-ponderance in the area of scriptural exegesis. This would be natural for a man whose writings were, for the most part, originally sermons, since a preacher would be commenting on biblical passages in a liturgical setting. Of these scriptural works all but one, the

Commentary on Luke, are devoted to the Old Testament, and nearly half of them focus on the book of Genesis, which was for the early Church a text of choice, offering rich opportunities for allegorizing. Almost none of the scriptural texts that Ambrose makes his own had ever before, to the best of our knowledge, been extensively treated in Latin (Hilary of Poitiers had commented on some of the same Psalms that Ambrose did). It is true that many, if not most, of Ambrose's ideas in interpreting the Scriptures are derived from Philo, Origen, Basil the Great and other Greek authors. Still, he reworked them as he saw fit and – whether reworked or not – transmitted these ideas to the West, where they were to exert an influence on Augustine and his successors.

Ambrose's threefold approach to the Scriptures – literal, moral/ ethical and allegorical/spiritual/mystical – is classic and had already been outlined by Origen a century and a half previously. These three ways of interpreting Scripture are not as frequently found together as one might have the impression that they would be from reading the prologue to the *Commentary on Luke*. The treatise *On Naboth*, for example, combines the literal and the moral: Ambrose recounts step by step the story of Naboth in 1 Kings 21 and draws from it a moral lesson on avarice. The treatise *On the Mysteries*, on the other hand, brings together the literal and the allegorical as Ambrose discovers in the history of the Old Testament mystical prefigurations of the sacraments of the Church. Although a spiritual meaning usually presupposes a literal one, which provides the basis and the point of departure for the more elaborate spiritual one, in some cases there is no literal meaning, or at least it is not alluded to. When Ambrose uses the Song of Songs in his work *On Virgins*, for instance, he does so without any reference to a possible literal signification; instead, he treats the Song of Songs as if it applied exclusively and quite naturally to the relationship between Christ and the virgin.

If Ambrose's exegetical works stand out by sheer weight of numbers, another set of writings attracts our attention for the same reason, even though their number is smaller: these are the treatises on virginity. Ambrose's fascination with virginity has already been mentioned (cf. pp. 17–18), and his four works on it represent a notable proportion of his output. Only Jerome, of the other great Latin Fathers of the Church, laid as much stress on this subject as he did.

The person who has an opportunity even cursorily to read

through Ambrose's writings, with their concentration on the deeper meanings of Scripture and the ideal of virginity, will catch a glimpse of the Bishop of Milan that is at least as authentic as that which shows him to be the great *Kirchenpolitiker* of the early Latin Church.

3

TRANSLATIONS

INTRODUCTION

The works that appear in translation here have been selected from among the many that Ambrose wrote because, it is believed, they will provide the reader with a reasonable grasp of his method and his concerns. The treatise *On Virgins* is included because Ambrose was one of Christian antiquity's most ardent promoters of virginity. *On Naboth* represents Ambrose's preoccupation with what we would today call social justice. The work *On the Mysteries* is a gem of early Christian baptismal literature, and it displays Ambrose in the guise of priest–liturgist. The prologue to the Lucan commentary focuses more specifically, of course, on exegesis, although hardly any of Ambrose's writings fail to manifest his exegetical style. Needless to say, examples of Ambrose's hymnody could not be omitted. His four undoubted hymns are presented here in a literal translation for the sake of retaining as much as possible of their imagery and theology; but for the sake of their poetry, with its sober majesty, the original Latin is given as well. Ambrose's two letters on the Altar of Victory, appearing on either side of the pagan Symmachus' *Appeal*, show the bishop in the role (not necessarily an attractive one to modern sensibilities) of politician, imperial tutor and uncompromising adversary of paganism.

Except for the prologue to the *Commentary on Luke*, these are translations of entire works. Abridgements and excerpts leave too much to the discretion of the person doing the abridging and excerpting, and they do not permit the reader to see the original author working out his thought in his own way, at his own pace.

As anyone who reads Ambrose will notice, he uses Scripture extensively. But often a passage that he cites, particularly from the

Old Testament, will appear unfamiliar to us. The reason for this is that Ambrose worked with various versions of the Bible that are no longer current and that contained variant readings; among these was the Greek translation known as the Septuagint. The scriptural texts that Ambrose cites have all been translated as they stand, including the variations. In the one or two cases where Ambrose quotes a text that does not even appear as such in the Scriptures as we know them today, an asterisk (*) has been placed with the citation.

ON VIRGINS

Introduction

This longest of Ambrose's ascetical treatises was probably published in 377, when its author had been a bishop for not quite three years, as we learn in 1.1.3 and 2.6.39. It is constructed out of at least two sermons – one by Ambrose himself, delivered on the feast of Saint Agnes (cf. 1.2.5), and the other by Pope Liberius, delivered on Christmas Day to Ambrose's sister Marcellina (cf. 3.1.1). Using these sermons, and perhaps a third, as a foundation, Ambrose produced a work that is comprehensive in its treatment of virginity and that easily ranks with the greatest writings of the Church Fathers on the topic.

The work is in three books, each of which has a distinct tone and purpose. The first effectively begins with an encomium of Saint Agnes and then quickly passes on to an encomium of virginity itself and to an exposition of what might be called the theory or theology of virginity. Some of the themes that are sounded here – most notably, perhaps, the comparison between virginity and marriage – were part of the stock in trade of ancient writers on virginity and the unmarried life. The second half of this first book is strongly christocentric: Ambrose portrays the virgin as the bride of Christ and, in striking fashion, finds in the passionate and erotic Song of Songs the analogue for the passionate but chaste relationship that he seeks to promote between Christ and the virgin.

The second book of the treatise is intended to illustrate the virginal life by offering models of it, as Ambrose himself mentions in 2.1.1–2. The primary model is Mary, the mother of Christ, to whom Ambrose devotes a significant amount of attention. Thecla, who was exceedingly popular in Christian antiquity (although mostly forgotten now), offers a second model, followed by an unnamed virgin of Antioch. The story of this anonymous virgin is told with a certain relish, and we would be justified in supposing that Ambrose was not only recounting an edifying tale for his readers' spiritual benefit but also catering to their adventurous and even romantic interests. The legend of Damon and Pythias that Ambrose inserts at the end of this story has to do, of course, not with virginity but rather with the self-sacrifice exemplified by the Antiochene virgin.

Finally, the third book reproduces, or claims to reproduce, Liberius' sermon and, that accomplished, turns to some practical aspects of virginity – reading, fasting, prayer and the expression of repentance through tears. A warning is also issued against dancing. In a kind of appendix, Ambrose takes up a suggestion of his sister Marcellina that he make a judgement on the permissibility of a virgin's committing suicide in order to avoid violation, and he shows himself to be sympathetic to such an act. The third book, then, in large part deals with particulars of virginity that were not raised in the previous two books.

The treatise has been translated from the critical edition of Egnatius Cazzaniga (1948). The Latin text is also to be found in PL 16.197–244 and CPS ser. lat. 6.15–163. There is an English translation in De Romestin 363–87 and in St Ambrose (1963: 17–76).

Book one

1.1. If, in keeping with the decree of heavenly truth, we are to give an account of every idle word that we have spoken (cf. Mat. 12:36), and if the servant who, like a fearful money-lender or avaricious property-owner, hides in the ground the talents of spiritual grace that were entrusted to him, which should have been distributed to the money-changers so that they would accumulate interest, incurs no small displeasure when his master returns (cf. Mat. 25:24–30), then rightly should we be fearful. Although our abilities are slight, none the less we are under a great obligation to pay out to the minds of the people the utterances of God that have been entrusted to us, lest the interest on our words be demanded of us, especially since the Lord requires of us not that we succeed but that we make an effort. This is why we decided to write down something, since there is more danger of embarrassment if our words are heard than if they are read, for a book feels no shame.

1.2. Although I distrust my own abilities, to be sure, none the less I am spurred on by tokens of the divine mercy and dare to give thought to a discourse, for when God willed it even an ass spoke (cf. Num. 22: 28–30). If an angel stands by me as I labor under the burdens of this world, I too shall open the mouth that has been closed for so long a time, for he who removed the hindrances of nature in the case of that ass can remove those of inexperience as well. In the ark of the Old Testament the priest's staff blossomed (cf. Num. 17:23): it is easy for God to bring forth flowers in his holy Church from our knotty wood also. Why should we despair that the Lord would speak in human beings when he spoke in thornbushes (cf. Exod. 3:4)? God did not disdain a bramblebush. If only he would cast light on my thorns too! Perhaps there will be those who will be surprised by a light shining even in our thornbushes, there will be those whom our thorns do not prick, there will be those whose shoes will be loosed from their feet when they hear our voice from the bramblebush, so that as their mind strides forward it may be freed from bodily hindrances.

But this is what holy men deserve.

1.3. If only Jesus would give me some slight notice as I lie under that still barren fig tree (cf. John 1:48)! Our fig tree too might bear fruit after three years (cf. Luke 13:6–9). But why should sinners be so hopeful? If only that gospel cultivator of the Lord's vine, who has perhaps already been ordered to cut down our fig tree, would hold off from doing so for this year as well, while he digs around it and lays on a basketful of dung, in case he should raise up a needy man from the earth and lift up a poor man from the dung (cf. Ps. 113:7)! Blessed are those who tether their horses under the vine and the olive trees (cf. Gen. 49:11), devoting the course of their labors to peace and joy. The fig tree – that is, the seductive itching of the world's pleasures – still overshadows me; it is of modest height, easily broken when worked at, too immature to use, and barren of fruit.

1.4 Perhaps there is someone who will wonder why I dare to write when I am unable to speak. But if we reflect on what we have read in the gospel writings and in priestly deeds, and if the holy prophet Zechariah is an example to us (cf. Luke 1:62–63), he will find that there are things which speech cannot disclose but which a pen can write. If John's name restored his father's voice (cf. Luke 1:64), neither must I, mute as I am, despair of receiving back my voice if I speak forth Christ, even though no one, in the words of the prophet, can recount his generation (cf. Isa. 53:8). And therefore as the Lord's servant I shall extol his household, for the unsullied Lord has dedicated to himself an unsullied household even in this body that is full of the offscourings of human frailty.[1]

2.5. So far, so good, for since today is the birthday of a virgin it is right to speak of virgins, and this book has its origin in my preaching.

It is the birthday of a virgin: let us follow her chastity. It is the birthday of a martyr: let us immolate victims. It is the birthday of Saint Agnes:[2] let men marvel, let children not despair, let the married be amazed, let the unmarried imitate. But what can I say worthy of her whose very name was not devoid of the glow of praise?[3] She had devotion beyond her years and virtue beyond her nature, so that it seems to me that she had not a human name but a presage of martyrdom by which she showed what she was to be.[4] Yet I have the means to be supplied with help.

2.6 The word 'virgin' is an indication of modesty. I shall invoke the martyr, I shall extol the virgin. That panegyric is not long enough which is not exotic but ready to hand. Away with genius, then, and let eloquence be stilled! A single word is commendation. It is this that the old, the young and children intone. There is none more praiseworthy than the one who can be praised by all. There are as many heralds as there are persons who proclaim the martyr when they speak.

74

2.7 [Agnes] is reported to have undergone martyrdom at the age of twelve. What cruelty is more hateful than that which did not spare the most youthful age! Or, rather, great was the power of the faith which bore witness even at that age. Was there room for a wound on her little body? But she who had no spot to receive the blow had the means to conquer the blow. Girls of that age, in fact, cannot endure even the stern faces of their parents, and when they are pricked by a pin they are likely to weep as if they had been inflicted with wounds. She was unafraid of the executioners' blood-stained hand, unmoved by the clumsy hauling of the clanking chains, as yet ignorant of death but ready to offer her whole body to the furious soldier's sword and, if she were to be dragged against her will to the altar, ready to stretch out her hands to Christ in the midst of the flames and to signal the victory of her conquering Lord in the sacrilegious firepans themselves, ready to insert her neck and her two hands into bonds of iron, although no bonds could confine such delicate limbs.

2.8 A new kind of martyrdom was this: not yet fit to suffer, she was already ripe for victory. Struggling with difficulty but easily crowned, she became a teacher in virtue while bearing the disadvantage of youth. No bride would hasten to her wedding as joyfully as the virgin proceeded with lively step to the place of her torture, her head adorned not with curls but with Christ, encircled not with flowers but with virtue. Everyone wept, but she herself was dry-eyed. Many were amazed that she was so careless of her life, which she was going to give away as if it were already over, even though it had hardly begun. All were astonished that she was already a witness to the Deity when she could not serve as her own witness on account of her youth. She bore credible testimony with respect to God, although she still could not bear credible testimony with respect to a human being, because what is beyond nature belongs to the author of nature.

2.9 With what terror the executioner behaved in order to frighten her, with what flattery he sought to persuade her! How many yearned for her to come to them in marriage! But she said: 'It would be an insult to my bridegroom for me to desire to be attractive. Let him take me who was the first to choose me. Why do you delay, executioner? Let my body perish. I do not want what eyes can love.' She stood, she prayed, she bowed her neck. You could see the executioner tremble as if he himself had been condemned, his hand shake, his face grow pale as he feared for another's distress, although the girl did not fear for her own.

You have, then, a twofold martyrdom in one victim – that of modesty and that of religion. She both remained a virgin and obtained martyrdom.

3.10 The love of chastity, and you too, holy sister (even though you are silent because of your subdued way of life), now beckon us to say something about virginity, lest what is one of the principal virtues seem to be slighted by a cursory treatment. For virginity is not praiseworthy because it is found in martyrs but because it itself makes martyrs.

3.11 But who can grasp with human understanding what does not fall under the laws of nature, and who can express in ordinary words what stands outside the order of nature? What is to be imitated on earth has its origin in heaven. Not without reason has she who has found a bridegroom for herself in heaven sought for herself a way of living from heaven. Going beyond the clouds, the lower atmosphere, the angels and the stars, she has found the Word of God in the very breast of the Father and seized upon him with her whole heart. Who, after all, having once found so great a good, would abandon it? For 'your name is ointment poured out; therefore the maidens have loved you and drawn you' (S. of S. 1:2). It is not merely I who have said that those who 'do not marry and are not given in marriage shall be as angels in heaven' (Matt. 22:30). Let no one be surprised, then, if those who are coupled with the Lord of angels are compared to angels. Who would deny that it is from heaven that this life has sprung which we do not see frequently on earth until God came down into these members of an earthly body? It was then that a virgin conceived in her womb 'and the Word became flesh' (John 1:14) so that flesh might become God.

3.12 Suppose someone were to say that Elijah was without lust as well and did not engage in sexual intercourse. That is the very reason why he was snatched up to heaven in a chariot (cf. 2 Kgs. 2:11), why he appears with the Lord in glory (cf. Matt. 17:3) and why he is to precede the Lord when he comes (cf. Mal. 4:5). And there is Miriam too, who with her timbrel led the dancing with virginal modesty (cf. Exod. 15:20). But consider what she represented then. Was it not the Church, which as a virgin was, through the unsullied Spirit, coupled with the devout assemblies of the people so that they might chant divine songs? We also read that virgins were assigned to the Temple at Jerusalem[5]. But what does the Apostle say: 'These things happened to them as a prefiguration' (1 Cor. 10:11), as signs of future events (cf. Col. 2:17), for there is a prefiguration in few things, but there is life in many.

3.13 But, after the Lord entered into this body and joined the Deity to a body without any stain of confusion, this custom characteristic of the heavenly life spread throughout the world and implanted itself in human bodies. It is this that the angels who minister upon the earth declared would come to be, which would offer to the Lord the obedient service of an unsullied body. This is that heavenly army which the host of praising angels prophesied would exist on earth. We have, then, the authority of antiquity from ages past and the fullness of profession from [the time of] Christ.

4.14 This is not at all something that I have in common with the pagans; it is not practiced by the barbarians, nor is it habitual among other living beings. Even though our lives are sustained by the very same air as theirs is, even though we share the common features of an earthly body and do not differ in the way that we beget offspring, still in this alone we reject the reproach that our natures are similar, because virginity is affected by the pagans but violated once it has been consecrated, is attacked by the barbarians, and is unknown to the rest.

4.15 Who would allege to me that the Vestal Virgins and the priestesses of the Palladium[6] are praiseworthy? This sort of modesty, which is prescribed not for perpetuity but up to a certain age, is a matter not of virtuousness but of years. Such chastity is all the more impudent when its deflowering is put off to a riper age. They themselves teach their virgins that they must not persevere; nor can they when they have placed a limit to virginity. What sort of religion is that, where young women are commanded to be chaste and old women to be unchaste? But she who is restrained by law is not chaste, nor is she unchaste who is let go by the law. What mysteries are these, and what virtuousness, where chastity is imposed as a requirement and licence is given to wantonness! For neither is she chaste who is compelled by fear, nor is she honorable who is motivated by gain, nor is that chastity which is exposed to the daily insult of roving eyes and harassed by brazen stares. Exemptions are bestowed on them and rewards are offered to them, as if the sale of chastity were not the greatest sign of impudence. What is promised for a price is absolved for a price, given up for a price, has a price put on it. She who is accustomed to selling her chastity cannot buy it back.

4.16 And what is there to be said of the Phrygian rites[7] in which unchastity is a discipline (and, if only it were of the frailer sex!)? What about the orgies of Liber,[8] where the mystery of religion is a goad to wantonness? What kind of life must the priests have there, where the debauchery of the gods is worshiped! These religions, then, have no virgins.

4.17. Let us see if perhaps in fact the precepts of philosophy, which is in the habit of claiming for itself teaching authority with respect to all the virtues, have produced any [virgins]. There is a certain Pythagorean virgin who is celebrated in story. When she was forced by a tyrant to disclose a secret, she is said to have bitten off a piece of her tongue and spat it in the tyrant's face, lest she permit a confession to be wrung from her even by torture; thus he who would not cease his interrogations had no one to interrogate.

4.18. Yet that same woman who could not be overcome by torture was overcome by lust, and with a strong spirit but a swelling womb she set an example by silence and was a wastrel with her chastity. She who was able to conceal a secret in her mind, then, did not conceal the dishonor of her body. She overcame nature, but she did not observe discipline. How she might wish the seriousness of her modesty to appear in her voice! And perhaps she was instructed in patience so that she would reject sin. She was not victorious in every respect, then, for the tyrant found what he was not asking for although he could not find what he was asking for.[9]

4.19. How much stronger are our virgins, who overcome even the powers that they do not see and who are victorious not only over flesh and blood but even over the very prince of the world and ruler of this age (cf. Eph. 6:12, John 12:31)! Agnes was young in years, to be sure, but mature in virtue. Her triumph was more manifold, her steadfastness more dauntless. She did not hold her tongue because of fear but restrained it for the sake of victory, for she had nothing that she was afraid to have known, since her confession was not criminal but religious. And so, while the former merely kept a secret, the latter bore witness to God, whom she confessed by her very being inasmuch as one of her age was not yet allowed to testify.

5.20. In panegyrics it is customary to praise native land and parents, so that by recalling the author of life the dignity of the offspring might be magnified. Although I myself have not undertaken a panegyric of virginity but rather an explanation of it, none the less I consider it apropos to mention what its native land is and who its author is.

First, let us determine where its native land is. If by native land we

78

mean birthplace, then chastity's native land is assuredly in heaven. And so it is a stranger here but at home there.

5.21. But what is virginal chastity if not a purity untouched by contamination? And whom could we consider its author if not the unsullied Son of God, whose flesh saw no corruption and whose divinity knew no contamination?

See, then, how great the merits of virginity are. Christ was before the virgin, Christ was from the virgin. He was born of the Father before the ages, to be sure, but he was born of the virgin on account of the ages. The former was natural to him, the latter was for our sake. He was always the former, he willed the latter.

5.22. And notice another of virginity's boasts. Christ is the bridegroom of a virgin and, if it can be said, Christ is the bridegroom of virginal chastity, for virginity is of Christ, but Christ is not of virginity. He is a virgin, then, who married [us]; he is a virgin who bore us in his womb; he is a virgin who brought us forth; he is a virgin who nursed us with his own milk. Of [this virgin] we read: 'What great things has the virgin of Jerusalem done! Teats shall not lack from the rock, nor snow from Lebanon, nor shall the water turn aside that is borne by the strong wind' (Jer. 18:13–14). Who is this virgin who is watered by the springs of the Trinity, to whom water flows from the rock, who does not lack teats and whose honey pours forth? 'But,' according to the Apostle, 'the rock is Christ' (1 Cor. 10:4). Therefore teats are not lacking to Christ, nor brightness to God, nor a river to the Spirit. For this is the Trinity, Father, Christ and Spirit, which waters its Church[10]

5.23. But now let us go from the mother to the daughters. 'Concerning virgins' says the holy Apostle, 'I have no command from the Lord' (1 Cor.7:25). If the teacher of the Gentiles had none, who could have any? And indeed he had no command, but he did have an example. For virginity cannot be commanded, but it can be wished for, inasmuch as the things that are above us are a matter of desire rather than of instruction. 'But I wish you' he says, 'to be without concern. For he who is without a wife is concerned about the things of the Lord, how to please God, and the virgin thinks about the things of the Lord, that she might be holy in body and spirit. For she who is married thinks about the things of the world, how to please her husband' (1 Cor. 7:32, 34).

6.24. By no means am I advising against marriage, but I am expatiating upon the benefits of virginity. 'The one who is weak,' says [the Apostle], 'should eat vegetables' (Rom. 14:2). It is one thing that I demand and another that I admire. 'Are you bound to a wife? Do not seek to be freed. Are you free of a wife? Do not seek a wife' (1 Cor. 7:27). This command is for those who are married. But what does he say about virgins? 'And the one who marries his virgin does well, and the one who does not marry her does better' (1 Cor. 7:38). The one does not sin if she marries; the other, if she does not marry, is immortal. In the one case there is a remedy for weakness, while in the other there is the glory of chastity. The one is not at fault, while the other is praiseworthy.

Let us compare, if you will, the advantages of married women with the very least advantages of virgins.

6.25. Although a noble woman may boast of her fruitful womb, the more she has borne the more she labors. Let her calculate the consolations that her children give her, but let her also calculate her trials. With marriage comes lamentation. How many are the desires that are wept over! She conceives and is heavy with child. Fruitfulness introduces a burden, in fact, before it produces progeny. She bears and is sick. How sweet are the offspring that begin in uncertainty and that end up in uncertainty, promising pain before pleasure! What she has gotten is fraught with uncertainty, nor is it possessed by her own choice.

6.26. What shall I say about the trials of nursing, training and marrying? These are the troubles of the happy! A mother has heirs, but she increases her sorrows. For one ought not to speak of adversity, lest the souls of the holiest parents be made to shudder. See, my sister, what a serious thing it is to undergo what ought not to be heard! And all of this is in the present age. But the days will come when they will say: 'Blessed are the barren and the wombs that have not borne' (Luke 23:29). For the children of this age are begotten and beget, but the daughter of the kingdom keeps her distance from the desire of man and from the desire of the flesh (cf. John 1:13) 'so that she might be holy in body and in spirit' (1 Cor. 7:34).

6.27. What point is there in going over women's heavy service and the slavery that binds them to their husbands, since God commanded them to serve before he did slaves (cf. Gen. 3:16; 1 Tim. 6:1)? I pursue these matters so that they might comply more willingly – they whose reward is love if they are upright, but who will be punished for wrongdoing if they are not upright.

6.28. From this there arise certain provocations to vice. For example, they paint their faces with far-fetched colors in their fear of displeasing their husbands, and with adulterated countenances they ponder how to adulterate their chastity. What madness is this, to change nature's likeness, to seek a painted countenance and, fearful of their husbands' judgement, to surrender their own! For she who desires to change what is natural is the first to declare against herself. And so, in striving to please someone else she first displeases herself. What truer judge of your unsightliness, which you fear to be seen, do we need, O woman, than you yourself? If you are beautiful, why are you hiding? If you are unsightly, why do you pretend to be attractive and allow neither yourself nor anyone else the favor of overlooking the matter? For he may love another woman, but you yearn to please another man. And you are angry if he should love another woman who is being taught to commit adultery against you! You are a bad teacher when it comes to being wronged. Even she who works for a pimp shuns flattering ways, and, however vile a woman she may be, none the less she does not sin against anyone else. But [the woman of whom I am speaking] sins against herself. More tolerable, nearly, are crimes of adultery, for in that case chastity is being adulterated, whereas in this case it is nature itself.

6.29. What price must one pay now so that even a beautiful woman may not be displeasing! Here costly necklaces hang from her neck, there her gold-spun garment is dragged through the dirt. Was her charm purchased, then, or did she already possess it! What about the various alluring scents that are used, too, the ears that are heavy with gems and the different color that is applied to the eyes? What is still her own when so much has been altered? How can a woman take leave of her senses and believe that she is alive?

6.30. But you, blessed virgins, who know not such great torments rather than ornaments, whose bashful countenances are suffused with holy modesty and whose adornment is a decent chastity, must not be enslaved to the glances of men and consider your merits from the perspective of others' waywardness. You yourselves, in fact, have your own soldierly charm, in which beauty of virtue and not of body shines forth. Age cannot extinguish it, nor death snatch it away, nor sickness ruin it. Of this beauty the sole judge to be sought is God, who loves the more beautiful souls even in the less beautiful bodies. You do not know the burden of the womb or the pains of childbirth, and yet more numerous are the offspring of a devout mind, which is fruitful in progeny and considers everyone her child, and which knows nothing of orphans but does have descendants.

6.31. You are like the holy Church, which is unsullied by

81

intercourse, fruitful in bearing, a virgin in chastity and a mother in offspring. And so she bears us as a virgin who has been impregnated not by a man but by the Spirit. As a virgin she brings us forth not with bodily suffering but with angelic rejoicing. As a virgin she nurses us not with the milk of the body but with that of the Apostle, which he gave to drink to a people of tender age who were still maturing (cf. 1 Cor. 3:2). What married woman, then, has more children than the holy Church? She is a virgin in her sacraments and a mother to her people, whose fruitfulness Scripture itself testifies to when it says: 'For more are the sons of the forsaken than of her who has a husband' (Isa. 54:1). Ours has no husband, but she does have a bridegroom because – whether as the Church in the midst of the peoples or as the soul in individuals – she is wedded to the Word of God as to an eternal bridegroom without endangering her chastity, and she is barren of injury and pregnant with reason.

7.32. You have heard, O parents, in what virtues you ought to raise and with what discipline you ought to instruct your daughters, so that you may have ones by whose merits your own sins may be forgiven. A virgin is a gift of God, a protection for her family, a priesthood of chastity. A virgin is an offering for her mother, by whose daily sacrifice the divine power is appeased. A virgin is the inseparable daughter of her parents, who neither troubles them about a dowry, nor abandons them by a leavetaking, nor offends them by a wrongdoing.

7.33. But suppose that someone desires to have grandchildren and to be called a grandparent. First he surrenders his own children while searching for others', and then he starts being defrauded of certain hope, only to have it replaced with uncertainty. He gives his own property and more is asked of him; if he does not provide a dowry, it is demanded of him; if he lives for a long time, he is a burden. This is purchasing a son-in-law, not acquiring one, who would make the girl's parents pay merely for looking at her. Was she carried in the womb for so many months only to be handed over to someone else's authority? Thus the upbringing of a well-bred virgin is undertaken only so that she may be all the more quickly removed from her parents.

7.34. Someone might say that I am discouraging marriage. But I encourage it and condemn those who are in the habit of discouraging it, since I am accustomed to cite the marriages of Sarah and Rebekah and other women of ancient times as instances of extraordinary virtue. For the one who condemns matrimony condemns children as well and also condemns human society from its first generation to its last. For how could generation succeed generation down through the ages unless the grace of marriage sparked the effort to beget offspring? And how could one commend the fact that the unsullied Isaac went to the altar of God as the victim of his father's devotion (cf. Gen. 22:1–14), or that Israel, while in a human body, saw God and gave a religious name to the people (cf. Gen. 32:29–31), if he condemns the fact that they were born? The sacrilegious persons [who say such things] have a point, which in this regard is approved even by those who are wisest – namely, that in condemning marriage they confess that they themselves ought not to have been born.

7.35. I am not discouraging marriage, then, if I enumerate the benefits of virginity. This latter, to be sure, is the work of a few, while the former is of all. Virginity cannot exist unless there is the possibility of being born. I am comparing good things with good things, so that what is superior may be that much more apparent. It is no judgement of mine that I am adducing; rather I am repeating the one that the Holy Spirit proclaimed through the prophet: 'Better,' he says, 'is barrenness with virtue' (Wisd. 4:1).

7.36. For the first thing that women who are to be married desire more than anything else is that they may boast of the beauty of their bridegroom. In this they inevitably confess that they are not the equals of the holy virgins, to whom alone it may justifiably be said: 'More beautiful than the sons of men, grace is poured forth on your lips' (Ps. 45:2). Who is this bridegroom? He is not one given to base inclinations or proud because of empty wealth, but his 'throne is forever' (Ps. 45:6). 'The daughters of kings are in his train. At his right has stood the queen in gold raiment, girt about with many virtues. Listen, then, O daughter, and see your father's house, for the king has desired your beauty, because he is your God' (Ps. 45:9–11).

7.37. Notice how much, according to the testimony of divine Scripture, the Holy Spirit has conferred upon you – a kingdom, gold and beauty: a kingdom, both because you are the bride of the eternal king and because you manifest an unconquerable soul and are not held captive by seductive pleasures but rule them like a queen; and gold, because just as that material is more precious when it is tried by fire, so the charm of the virginal body acquires an increase of loveliness after having been consecrated to the Divine Spirit. As far as beauty is concerned, who can think of a greater comeliness than that of her who is loved by the king, approved by the judge, dedicated to the Lord and consecrated to God, who is always a bride and always unwedded, so that her love is unending and her chastity unharmed?

7.38. This, this is indeed true beauty, which wants for nothing and which alone deserves to hear from the Lord: 'You are all beautiful, my beloved, and there is no blemish in you. Come hither from Lebanon, my bride, come hither from Lebanon. You shall pass and pass through from the beginning of faith, from the top of Sanir and Hermon, from the dens of the lions and from the mountains of the leopards'(S. of S. 4:7–8). In these words is described the perfect and unblemished beauty of the virginal soul, which is consecrated at the divine altar in the midst of the haunts and dens of spiritual beasts, not moved by transient things but intent, through the mysteries of God, upon being worthy of the beloved, whose breasts are full of gladness.

7.39. 'For wine gladdens the heart of man' (Ps. 104:15). 'And the fragrance of your garments,' it is said, 'surpasses every spice' (S. of S. 4:10). And further: 'And the fragrance of your garments is like the fragrance of Lebanon' (S. of S. 4:11). Notice the development, O virgin, that you are demonstrating to us. For the first fragrance of yours 'surpasses every spice' that was placed in the Savior's tomb, and it spreads its aroma upon the dead members of the body and upon the pleasures of its members that have expired. The second fragrance of yours, 'like the fragrance of Lebanon,' breathes forth the purity of the Lord's body thanks to the flower of virginal chastity.

8.40. And so, let your works be like honey from the comb, for worthy is the virginity that recalls the bees and that is as industrious, as modest and as continent as they are. The bee feeds on dew, knows nothing of copulation, and produces honey. As for the virgin, her dew is the divine discourse, because the words of God come down like dew (cf. Isa. 45:8). The virgin's modesty is her inviolate nature. What the virgin begets is the fruit of her lips, devoid of bitterness, rich in sweetness. Her toil is in common, and common is her fruit.

8.41. How I would wish you, O daughter, to be an imitator of this little bee, whose food is dew, whose mouth begets offspring, whose work is accomplished by its mouth! Imitate her, O daughter. Let your words not serve to veil anything deceitful, let them not cover over anything fraudulent, so that they may be pure and full of gravity. Let your mouth bring forth for you, as well, the everlasting posterity of your merits.

8.42. May you gather not for yourself alone but for many others (for how do you know when your soul may be demanded of you?), so that when you leave behind your granaries piled high with grain, which will add nothing either to your material well-being or to your merits, you may not be snatched away to a place where you cannot bring your treasure (cf. Luke 12:16–21). Be rich, therefore, for the sake of the poor, so that those who share your nature may share your wealth too.

8.43. Let me also point out to you the flower that you must browse upon. It is the very one that says: 'I am the flower of the field and the lily of the valleys, like a lily in the midst of thorns' (S. of S. 2:1–2). From this it is clear that virtue is surrounded by the thorns of evil spirits, such that no one may pluck its fruit unless he approaches it with caution.

8.44. Take up wings, then, O virgin, but let them be those of the spirit, so that you may soar above the vices if you yearn to touch Christ. 'He dwells on high and looks upon what is lowly' (Ps. 113:5), and 'his appearance is like' a cedar 'of Lebanon' (S. of S. 5:15) whose crown is in the clouds and whose roots are in the earth. For his origin is from heaven, but those parts of his that are deep in the earth have produced fruits that are very near to heaven. Search carefully for this flower, which is so good, lest you overlook it in the valley of your heart, for its fragrance is often caught in the lowliest places.

8.45. It loves to spring up in gardens, where Susanna found it as she walked about – she who was prepared to die rather than be violated (cf. Sus. 13:7, 23). What these gardens are [the Lord] himself explains when he says: 'A garden enclosed is my sister, my bride, a garden enclosed, a fountain sealed' (S. of S. 4:12). Thus in gardens of this sort the water of the pure fountain reflects the image of God that is impressed by its seals, so that its streams are not muddied by the wallowing of spiritual beasts.[11] The modesty that is fenced about by the wall of the Spirit is closed off so that it might not be exposed to violation. And so, like a garden inaccessible to intruders, it is redolent of the vine, emits the fragrance of an olive tree, and bursts with roses, so that on the vine religion may grow, on the olive tree peace, and on the rosebush the purity of sacred virginity. This is the fragrance that the patriarch Jacob emitted when he merited to hear: 'Behold, the fragrance of my son is like the fragrance of a fertile field' (Gen. 27:27). For although the field of the holy patriarch was fertile with nearly every fruit, nevertheless it produced fruits with more of an effort, whereas this one produces flowers.

8.46. Gird yourself, then, O virgin, and, if you wish this sort of garden to bloom for you, enclose it with the precepts of the prophets. 'Set a guard at your mouth and a door at your lips' (Ps. 141:3). Thus you will also be able to say: 'As an apple tree among the trees of the wood, so is my beloved in the midst of the sons. I took delight in his shadow, and I sat, and his fruit was sweet in my throat' (S. of S. 2:3). 'I found him whom my soul loved; I held him and I would not release him' (S. of S. 3:4). 'Let my beloved come down into his garden and eat the fruit of his fruit trees' (S. of S. 4:16). 'Come my beloved, let us go into the field' (S. of S. 7:12). 'Set me as a seal upon your heart and as a signet upon your arm' (S. of S. 8:6). 'My beloved is white and ruddy' (S. of S. 5:10).

For it behoves you, O virgin, to know fully him whom you love and to recognize in him the whole mystery of his unbegotten divinity and of the body that he assumed.[12] Rightly is he white, because he is the brightness of the Father (cf. Heb. 1:3), and ruddy, because he is the offspring of a virgin. The color of both natures shines and shimmers in him. Realize, though, that the signs of divinity in him are more ancient than the sacraments of his body[13] because he did not take his start with the virgin; rather, he who already existed came into the virgin.

8.47. He who was stretched out [on a cross] by the soldiers, he who was wounded with a lance in order to heal us by the blood of his sacred wound, will most certainly reply to you (for he is 'meek and lowly of heart' [Matt. 11:29] and 'charming in countenance' [Gen. 39:7]): 'Rise up, O north wind, and come, O south wind, blow upon my garden and let my spices flow forth' (S. of S. 4:16). For in every corner of the globe the fragrance of sacred religion has increased, where the members of the beloved virgin have emitted their aroma. 'You are as lovely as a good reputation, my beloved, as beautiful as Jerusalem' (S. of S. 6:4). It is not, then, the beauty of a frail body, which will perish through disease or old age, but the reputation for a meritorious goodness, which is subject to no vicissitudes and will never die, which is the virgins' ornament.

8.48. And since you are worthy now to be placed on the same footing with the heavenly beings whose life you live on earth, rather than with humans, accept from the Lord the commands that you are to observe. 'Set me,' he says, 'as a seal upon your heart and as a signet upon your arm.' In this way clearer proofs of your wisdom and of your deeds may be manifested, in which Christ, who is the image of God, may shine forth – he who is on a par with the

Father's nature and is the complete expression of everything that he has received from the Father of Deity. Hence also the Apostle Paul says that we have been sealed in the Spirit (cf. Eph. 1:13) because we possess the image of the Father in the Son, and we possess the seal of the Son in the Spirit. We who have been sealed with this Trinity should pay careful attention lest either loose behavior or any fraudulent adulteration unseal the pledge that we have received in our hearts.

8.49. But let this fear cease to exist in the holy virgins, for whom at the very beginning the Church provided great safeguards. She [i.e., the Church] who is solicitous for the well-being of her tender offspring herself grows like a wall, with abundant breasts like towers (cf. S. of S. 8:9), until the attack of the besieging enemy is over and she has obtained peace for her robust child through the protection of her motherly strength. Hence also the prophet says: 'Let there be peace in your strength and abundance in your towers' (Ps. 122:7).

8.50. Then 'the Lord of peace' (2 Thess. 3:16) himself, after having embraced in his strong arms the vineyards entrusted to him and looked upon his vines as they flourish, will with a protective gaze moderate the breezes [blowing] on the young fruits, as he himself testifies when he says: 'My vineyard is in my sight. There are a thousand for Solomon, and two hundred who care for his fruit' (S. of S. 8:12).

8.51. Previous to that it said: 'There are sixty strong men round about his offspring, armed with drawn swords and trained in military discipline' (S. of S. 3:7–8). Here it is a thousand two hundred: the number has grown where the fruit has grown, because the holier one is the more protected one is. Thus the prophet Elisha indicated that hosts of angels were with him to defend him (cf. 2 Kgs. 6:17); thus Joshua, son of Nun, recognized the captain of the heavenly army (cf. Josh. 5:14). Those, then, who can protect the fruit in us can also fight on behalf of us. But for you, holy virgins, there is special protection – you who with undefiled chastity are in attendance at the Lord's sacred bedchamber. It is not surprising that the angels fight on behalf of you who fight to maintain an angelic way of life. Virginal chastity is worthy of the protection of those whose life it is worthy of.

8.52. And why should I pursue the praise of chastity at greater length? Chastity has even produced angels. The one who has kept it is an angel, the one who has lost it is a devil. It is from this, in fact, that religion has taken its name. The virgin is one who is wedded to

God, the harlot is one who has made gods. What shall I say about the resurrection, whose rewards you already hold? 'In the resurrection,' we are told, 'they neither marry nor are given in marriage, but they are like the angels in heaven' (Matt. 22:30). What is promised to us is already yours, and the object of our longings is a commonplace for you. You are of this world and you are not in this world. The world has merited to have you, but it has been unable to keep you.

8.53. How remarkable it is that angels have fallen from heaven to earth on account of their intemperance (cf. Gen. 6:1–4), and that virgins have passed from earth to heaven on account of their purity!

Blessed virgins, whom the allurement of bodies does not disturb and whom the swill of pleasure does not cause to slip! A frugal diet and abstemious drinking habits, which teach them to be ignorant of the causes of vice, teach them to be ignorant of vice. What causes sin has frequently deceived even the righteous. Thus the people of God denied God after they sat down to drink (cf. Exod. 32:6). Thus Lot was unaware and endured it when his daughters slept with him (cf. Gen. 19: 31–35). Thus long ago the sons of Noah, walking backwards, covered over their Father's private parts, which the impudent one looked at, while the one who was most modest blushed and the one who was respectful covered them over, since he would have been shocked if he himself had looked as well (cf. Gen. 9:20–24). So great is the power of wine that wine could denude him whom the floods did not denude.

9.54. What is this! How fortunate it is that no desire for possessing inflames you! A poor person begs for what you have, but what you do not have he does not demand. The fruit of your toil is a treasure for the needy, and if two small coins are all that you have, it is wealth on the part of the giver (cf. Luke 21:1–4).

Listen, then, O sister, to what you are missing. It is not my role to teach or yours to learn what you should beware of, for perfect virtue does not usually desire instruction but itself educates. You see that the woman who sets out to be pleasing goes about like a float at a parade, making herself the object of everyone's glance and talk. Her very attempt to please makes her unattractive, for she displeases the people before she pleases her husband. In you, though, an unconcern for comeliness is the more becoming, and the very fact that you are unadorned is an ornament.

9.55. Observe the ears torn with wounds and pity the neck weighed down with burdens. The differences among the metals do not lighten the pain. In one case a chain binds the neck, in another it is fetters that confine the foot. It makes no difference whether a body be burdened by gold or by iron. Thus the neck is pressed down, thus the steps are made heavy. No price is too high, except that you women are afraid that your pain will disappear. What matters it whether someone else's judgement or your own condemns you? You are even more wretched than those who have been condemned by civil law, because they yearn to be set free, whereas you yearn to be bound.

9.56. And how wretched it is when a marriageable woman is put up for sale as if she were a slave, so that the highest bidder may purchase her! Yet slaves are better off, for they often choose their masters. It is a crime for an unmarried woman to make a choice and a reproach if she does not. However charming and attractive she may be, she both desires and fears not to be seen: her desire is to be sold more dearly, her fear is that being seen itself may be unbecoming. But how many absurd desires and fearful uncertainties she experiences over the outcome of her wooing: perhaps a poor man will mock her, for example, or a rich man scorn her, or a handsome man laugh at her, or a man of rank spurn her.

10.57. Suppose someone were to say: 'You sing the praises of virginity to us every day.' What am I to do if I sing the same thing over and over again every day without any success? But that is not my fault. Virgins come from Piacenza to be consecrated; they come from Bologna, they come from Mauretania to receive the veil here. It is a remarkable thing that you see: I preach here and I am persuasive elsewhere. If this is the way it is, we should preach elsewhere in order to persuade you.

10.58. Why is it that those who do not hear me are moved, while those who do hear me are unmoved? For I have known many women who wished to be virgins and were prevented from proceeding by their mothers and – what is worse – by widows. To them my words are addressed here: If your daughters wanted to love a man, according to the law they would be able to choose whom they wanted. Are they allowed to choose a man, then, and not allowed to choose God?

10.59. You may see how sweet the fruit of chastity is when it has made a favorable impression even upon barbarians. From the remotest parts of Mauretania and beyond virgins are drawn here in their longing to be consecrated, and, although all their families are in chains, still chastity knows no chains. She who grieves over the injustice of her servitude professes the kingdom of eternity.[14]

10.60. What shall I say of the virgins of Bologna? They are a multitude, fertile in chastity, who have renounced worldly pleasures and dwell in the sanctuary of virginity. Without sexual mates, but mated by purity, they have attained to the number of twenty and to the hundredfold fruit (cf. Matt. 13:23), and, as soldiers of an indefatigable chastity, they have abandoned their parents' hearth and make for the tents of Christ. Now they sound forth with spiritual canticles, now they provide for their sustenance by their labor, and by their own hand they seek to obtain the means for their generosity.

10.61. Once they have gotten wind of a virgin that should be tracked down (for they go after the game of chastity, which they seek out more than anything else), they pursue their hidden prey with the greatest care all the way to her very den. Or, if the flight of one of them seems to be freer, you may mark all of them rising in full feather, flapping their wings and breaking into applause as in a chaste chorus of purity they circle round the flier until, delighting in that white troop and having forgotten their father's house (cf. Ps. 45:10), she attains to the regions of purity and the vision of chastity.

11.62. It is a good thing, then, if a virgin's parents make an effort to encourage her to be pure, but it is still more glorious if the flame of a tender age betakes itself of its own free will, even without the support of its elders, into the blaze of chastity. Parents will refuse a dowry, but you have a wealthy bridegroom and, content with the riches of his ancestral inheritance, you shall not want for gain. How much more excellent is chaste poverty than a large dowry!

11.63. And yet, who have you ever heard was deprived of her lawful inheritance on account of her pursuit of chastity? Parents may object, but they want to be won over. At first they resist because they fear to give credence; they are frequently angry so that you may learn to stay your course; they threaten disinheritance in order to find out if you are able to allay your fear of the world's condemnation; they coax you with refined enticements in order to see if the lure of different pleasures might not make you more pliable. You are being tested, O virgin, as you undergo constraint. And these first struggles are the ones set for you by your parents' anxious wishes. Conquer your family feeling first, young woman; if you conquer your home, you will conquer the world as well.

11.64. But suppose that the loss of your inheritance is a threat to you. Does not the future reign of heaven make up for the loss of empty and perishable wealth? Yet, if we are to believe the heavenly words, 'there is no one who has left home or parents or brothers or

wife or children on account of the kingdom of God who shall not
receive sevenfold in the present time alone, but in the age to come
shall possess eternal life' (Luke 18:29–30, modified by Sir. 35:10).
Place your faith in God. You who entrust your money to human
beings, lend to Christ. The trustworthy guardian of the hope that
you have deposited will pay back the talent of your faith with multiplied interest (cf. Matt. 25:14–30). Truth does not fail, righteousness
is not confining, virtue does not deceive. But if you do not put faith
in Scripture, at least put faith in examples.

11.65. Not so long ago, within our memory, a young woman of
distinction by the world's standards, but now more distinguished in
God's sight, sought refuge at the sacred altar when she was being
urged to marry by her relatives and kinsfolk. For where better for a
virgin to go than where the sacrifice of virginity is offered? Nor,
indeed, was this the end of her boldness. She stood by the altar of
God, an offering of purity, a victim of chastity, now putting the
priest's hand on her head and beseeching his prayers, now impatient
at the justifiable delay and placing her head under the altar while
saying: 'Could there be a better veil for me than the altar, which
makes holy the veils themselves? More fitting is the bridal veil upon
which Christ, the head of all things (cf. Eph. 1:10), is daily consecrated.[15] Why are you upset, my kinsfolk? Why do you trouble
yourselves by continuing your matchmaking? I have already been
provided for. Are you offering me a bridegroom? I have found a
better one. Extol whatever riches he has, boast of his distinction,
talk up his power: I have one who is without compare – rich in the
world, powerful in authority, distinguished in heaven. If you have
one such, I will not turn him down. If you have not found him, you
are not acting to my benefit, my relatives, but behaving grudgingly.'

11.66. While the others kept silent, one man burst out: 'What if
your father were alive? Would he allow you to remain unmarried?'
Whereupon she replied with more religious devotion than family
feeling: 'Perhaps he died so that no one would be able to put anything in my way.' By his own death soon after that man showed that
this response regarding the father was a prophecy concerning himself. So the others, who had tried to stand in her way, feared the
same thing for themselves and began to be favorably disposed, and
her virginity did not bring upon her the loss of what was owed her
but even made a gain in terms of her purity.

Young women, you have the reward of your devotion. Parents,
take heed of the example of an offense.

Book two

1.1. In the previous book we wanted – although in fact we were not capable of it – to explain how great the gift of virginity was, so that the heavenly grace of the gift might of itself attract the reader. In the second book it would be fitting for the virgin to be initiated and, as it were, educated in the teachings of the appropriate precepts.

1.2. But inasmuch as we are feeble in counseling and unequal to teaching (for the one who teaches must surpass the one who is taught), we have decided, lest we appear to have abandoned the project that we began or to have taken too much upon ourselves, that she should be instructed by examples rather than by precepts. In any event, more progress may be made by way of example, because what has already been done is not considered difficult, what has been judged good is considered beneficial, and what has been successively passed on to us as a kind of legacy of our forebears' virtue is considered to be a matter of religion.

1.3. But if anyone charges us with presumption, he should make the charge of earnestness instead, because in fact I did not think that what the virgins asked for should be denied them. For I preferred to run the risk of immodesty than to be heedless of the desire of those whose efforts our God himself approves of with kindly indulgence.

1.4. Nor can this be seen as presumption because, when they had the means to learn, they sought my love rather than my teaching; and my earnestness can be excused because, although they had a martyr's authority regarding the observance of this discipline,[16] I did not judge it superfluous for them to be coaxed by our discourse into embracing their profession. He who corrects vices with severity can teach easily, but we, who are unable to teach, coax.

1.5. And because many of those who were absent wanted to have our discourse at hand, I put together this volume so that, while holding the book of my words addressed to them, they might not think that he whom they held was absent.

But let us proceed with what we had in mind.

2.6.[17] Let, then, the life of Mary represent virginity for you, set forth as it were in a portrait, from which, as if from a mirror, the beauty of chastity and the shape of virtue will shine out. From this source you may draw patterns of life that show, in the form of examples, clear teachings on upright behavior, what you ought to correct, what to flee from, what to hold onto.

2.7. The ardor to learn is first stirred up by the nobility of the teacher. What could be nobler than the mother of God? What could be more splendid than she whom splendor chose (cf. Heb. 1:3), what more chaste than she who brought forth a body without contaminating her body? And what is there to say about her other virtues? She who defiled no sincere affection with any corrupt guile was a virgin not only in body but also in mind. Humble of heart (cf. Matt. 11:29), serious in speech, prudent of spirit, sparing of words, devoted to reading, placing her hope not in uncertain riches (cf. 1 Tim. 6:17) but in the prayers of the poor, intent on work and modest in discourse, she was accustomed to seek not man but God as the judge of her soul, to slander no one, to wish everyone well, to stand up in the presence of her elders, not to look askance at her equals, to flee pride, to pursue reason and to love virtue. When did she offend her parents by so much as a glance? When did she argue with her kinsfolk? When did she disdain the humble? When did she laugh at the feeble? When did she shun the needy – she who was accustomed to go only to those gatherings of men that mercy would not blush at nor modesty pass by? There was nothing harsh in her eyes, nothing forward in her words, nothing unbecoming in her behavior. Her gestures were not abrupt, her gait was not slack, her voice was not pert: her bodily appearance itself was the image of her soul and an indicator of her virtuousness. A good house, indeed, ought to be recognizable from its very threshold and, when one first enters, it should be evident that no darkness lies hidden within. Thus our soul, unencumbered by any bodily restraints, should shine without like the light of a lamp placed within.

2.8. What is there to be told, then, about her sparing use of food or the abundance of her labors? The one exceeded nature, the other barely attended to nature; there were no intervals, and days of fasting were joined one to the other. And whenever she chose to eat, her food was usually what was at hand, which would keep her alive but not cater to pleasure. Sleeping was a necessity rather than a desire, but, even so, as her body rested her soul was alert: often in her sleep she either went over what she had been reading or continued what had been interrupted by sleep or made plans or arranged what had to be done.

2.9. Leaving her home was something unknown to her, except when she went to church,[18] and that she did with her parents or kinsfolk. Toiling in the recesses of her home or pressed upon by the crowd in the marketplace, yet with no better guide than herself, dignified in her gait and her countenance, with each step that she took she grew in grace. Although a virgin may have others to look out for her body, she herself must look out for her own behavior. There will be many from whom she may learn, but she who has virtues as her instructors must teach herself, for whatever she may have done serves as a lesson. Thus Mary paid heed to everyone as if she were being advised by many; thus she fulfilled all the obligations of virtue, not so much to learn as to teach.

2.10. It is as such that the evangelist has portrayed her, as such that the angel found her (cf. Luke 1:26–38), as such that the Holy Spirit chose her. What point is there in dwelling on details – that her parents loved her, that strangers praised her, she who was worthy of bearing the Son of God? At the very approach of the angel she was to be found at home, in seclusion, with no companions, lest anyone distract her attention, lest anyone disturb her, for she whose thoughts served as good companions did not desire female companions. Indeed, she even seemed to herself to be less alone when she was alone, for how could she be alone in the presence of so many books, so many archangels, so many prophets?

2.11. And so too, when Gabriel visited her, he found her, and Mary took fright at the angel as if at a man, having been surprised at his appearance, but when she heard his name she recognized it as not unknown. She who was no stranger to angels was a stranger to men, so that you might acknowledge her devout ears and her chaste eyes. Then when she was greeted she kept silent, but when she was addressed she responded, and she who at first had been disturbed afterwards promised compliance.

2.12. How considerate she was to her kinsfolk the divine Scripture attests. For she humbled herself the more when she knew that she had been chosen by God, and at once she set out for her kinswoman in the mountains (cf. Luke 1:39) – not, indeed, in order to believe through sight what she already believed through prophecy, for, as it says: 'Blessed are you who have believed' (Luke 1:45). And she stayed with her for three months (cf. Luke 1:56). It was not belief that was being cultivated over such a length of time; it was a matter, instead, of showing love. And this happened after the boy, enabled by devotion rather than by nature, leapt in his mother's womb and greeted the mother of the Lord (cf. Luke 1:41, 44).

2.13. Then, when so many wonders followed, when the barren woman gave birth (cf. Luke 1:57), the virgin conceived, the dumb man spoke (cf. Luke 1:64), the magi adored (cf. Matt 2:11), Simon waited (cf. Luke 2:25–35), and the stars made their announcement (cf. Matt. 2:2?), Mary, who was disturbed at the outset but undisturbed by these marvels, 'kept all these things,' it says, 'in her heart' (Luke 2:19). Although she was the mother of the Lord, still she desired to learn the precepts of the Lord, and she who had begotten God still yearned to know God.

2.14. What about her going to Jerusalem every year, too, for the solemn day of Passover, and her going with Joseph (cf. Luke 2:41)? In the virgin purity is the companion of each of her virtues, wherever she may be. This particular one must be in the virgin, or else there can be no virginity. Nor did Mary go to the Temple, then, without purity as her companion.

2.15. This is the portrait of virginity. For such was Mary that her life alone is a lesson for all. If, then, the model is not displeasing, let us approve of the deed in such a way that whoever yearns for [Mary's] reward for herself imitates her example. How many kinds of virtue are apparent in one virgin! The solitude of modesty, the ensign of faith, the obedience of devotion! She was a virgin within the home, a companion in service, a mother at the Temple.

2.16. O how many virgins will she meet, how many will she embrace and draw to the Lord as she says: 'She has been faithful to her marriage with my Son, she has maintained her bridal bed with an unstained chastity!' In the same way the Lord himself will greatly commend them to his Father, repeating these words of his: 'Holy Father, these are the ones whom I kept for you, on whom the Son of Man lay his head as he rested (cf. Matt. 8:20). I ask that where I am they also may be with me. But it must not be so for them alone, since they have not lived for themselves alone: let this one redeem her parents and that one her brothers. Righteous Father, the world has not known me, but these have known me, and they have not desired to know the world.' (cf. John 17:24–25).

2.17. What a display there will be, how great will be the joy of the applauding angels when one who has lived the heavenly life in this world merits to dwell in heaven! Then Mary herself, taking up the timbrel, will rouse the choirs of virgins who are chanting to the Lord because they have passed through the sea of this world, untouched by worldly tempests (cf. Exod.15:20). Then will each one exult and say: 'And I shall go to the altar of my God, to the God who rejoices in my youth' (Ps. 43:4). 'I shall offer to God a sacrifice of praise and pay my vows to the Most High' (Ps. 50:14).

2.18. For I would not doubt that these altars are accessible to you whose souls I would confidently call altars of God, upon which Christ is daily sacrificed for the redemption of your body. For if a virgin's body is a temple of God, what is her soul, which, when the ashes of its members, so to speak, have been stirred by the hand of the eternal priest, exhales the warmth of the divine fire once it has been covered over again? Blessed are you virgins who breathe out such immortal grace, as gardens do with flowers, as temples do with devotion, as altars do with a priest!

3.19. Let the holy Mary, then, shape you a lesson for living. Let Thecla instruct you in sacrifice.[19] When she had shunned marital intercourse and been condemned by her husband's rage, she altered the nature even of wild animals, which respected her virginity. For, having been readied for the beasts, when she had refused the glances of men and was offering her very vitals to a savage lion, she caused those who had looked with unchaste eyes to look again with chaste ones.

3.20. There they saw the beast crouched on the ground and licking her feet, giving silent witness that it could not violate a virgin's sacred body. The beast, then, was reverencing its prey. Oblivious of its own nature, it had put on ours, which men had abandoned. You could see, by a certain exchange of natures, men goading a beast who were clothed in animal savagery, and the beast, eagerly kissing the virgin's feet, teaching men how they should behave. So admirable is virginity that even lions marveled at it. Food did not move them, although they were unfed; violence did not get the better of them, although they were unpredictable; rage did not exasperate them, although they were stirred up; their instincts did not entrap them, although that was their way; their nature did not possess them, although they were savage. In adoring a martyr they taught what it meant to be religious. They even taught chastity inasmuch as they kissed nothing but the virgin's feet while, as it were, lowering their eyes modestly to the ground, lest any male, even a beast, see a virgin naked.

3.21. Someone might well say: 'Why have you proposed the example of Mary, as if there were anyone who could imitate the mother of the Lord? Why even Thecla, whom the teacher of the Gentiles instructed?' Let me offer you a recent example of this sort, then, so that you may realize that the Apostle was the teacher not just of one but of all.

4.22.[20] Not long ago there was a certain virgin at Antioch who kept from public view. But the more she avoided the gaze of men, the more she inflamed them. For a beauty that is heard of but not seen is all the more desirable by reason of two spurs to passion – love and knowledge – as long as nothing displeasing is encountered and it is thought that something pleasing is there, which the scrutinizing eye does not catch sight of but the yearning soul longs for. And so, lest passions feed any longer on the hope of possession, the holy virgin declared her chaste celibacy, thus extinguishing the fires of the unrighteous. The result was that she was no longer loved; instead she was betrayed.

4.23. Now there was a persecution. The maiden was unable to flee, and, very much afraid that she would meet those who were preying on her chastity, she prepared her soul for virtue, being so religious that she might not fear death and so pure that she might expect it. The day of her crown arrived. Everyone was tense with expectation. The young woman was brought forth, having declared herself ready to fight for both chastity and religion. But when they saw the firmness of her profession, her concern for her purity, her readiness to suffer and her modesty in the face of their stares, they began to reflect how they might strike at her religion by way of her chastity so that, once having removed what was more important, they might also snatch away what they had left. They ordered the virgin either to offer sacrifice or to be sent to a brothel.

4.24. (How can gods be worshiped who avenge themselves in such a way, and how can they live who make such judgements?) At this the young woman, not in doubt as to her religion but fearing for her chastity, said to herself: 'What shall I do? Today I shall be either a martyr or a virgin. One of the two crowns is begrudged us. But the title of virgin has no meaning where the author of virginity is denied. For how can you be a virgin if you devote yourself to a prostitute? How can you be a virgin if you love adulterers? How can you be a virgin if you seek love? It is more tolerable to have a virgin mind than virgin flesh. Both would be good if it were possible. If it is not possible, let us at least be chaste for God and not for man. Rahab too was a prostitute, but after she believed in God she found salvation (cf. Josh 2:1–21, 6:17–25). And Judith adorned herself in order to please an adulterer. Yet, because she did this for the sake of religion and not for love, no one judged her an adulterer. (Cf. Judith 10:3–4, 13:16). The case turned out well. For if she who committed herself to religion preserved both her purity and her native land, perhaps we too, by preserving our religion, can also preserve our chastity. But, if Judith had chosen to set her purity above her

97

religion, she would have lost her native land and then her purity as well.'

4.25. And so, having reflected on examples such as these, she at once took to heart the words of the Lord in which he says: 'Whoever loses his soul for my sake shall find it' (Matt. 10:39). And she wept and was silent, lest an adulterer so much as hear her speaking, and she chose not to do harm to her purity but refused to do harm to Christ. Consider whether she who did not submit her voice to adultery would have been able to submit her body to adultery. '

4.26. All at once my discourse is ashamed and fears, as it were, to enter upon and relate the wicked course of events. Stop your ears, virgins of God: a young woman of God is being led to a brothel. But open your ears, virgins of God: a virgin can be made to prostitute herself but she cannot be made to commit adultery. Wherever a virgin of God is, there is a temple of God. Brothels not only do not bring chastity into disrepute, but chastity even does away with the disrepute of a place.

4.27. A huge crowd of curiosity seekers surged towards the bordello. (Learn the miracles of the martyrs, holy virgins, but unlearn the vocabulary of these places.) The dove was shut up inside, while outside the hawks were loud, contending among themselves as to who would be the first to seize the prey. She, however, raised her hands to heaven, as if she had come to a house of prayer and not to a den of wantonness, and said: 'O Christ, you tamed savage lions for the virgin Daniel's sake (cf. Dan. 6:22): you can also tame the savage minds of human beings. Fire turned to dew upon the Chaldeans (cf. Dan. 3:27) and water stood still for the Jews (cf. Exod. 14:22) not of their own nature but by your mercy. Susanna knelt down for punishment and triumphed over the adulterers (cf. Sus. 13:44–63). The hand that violated the gifts of your temple withered up (cf. 1 Kgs. 13:4); now your temple itself is being threatened. Do not allow the sacrilegious unchastity, you who did not allow the thievery. May your name also be blessed now, so that I who have come to a place of defilement may depart a virgin.'

4.28. She had hardly completed the prayer when all of a sudden a man with the appearance of a fearsome soldier burst in. How the virgin trembled before him to whom the trembling people gave way! But she was not forgetful of what she had read. 'And Daniel,' she said, 'arrived as Susanna was about to be punished, and by himself he freed her whom the people had condemned. A sheep too may lie hidden in this lair of wolves. Christ, who even has his legions (cf.

Matt. 26:53), has his soldiers as well. Or perhaps the executioner has come in. Do not be afraid, my soul: he is used to making martyrs.' O virgin, 'your faith has saved you' (Luke 8:48).

4.29. The soldier said to her: 'I beg you not to fear, my sister. I have come here as your brother to save my soul, not to destroy it. Heed me, so that you may be spared. Having come in as an adulterer, I shall, if you wish, go out as a martyr. Let us exchange our clothing; yours fits me and mine fits you, but both fit Christ. Your garb will make me a true soldier; mine will make you a virgin. You will be clothed well and I shall be stripped better, so that the persecutor may recognize me. Put on the garment that will hide the woman and hand over the one that will consecrate the martyr. Wear the cloak that will hide the virgin's body and preserve her purity. Put on the cap that will cover your hair and conceal your face. Those who have gone into a brothel are usually embarrassed. Once you have gone out, never look back. Remember Lot's wife: she lost her natural condition because, even though her eyes were chaste, she looked upon lewd men (cf. Gen. 19:26). Do not fear that something may be lacking to the sacrifice. I myself am offering a sacrifice to God on behalf of you, and you are doing so on behalf of me, a soldier of Christ. You have accomplished much in the service of chastity, which fights for an everlasting gain. You have the "breastplate of righteousness" (Eph. 6:14), which encloses the body and provides a spiritual defense, "the shield of faith" (Eph. 6–16), which prevents one from being wounded, and "the helmet of salvation" (Eph. 6:17), for Christ is where the protection of our salvation is, because the man is the head of the woman (cf. Eph. 5:23), and Christ is of the virgin.'

4.30. While saying this he removed his cloak, which was a garment that until this time was suspected of being that of a persecutor and an adulterer. The virgin offered her neck, the soldier his cloak. What a festival there was, and what grace, when they contended for martyrdom in the brothel! A soldier and a virgin – that is, persons unlike in nature but alike in God's mercy – were brought together so that the prophecy might be fulfilled: 'Then wolves and lambs shall pasture together' (Isa. 65:25). See! the lamb and the wolf not only pastured but were even sacrificed together.

What else is there to say? When she had changed her clothing the maiden flew out of the snare, but no longer with her own wings inasmuch as she was borne by spiritual ones. And – what had never been seen before – she left the brothel a virgin, but Christ's.

4.31. Those, however, who were looking with their eyes but did not see (cf. Matt. 13:13), were like wolves overpowering a lamb, raging at their prey. One who was less modest went in. But when with his eyes he had grasped the situation he said: 'What is this? A maiden went in but a man is here. This is not that famous story of the hind substituted for the virgin.[21] Rather it is a case of a maiden being transformed into a soldier. I had heard and did not believe that Christ changed water into wine (cf. John 2:1–10), but now he has begun to change sexes as well. Let us get out of here while we still are what we are. Have I myself, who see something else than I can believe, been changed too? I came to a brothel, I see a pledge.[22] And yet I shall depart changed, I shall go out chaste – I who came in unchaste.'

4.32. When the facts were discovered (because a crown was owed to so great a victor), he who had been seized in place of the virgin was condemned in place of the virgin. Thus it was not just a virgin but martyrs as well who came out of the brothel. It is told that the maiden ran to the place of execution and that both contended over their death, he saying: 'I have been ordered to be killed; when the sentence was applied to me it no longer pertained to you,' and she crying out: 'I did not choose you as a bondsman against my death but as a protector of my purity. If it is my purity that is being sought after, your obligation remains. But if it is my blood that is demanded, then I want no one to assume liability for me; I have the means to pay my debt. The sentence was pronounced against me that was pronounced for me. Certainly, if I had made you financially liable for me and in my absence a judge had awarded your property to my creditor, the same sentence would be appropriate for me: I would meet your bond with my wherewithal. If I were to refuse, who would think me unworthy of a fitting death? How much greater is the loan when it is a question of life and death! Let me die innocently that I may not die wickedly. There is no middle ground here: today I shall be either guilty of your blood or a martyr in my own. If I came back quickly, who would dare exclude me? If I delayed, who would dare absolve me? As one who is guilty not only of her own flight but also of another's murder I am all the more subject to the laws. My body, which would not endure dishonor, can endure death. A virgin has a place to bear a wound, even if she had no place to bear an affront. I have resisted the disgrace, but I have not ceded my martyrdom to you. I have changed my clothing, not my profession.

If you snatch death from me, you have not saved me but defrauded me. Take care, I beg you, not to contend with me, take care not to dare to stand in my way. Do not remove the benefit that you have conferred. If you deny me this sentence you are restoring the previous one, for one sentence is changed by a previous sentence. If I am not bound by the more recent one, then I am bound by the previous one. We can both satisfy our sentence if you allow me to be killed first. Upon you they can carry out no other punishment, but in the case of a virgin her purity is punishable. And so you will be the more glorious if you are seen to have made a martyr out of an adulteress than to have saved an adulteress from martyrdom.'

4.33. What do you think happened? The two contended and both were victorious, and their crown was not divided but joined. And so the holy martyrs bestowed benefits on one another: one began and the other concluded their martyrdom.

5.34.[23] The schools of the philosophers, for their part, boast to the skies of the Pythagoreans Damon and Phintias. One of them, when he was condemned to death, asked for time to attend to his obligations. The tyrant, however, who was a very shrewd man, judged that he might not be able to find him, and he asked him to supply a stand-in who would be slain if he himself were to delay. Which of the two was the more noble I do not know. Both were noble. One found a bondsman against his death, the other offered himself. And so, when the guilty one was late for his execution, the one who bore liability for him accepted his death with utter composure. As he was being led off, his friend returned, substituted his own neck and yielded himself to the executioner. Thereupon the tyrant, astonished that friendship was dearer to philosophers than life, asked that he himself might enjoy the friendship of those whom he had condemned. So great was their virtue that it swayed even a tyrant!

5.35. This is worthy of praise, but it is less so than the case that we previously cited. For in the one instance they were both men; in the other, one was a virgin, who first overcame her sex. The ones were friends, the others unacquainted. The ones offered themselves to a single tyrant, the others to many and even crueler tyrants, for he was merciful but they were murderers. In the case of the former there was a legal obligation upon the one, whereas in the case of the latter the decision of both was free. The latter were the wiser because the joy of friendship was the goal of the others' pursuit, whereas theirs was the crown of martyrdom, for they contended for human beings, but the latter for God.

5.36. And since we mentioned that king,[24] it is appropriate to tell what he thought of his gods, so that you may better judge how weak they are when their own partisans mock them. For, when he entered the temple of Jupiter, he ordered that the gold cloak which covered his statue be taken off and a wool one be put on it, saying that gold was cold in the winter and heavy in the summer. So he made a mockery of his god by thinking that he could put up with neither heaviness nor cold. Likewise, when he saw a gold beard on Aesculapius, he commanded it to be removed, declaring it incongruous that the son had a beard while his father Apollo still had none. In the same way, he took the gold libation bowls from the statues that had them, alleging that he should accept what the gods gave. As he said: 'These are the offerings of human beings, made with the intention of our obtaining what is good from the gods. Nothing, however, is better than gold. If it is bad, though, the gods ought not to have it; but, if it is good, human beings, who know how to make use of it, are more entitled to it.'

5.37. Thus they were mocked, so that neither was Jupiter able to defend his cloak nor Aesculapius his beard, nor had Apollo yet attained puberty, nor were all those who are called gods able to get back the libation bowls that they were holding. It was not so much that they feared the crime of theft as that they had no feeling. Who, then, would worship those who can neither defend themselves like gods nor hide themselves like human beings?

5.38. But in the temple of our God, when Jeroboam, the very wicked king, removed the gifts that his father had put there and was pouring out libations to idols on the holy altar, the hand that he stretched out withered up, and the idols of his that he called upon were of no help to him. Then he turned to the Lord and pleaded for pardon, and at once his hand, which had withered up in sacrilege, was healed by true religion. (Cf. 1 Kgs. 12:26–13:6.) It was a very timely example of both the divine mercy and the divine wrath at work in one person when his hand was suddenly rendered useless as he offered sacrifice, but that he was pardoned when he repented.

6.39. I have prepared these small gifts for you, holy virgins, although I have not even been a bishop for three years and am uninstructed by experience; still, I have been educated by your way of life. For how could such wide experience as this have come about at so young an age in terms of formal religion? If you see any flowers [in my discourse], gather and collect them from the bosom of your own lives. These are not precepts for virgins but examples from virgins. Our discourse has painted a picture of your virtue, and you may see the outline of your dignity reflected back, as it were, in the mirror of this talk. Whatever is fragrant in this book is yours; to the degree that there is any grace in my thoughts, it is you who have inspired it. And because there are as many opinions as there are people, if there is anything refined in this talk of ours, let everyone read it; if there is anything astringent, let the more mature try it; if there is anything pure, let it cleave to your hearts and color your cheeks; if there is anything flowery, let the flowery age [of youth] not reject it.

6.40. We ought to stir up the love of the bridegroom, for it is written: 'You shall love the Lord your God' (Deut. 6:5). At weddings we should adorn our hair with at least some ornaments of speech, for it is written: 'Clap your hands and stamp your feet' (Ezek. 6:11). We should spread the everlasting marriage beds with roses. Even in these temporal unions the bride is acclaimed before being issued commands, lest harsh commands cause her offense before love be fostered by caresses and be firmly implanted.

6.41. Colts in all their vigor learn to love the sound of clapping near their necks, so that they will not refuse the collar; then they are broken in by endearing words rather than by the disciplinary lash. But once they have submitted their necks to the collar, then the rein holds them in check, the spur urges them on, their team members pull them along and their mates encourage them. In the same way our virgin must first frisk about with a devout love, look with wonder from the very threshold of marriage upon the gold couches of the heavenly nuptials, see the doorposts festooned with wreathes of greenery and drink in the charm of the chorus performing within. Thus, after having been called, she will not withdraw herself from the Lord's yoke before she has given her obedience.

6.42. 'Come hither from Lebanon,' then, 'my bride, come hither from Lebanon: you shall pass over and shall pass through' (S. of S. 4:8). Quite frequently should we sing this verse, so that she who has been called may at least harken to the Lord's words even if she gives no credence to human words. This is not a teaching that we have invented but one that we have received. The heavenly doctrine of the mystical hymn has taught this as follows: 'Let him kiss me with the kisses of his mouth, because your breasts are better than wine and the odor of your ointments is better than any spice; your name is ointment poured out' (S. of S. 1:1–2). The whole passage that speaks of these delights has the ring of play to it; it stirs up acclamation and arouses love. 'On that account,' it says, 'the maidens have loved you and drawn you. Let us run after the odor of your ointments. The king has led me into his inner chamber' (S. of S. 1:3). She begins with kisses so that she may attain to the inner chamber.

6.43. And so well does she endure hard labor and the practice of virtue that she may unlatch the bolt with her hand, go out into the field and remain in strongholds, although in the beginning she ran after the odor of his ointment. Soon, when she has entered the inner chamber, the ointment will be changed to strongholds. See then where she will go: 'If there is a wall,' it says, 'we shall build silver towers upon it' (S. of S. 8:9). She who used to play with her kisses is now building towers. Thus, turreted with the precious fortifications of the saints, she will not only repel hostile invasions but also provide trusty defences for good merits.

Book three

1.1. Now that we have arranged what we had to say in two earlier books, it is time, holy sister, to reflect upon those precepts of Liberius[25] of blessed memory, which you are accustomed to discuss with me. For as the man is holier his discourse will be all the more pleasing. For when on the birthday of the Savior you were making profession of your virginity at the tomb of the apostle Peter[26] by changing your garb (and what day could have been better than that on which a virgin acquired offspring?[27]), and numerous young women of God were also present, vying among themselves for your companionship, he said: 'My daughter, you have desired an excellent marriage. You see how many people have come together for the birthday of your bridegroom, and no one departs unfed. He is the one who, when he was invited to a wedding feast, changed water into wine (cf. John 2: 1–10). Upon you too, who were formerly subject to the base elements of material nature, he bestows the pure sacrament of virginity.[28] He is the one who fed four thousand people in the desert with five loaves and two fishes (cf. Matt. 14:15–21; 15:32–39). He could have fed more if there were more at the time who should have been fed. And he has called many to your wedding, but now it is not barley-bread that is served but his body from heaven.

1.2. 'Today, indeed, as far as his humanity is concerned, he was born a man of a virgin, but before all things he was begotten of the Father. In his body he recalls his mother, in his power his Father. He is only-begotten on earth, only-begotten in heaven, God from God, the offspring of a virgin, the righteousness of his Father, power from power, light from light, not unequal to his begetter, not divided in power, not confused when the word is projected or uttered, as if mixed with the Father, but as distinct from the Father by reason of the law of generation. It is he who is your beloved (cf. S. of S. 4:16), without whom there would be neither the things of heaven nor the things of the sea nor the things of earth. He is the Father's good word, which, it says, "was in the beginning" (John 1:1); there you have his eternity. "And he was," it says, "with the Father" (John 1:1); there you have his power, indistinguishable and inseparable from the Father. "And the word was God" (John 1:1); there you have his divinity. From this summary you must draw your faith.

1.3. 'Love him, O daughter, because he is good. For "no one is good but God alone" (Luke 18:19). For if there is no doubt that the

Son is God, and that God is good, then there is no doubt at all that God the Son is good. Love him, I say. He it is whom the Father begot as eternal before the morning star (cf. Ps. 110:3), whom he brought forth as his Son from his bosom, whom he uttered as his word from his heart (cf. Ps. 45:1). He it is in whom the Father was well pleased (cf. Matt. 17:5). He is the Father's arm, because he is the creator of all things; the Father's wisdom, because he has come forth from the mouth of God; the Father's power, because in him the fullness of Deity dwells bodily (cf. Col. 2:9). Him the Father so loves that he bears him in his bosom, places him at his right hand, calls him his wisdom and recognizes him as his power.

1.4. 'If, then, Christ is the power of God, is God ever without his power? Is the Father ever without his Son? If he is of course always a Father, then of course there is always a Son as well. He is, therefore, the perfect Son of a perfect Father. The one who disparages his power disparages him whose power he is. Perfect Deity does not allow for inequality. Love, then, him whom the Father loves; honor him whom the Father honors. For "whoever does not honor the Son does not honor the Father" (1 John 5:23), and "whoever denies the Son does not have the Father" (1 John 2:23). Let that be enough concerning faith.

2.5. 'But sometimes, even though faith may be secure, youth is uncertain. Use, then, a little bit of wine lest you contribute to bodily illness (cf. 1 Tim. 5:23), but not so that you arouse wantonness, for together the two, wine and youth, kindle a fire. Let fasting also rein in your tender age, and let a sparing approach to food confine your untamed desires as if by chains. Let reason serve to restrain you, hope to pacify you, fear to check you. For one who knows nothing of moderation is as if seized by horses; he is tossed about, trampled upon, mangled and afflicted by his untamed desires.

2.6. 'This is related to have happened once to a youth who was in love with Diana.[29] The story, however, is colored with poetic lies. Neptune, for example, griefstricken because his rival was preferred, is said to have loosed madness upon his horses, and for that reason his power is praised as great – not because he overcame the young man by strength but because he deceived him with a trick. Hence also they have instituted a yearly sacrifice to Diana, in which a horse is immolated at her altar. She who could love a person who did not love her, which is something that even prostitutes are usually ashamed of, is called a virgin!

'But, as far as I am concerned, even if they are fables, let them have authority because, although each of them was wicked, still it is less wicked that a youth would have been so inflamed with love for an adulteress as to die than that two gods, as they tell the story, would have contended in adultery, and that Jupiter would have avenged the grief of his prostituted daughter upon the adulterer's physician because he had healed the wounds of the one who had committed adultery in the woods with Diana – an excellent hunter, to be sure, not of beasts but of lusts (but also of beasts), so that she hunts naked.

2.7. 'Let them give Neptune, then, dominion over madness in order to add to him the crime of an unchaste love. Let them give Diana rule over the woods where she dwelled in order to confirm the adultery that she committed. Let them give Aesculapius the restoration of the dead so long as they confess that he himself, when struck by thunderbolts, did not escape [death]. Let them even give Jupiter the thunderbolts that he never had so long as they testify that he did have disgraceful behavior.[30]

2.8. 'But let us turn from fables to the task that we have set ourselves. I consider that in fact you should use sparingly all foods that produce heat for the body, for meat even brings down eagles in flight. In you yourselves there is that interior eagle of which we read: "Your youth shall be renewed like an eagle" (Ps. 103:5). As it holds to its lofty course, swift in its virgin flight, let it know of no longing for superfluous meat.

'The crowds at banquets are to be avoided, and formal calls are to be shunned.

3.9. 'I would like visits among the young to be infrequent, unless they be made to one's parents or those of equal status. For chastity is worn away by such duties, imprudence makes its appearance, laughter resounds and modesty disappears under the guise of sophistication. Not to carry one's part in a conversation is considered immaturity, but to converse is to engage in lies. It is better for a virgin to be parsimonious with her words than to abound in wickedness. For if women are ordered even to be silent in church concerning divine matters and to ask their husbands at home (cf. 1 Cor. 14:34–35), how cautious do we think virgins should be, in whom modesty is an adornment of their age and silence a recommendation of their modesty?

3.10. 'Is it an insignificant example of modesty that Rebekah put on a veil when she came to her espousals and saw her bridegroom, lest she be seen before she was married (cf. Gen. 24:64–65)?

107

Certainly the beautiful virgin feared not for her beauty but for her modesty. What about Rachel? How she wept and groaned when a kiss was wrung from her! Nor would she have ceased weeping except that she recognized her relative. (Cf. Gen. 29:11–12.) In this way she observed the duty of modesty while not neglecting the warmth of family ties. If a man is told: "Do not look at a virgin, lest she cause you to fall" (Sir. 9:5), what is to be told a consecrated virgin who, if she is in love, sins in her soul, and, if she is loved, sins in deed?

3.11. 'The virtue of keeping silent is highly important, especially in church. Let not a word of the divine readings[31] escape you; if you would apply your ear, suppress your tongue. You should let no word come from your mouth that you would wish to revoke, but you should be quite restrained in your willingness to speak. Indeed, there is much sin in talkativeness (cf. Prov. 10:19). To the murderer it was said: "You have sinned, be still" (Gen. 4:7), lest he sin the more. But to the virgin it must be said "Be still, lest you sin." For Mary, as we read, "stored up in her heart everything" (Luke 2:19) that was said of her son. And you, when anything is read in which Christ is either announced as about to come or shown to have come, must not make a disturbance by talking; instead, pay attention. Is there anything more disgraceful than that the divine utterances should be drowned out, so that they go unheard, are not believed and can reveal nothing, or that the sacraments[32] are proclaimed in the midst of a cacophany, so that the prayer which is offered for the salvation of all is impeded?[33]

3.12. 'The pagans tender the respect of silence to their idols. A well-known example bears this out:[34] When Alexander, the king of the Macedonians, was offering sacrifice, the flame caught the arm of the little barbarian boy who was kindling a fire for [the king] and scorched his body. But he remained immobile; he neither gave vent to his suffering with a groan nor displayed his pain with silent weeping. There was such a disciplined reverence in the barbarian boy that it overcame his natural inclinations. And it was not the gods that he feared, who were nothing, but the king. For what was there to fear in them who, had the same fire touched them, would have been burned?

3.13. 'How much better [an example) is it that a certain young man was ordered, while at his father's banquet, not to betray his meretricious amours with obscene gestures?[35] But you, virgin of God, "abstain from groaning, shouting, coughing and laughing"[36]

108

while at the mystery.[37] Can you not do at the mystery what he could do at a banquet? Let virginity be signaled first by the voice, let modesty close the mouth, let religion exclude weakness, let custom instruct nature. Her gravity is what should first announce a virgin to me – her obvious modesty, her sober gait, her chaste visage: let these tokens of purity precede the other indications of virtue. A virgin who is inquired after when she is seen is not sufficiently virtuous.

3.14. 'There is an oft-told tale about how, when the loud croaking of frogs was making it difficult for a religious gathering to hear, the priest of God ordered them to be quiet and to behave respectfully during the sacred prayer. Then, all at once, the overwhelming racket ceased. If the marshes keep silence, then, shall human beings not be silent? An irrational animal recognizes by reverence what it does not know by nature. Is the shamelessness of human beings so great that many of them pay less heed to the religion of their minds than they do to the wantonness of their ears?'

4.15. That is what Liberius of holy memory said to you. What for others is a major accomplishment in deeds is for you a fairly minor achievement in examples.[38] You have not only reached the level of all the disciplines by your virtue but by your striving have even gone beyond it. For we are commanded to fast, but on single days, whereas you spend an incalculable amount of time, nights and days in succession, without food, and if ever you are begged to take food and to lay down your book[39] for a moment you at once reply: 'Man does not live on bread alone but on every word of God' (Matt. 4:4). The food that you take is whatever is at hand, and your aversion to eating makes desirable not only fasting but also drinking plain water, weeping at prayer and falling asleep on your book.

4.16. These things are appropriate for one's younger years, until the mind has attained to a ripe age. But when a virgin has achieved the victory of a body that is under control, she should temper her efforts so that she may be spared to teach a younger generation. An old vine that was laden with fruitful shoots would quickly snap if it were not occasionally cut back. Yet as long as it is young it should be pruned lest it run wild with branches or, through an excessive fruitfulness, lose its strength and die. The good vinedresser works the soil surrounding the best vine, protects it from the cold and sees to it that it is not burned by the midday sun. He also tills alternating parcels of land or, if he does not let some go fallow, he varies his seed so that, by rotating his crops, his fields may rest. You also, as a seasoned virgin, should at least sow the hills of your heart with different seeds – at one time with mediocre sustenance, at another with harsher fasting, at still another with reading, then with work, and then with prayer. The variation of effort will thus serve as a beneficial pause.

4.17. The whole land does not produce [the same] harvest. Here vines rise upon the hills, there you may see purple olives and in another place fragrant roses. Often, too, the tireless husbandman leaves behind his plow and digs the earth with his fingers in order to plant flowers that are already rooted, and with the roughened hands that he uses to turn away the young bullocks fighting amid the vines he gently presses the udders of his sheep. It is better land, indeed, that produces a more abundant yield. You too, then, should follow the example of the good husbandman and not cleave your soil with constant fasting as with furrowing ploughshares. Let the rose of modesty and the lily of the spirit flourish in your gardens, and let banks of violets drink from the spring that is watered by the sacred blood.[40] What people say in ordinary language is that, if you want to do something abundantly, do not do it all the time. There should be something added to the days of Lent, but in such a way that nothing becomes a cause of ostentation rather than of religious devotion.

4.18. Let frequent prayer also commend us to God. For if the prophet who was preoccupied with the demands of his kingdom[41] said: 'Seven times a day I have praised you' (Ps. 119:164), what does it behove us to do, who read: 'Watch and pray, lest you enter into temptation' (Matt. 26:41)? Solemn prayers with thanksgiving should certainly be made when we arise from sleep, when we go out, when we are about to eat, when we have eaten, and at the hour of incense, when at last we are going to bed.[42]

4.19. But even in bed I want you to join psalms with the Lord's Prayer in frequent alternation, as also when you wake up and before drowsiness floods your body, so that at the very beginning of your repose sleep may find you free of care about worldly things and meditating upon divine ones. Even the man who gave philosophy itself its name used to order the flutist to play softer tunes, every day before he went to bed, so as to soothe his heart, which was anxious with worldly cares.[43] But he, like one who washes a brick, wished in vain to do away with worldly things by means of worldly things, for in seeking a respite through pleasure he besmeared himself with mud instead. We, however, once the filth of our early vices has been washed away, must cleanse ourselves within from every stain of flesh and mind.

4.20. Daily, too, before daybreak, we ought to make a point of going over the Creed, which is as it were the seal of our heart. Even when something frightens us we should have recourse to it in our soul. For when is the soldier in his tent or the warrior in battle without his military oath?

5.21. Now who would not understand the word that the holy prophet spoke for our instruction: 'Every night I shall wash my bed, I shall water my couch with my tears' (Ps. 6:6)? For if you understand 'bed' in a literal sense, it means that such an abundance of tears should be shed that the one who is making supplication washes his bed and waters his couch with his tears, for tears are present things, while recompense is in the future, because: 'Blessed are you who weep, for you shall laugh' (Luke 6:21). But if we take the prophetic word in reference to the body, we must wash away the sins of the body with the tears of repentance, for 'Solomon made himself a bed out of wood of Lebanon; its columns were silver, its frame was gold, its back was strewn with gems' (S. of S. 3:9–10). What is this bed except a symbol of our body? For by the gems, by reason of their brightness, the air is indicated; by the gold, fire; by the silver, water; and earth by the wood. Of these four elements the human body consists.[44] In it our soul reclines, if it is not deprived of rest because of the harshness of the mountains or the dryness of the ground but reposes supported by wood, far above the vices. Hence David says: 'The Lord will bring him help upon his bed of pain' (Ps. 41:3). For what could a bed of pain be if something that is senseless cannot feel pain? But a body of pain is like a body of death. 'Unhappy man that I am, who will free me from the body of this death?' (Rom. 7:24.)

5.22. And, since we introduced the verse in which we mentioned the Lord's body,[45] it should be remembered (lest perhaps it disturb a reader that the Lord took on a body of pain) that he was pained at and wept over the death of Lazarus (cf. John 11:33–35), that he was wounded during his sufferings, that water and blood came out of the wound (cf. John 19:34), and that he breathed forth his spirit (cf. John 19:30). The water was for washing, the blood for drinking and the spirit for resurrection. For the one Christ is for us hope, faith and charity – hope in the resurrection, faith in the washing and charity in the sacrament.[46]

5.23. Yet, as he took on a body of pain, so also he turned his bed in his weakness (cf. Ps. 41:3), in that he turned it to the advantage of human flesh. For weakness was abolished by his suffering, and death

111

by his resurrection. Even so, you ought to grieve over the world and to rejoice in the Lord (cf. Phil. 3:1, 4:4), to be sad for repentance (cf. 2 Cor. 7:9) and joyful for grace, although the teacher of the Gentiles (cf. 1 Tim. 2:7) also prescribed, in a salutary injunction, that we should weep with those who weep and rejoice with those who rejoice (cf. Rom. 12:15).

5.24. But the one who wishes to unravel this problem completely should have recourse to the same Apostle, for he says: 'Whatever you do, in word or in deed, do in the name of the Lord Jesus Christ, giving thanks to God the Father through him' (Col. 3:17). We should, therefore, refer all that we say and do to Christ, who produced life from death and created light from darkness (cf. Gen. 1:3). For a sick body is sometimes warmed with hotter objects and sometimes tempered with colder ones, and a change of remedies is salutary as long as it is carried out in accordance with a physician's orders, whereas, if this is done contrary to his directives, the illness increases. In the same way, whatever is decided upon by Christ, our physician, is a remedy, but whatever is used wrongfully is detrimental.

5.25. Joy, then, must be the product of a fully conscious mind – one that is not confused by coarse revelry and wedding tunes. For modesty is jeopardized and temptation lurks where extremes of dancing accompany pleasures. I desire the virgins of God to be removed from this. 'For no one,' as a certain teacher of worldly things has said, 'dances soberly unless he is crazy.'[47] If, in the view of worldly wisdom, the instigator of dancing is either drunkenness or madness, what are we to think of the warning – in the form of examples – of the divine Scriptures, where John, the forerunner of Christ, who was slain at the choosing of a dancer, is an example of the temptation of dancing being more harmful than the madness of sacrilegious rage (cf. Matt. 14:3–12)?

6.26. And since the memory of so great a man ought not to be evoked cursorily, it is apropos for us to advert to who and by whom and for what reason, how and at what time he was killed. The righteous man was killed by adulterers, and by the culprits the punishment for a capital crime was turned against its judge. Then, the dancer's reward was a prophet's death. Finally, in the midst of the banqueting and feasting, the order to carry out this cruel act was issued, and compliance in this fatal and shameful deed passed from the feast to the prison and back from the prison to the feast, which is something that would shock even the barbarians. How many crimes there were in this one evil act!

6.27. A feast marked by madness was heaped up with royal extravagances, and, when it was certain that a larger throng than usual had assembled, the queen's daughter, who had to be kept in a remote location, was brought forth to dance in the sight of the men. For what could be learned from an adulteress but the ruination of chastity? And what is such an incitement to wantonness as those things that, by reason of our coarse impulses, either nature hides or discipline veils, and to lay bare the secrets of the body, to flirt with the eyes, to turn the neck, to loosen the hair? Small wonder that the next step would be a crime against the Deity.

6.28. For how can modesty exist where there is dancing, shouting and noisemaking? Then the king, it says, was delighted and told the young woman that she could ask the king for whatever she wanted. He swore that, even if she asked for half his kingdom, he would grant it. See what worldly people themselves think of their worldly wherewithal, when for a dance even kingdoms are given away! But the young woman, advised by her mother, requested that the head of John be brought to her on a dish. When it says that 'the king was saddened' (Matt. 14:9) it implies not the king's repentance but a confession of iniquity, since the divine judgement customarily works in such a way that those who have done evil condemn themselves by their own admission. 'But on account of his guests' (ibid.), it says. What could be more disgraceful than to order that murder be committed lest one's guests be displeased? 'And,' it says, 'on account of his oath' (ibid.). O unheard-of conscientiousness! It would have been better had he broken his oath. That is why, with good reason, the Lord commands in the gospel that there should be no swearing, lest there be cause for perjury or a need to transgress one's oath. And so, lest an oath be violated, an innocent man was struck down. I know of nothing more horrifying. More tolerable are the perjuries of tyrants than their oaths.

6.29. Who, upon seeing the traffic between the banquet and the prison, would not think that the prophet had been commanded to be set free? Who, I say, upon hearing that it was Herod's birthday, that there was a ceremonial banquet and that the young woman had been given the right to choose whatever she wanted, would not believe that this was a mission bearing John's acquittal? What is there in common beween cruelty and pleasure, between violent death and wantonness? The prophet was taken away to be punished during a banquet, by an order issued during a banquet that he would not even have wished to be countermanded. He was slain by the sword, his head was brought out on a dish. This platter, from which an insatiable ferocity feasted, fit the cruelty.

6.30. See, O harshest of kings, a sight worthy of your banquet. Stretch out your hand lest anything be lacking to your savagery, so that streams of the holy blood may flow from between your fingers. And since your hunger cannot be sated by banquets, nor your thirst for unheard-of savagery quenched by goblets, drink the blood that is still flowing from the gushing veins of the severed head. Gaze upon the eyes that, even in death, bear witness to your wickedness and are repulsed by the sight of pleasure. Those eyes are shut not so much by the exigency of death as by a horror of wantonness. That golden mouth, now bloodless, whose judgement you could not endure, has grown silent, but it is still to be feared. Yet the tongue, which even after death is accustomed to fulfill the function of a living person, condemned the incest, albeit tremblingly.[48] This head was brought to Herodias, who rejoiced and exulted as if she had avoided judgement by butchering the judge.

6.31. What say you, holy women? Do you see what you should teach and also what you should unteach your daughters? Let her dance – but as the daughter of an adulteress. Let the woman who is modest and chaste, however, teach her daughters religion, not dancing. And you, grave and prudent men, learn also to shun the banquets of detestable persons; the feasts of the perfidious are like their judgements.

7.32.[49] Now, at the end of my discourse, as I spread my sails, you do well, holy sister, to raise the issue of what should be thought concerning the merits of those who have thrown themselves from heights or drowned themselves in a river in order not to fall into the hands of their pursuers, when divine Scripture forbids the Christian to use violence against himself.[50] And indeed, with respect to virgins placed in a situation of constraint, we have a clear judgement, since this is a case of martyrdom.

7.33. Saint Pelagia, who lived some time ago in Antioch, was barely 15 years old, a sister of virgins and a virgin herself. When the signal for persecution was first given she shut herself up at home, since she saw that she was surrounded by those who would rob her of her faith and her chastity. Her mother was away and she was bereft of her sisters' protection, but all the more filled with God. 'What shall we do,' she said, 'except be on the watch, O captive virginity? It is both my wish and my fear to die, because death is not something that we overtake but something that we accept. Let us die if that is permitted; but let us die even if they do not permit it. God is not offended by the remedy, and faith mitigates the misdeed. Certainly, if we should think of the full significance of the word, when is violence voluntary? It is violence, rather, to wish to die and not to be able. Nor do we fear the difficulty. For who is there who wishes to die and cannot, since there are so many ways that lead to death? Now will I overturn the sacrilegious altars by my own fall, and with my blood will I extinguish the blazing hearths. I do not fear that my hand will weaken and not follow through with the deed, that my heart will shrink from the pain. I will leave no sin to the flesh. I will not fear the lack of a sword. We can die by our own arms, we can die without benefit of an executioner, upon our mother's breast.'[51]

7.34. It is reported that she adorned her head and put on a wedding garment, so that you might say that she was going not to her death but to her bridegroom.

Now when the detestable persecutors saw the booty of purity that they had seized for themselves, they began to search for her mother and her sisters. They for their part, by a spiritual flight, were already holding the field of chastity when suddenly they were prevented from escaping and prepared for their crown by the approach of their persecutors on one side and by a rushing river on the other. 'What have we to fear?' they said. 'Here is water. Who will stop us from being baptized? (Cf. Acts 8:36.) This indeed is baptism, where sins are forgiven and a kingdom is obtained. This indeed is baptism, after which no one transgresses. Let the water take us that is accustomed to offer regeneration; let the water take us that makes virgins; let the water take us that opens heaven, that shelters the weak, that conceals death, that gives back martyrs. We beseech you, God, creator of all things: Do not allow the flood to disperse our bodies once they are deprived of life, nor let death separate our corpses when life did not separate our affections. Let there be one steadfastness, one death and one grave as well.'

7.35. Having said this, and having hitched up their dresses a little so as to protect their modesty while not impeding their movement, they joined hands as if they were dancing and advanced to the middle of the river bed, directing their steps to the spot where the water rushed all the more and the drop was steeper. Not one stepped back, not one slowed her pace, not one hesitated over her footing. They were anxious when they felt the ground or chanced upon a shallow place, and they were happy when it was deep. You

115

might have seen the loving mother tightening her grasp, rejoicing over her children and apprehensive of falling, lest the torrent sweep her daughters away from her. 'I offer these victims to you, O Christ,' she said, 'as guardians of chastity, guides of our journey, companions in suffering.'

7.36. But who could rightly marvel that such steadfastness was to be found among the living when even in death their bodies remained unmoved? The waters did nor strip their corpses, nor did the river's rushing current toss them about. Even the holy mother, though unconscious, still maintained her loving embrace, nor did she loosen in death the sacred grasp that she had tightened. Thus, having paid her debt to her religion, she died with a mother's love as her heir. For those whom she had joined together in martyrdom she claimed as her own even at the grave.

7.37. But why, sister, do I give you foreign examples when an inspired succession of chaste forebears has taught you, thanks to the presence of a martyr in your background.[52] For where did you learn when you did not have anyone from whom to learn, living in the country with no virgin for a companion and no teacher to instruct you? You have not acted as a disciple of virtue, because that cannot be the case without formal instruction, but as its heir.

7.38. How could it happen that Saint Soteris would not have begotten your spirit when she was the begetter of your line? In the days of persecution, after having been lifted to the pinnacle of suffering by the abuse of slaves, she gave her face – which, when the entire body is tortured, is usually untouched and looks upon the torment instead of suffering it – to the executioner. So strong and patient was she that, when she offered her tender cheeks to be punished, the executioner forsook his beating before the martyr surrendered to her wounds. Her face did not flinch, her countenance did not yield, lamentation did not overcome her nor did she give way to tears. Finally, when she had conquered the other kinds of punishment, she found the sword that she was searching for.

ON NABOTH

Introduction

This work, which may be datable to the late 380s, relies extensively on two sermons of Basil the Great – his sixth, *Against the Rich*, and his seventh, *On Avarice*. The drive of the treatise, its straightforwardness, its appeal to the emotions, its frequent use of direct address and its occasional lack of organization all suggest that it was originally a sermon or sermons, and that as such it may have undergone relatively little revision before having been published in its present form.

Ambrose uses both the account of Naboth's vineyard in 1 Kgs 21 and the parable of the rich fool in Luke 12:16–20 as his main scriptural texts, the latter of which serves as a kind of commentary on the former. Comparing the wealthy to the grasping King Ahab and the rich fool, he rebukes them for their heartless attitude toward the poor. Simultaneously he develops three notable ideas: that the earth and its resources are the common property of humankind; that almsgiving is of benefit to both rich and poor; and that avarice destroys not only those against whom it is directed but, even more so, those in whom it resides. These ideas were commonplaces in Christian antiquity, but rarely did other Western Fathers promote them as vigorously as did Ambrose in this writing.

On Naboth has been translated from the edition by Martin R.P. McGuire (ed.), *S. Ambrosii De Nabuthae*, pp. 46–103. The Latin text may also be found in PL 14.765–92 and CSEL 32.2.469–516. McGuire provides the sole English translation of the treatise.

1.1. The story of Naboth is an old one, but it is repeated every day. Who among the rich does not daily covet others' goods? Who among the wealthy does not make every effort to drive the poor person out from his little plot and turn the needy out from the boundaries of his ancestral fields? Who is satisfied with what is his? What rich person's thoughts are not preoccupied with his neighbor's possessions? It is not one Ahab who was born, therefore, but – what is worse – Ahab is born every day, and never does he die as far as this world is concerned. For each one who dies there are many others who rise up; there are more who steal property than who lose it. It is not one poor man, Naboth, who was slain; every day Naboth is struck down, every day the poor man is slain.

Seized by this fear, the human race is now departing its lands. Carrying his little one, the poor man sets out with his children; his wife follows in tears, as if she were accompanying her husband to his grave. Yet she who mourns over the corpses of her family weeps less because she [at least] has her spouse's tomb even if she has lost his protection; even if she no longer has children, she at least does not weep over them as exiles; she does not lament what is worse than death – the empty stomachs of her tender offspring.

1.2. How far, O rich, do you extend your mad greed? 'Shall you alone dwell upon the earth' (Isa. 5:8). Why do you cast out the companion whom nature has given you and claim for yourself nature's possession? The earth was established in common for all, rich and poor. Why do you alone, O rich, demand special treatment? Nature, which begets everyone poor, knows no wealthy, for we are not born with clothing or begotten with gold and silver. Naked it brings us into the light (cf. Job 1:21), wanting food, clothing and drink, and naked the earth receives us whom it brought forth, not knowing how to compass our possessions in the tomb. The narrow sod is equally spacious for poor and rich, and the earth, which did not contain the desires of the rich person when he was alive, now contains him entirely. Nature, then, knows no distinction when we are born, and it knows none when we die. It creates all alike, and all alike it encloses in the bowels of the tomb. What differences can be seen among the dead? Open up the earth and, if you are able, discern who is rich. Then clear away the rubbish and, if you recognize the poor person, show who he is apart, perhaps, from this one fact alone – that more things perish with the rich.

1.3. The silk raiment and wrappings woven with gold in which the body of the rich person is clothed are losses to the living and of no help to the dead. You are anointed, O rich man, and you stink. You ruin the beauty that belongs to others and acquire none for yourself. You leave behind heirs who fight among themselves. To your heirs, who fear to diminish or violate what has been left them, you leave behind an inherited responsibility rather than an open-ended benefit. If your heirs are frugal, they maintain it; if they are spendthrifts, they use it up. And so you either condemn your good heirs to constant anxiety or leave behind bad ones; wherefore let them condemn your deeds.

2.4. But why do you think that, as long as you are alive, you abound in all things? O rich man, you do not know how poor you are, how needy you seem to yourself – you who call yourself rich.

The more you have the more you require, and whatever you get hold of, you are still in need. Avarice is inflamed by money, not extinguished. Greediness has, as it were, certain steps, and as a person mounts them he hastens on to heights whence grave ruin awaits his downfall. Such a person was better off when he had less. In view of his possessions his requirements were modest, but with an increase of income there came a growth in greed. He does not want to be small in his wishes or poor in his desires. And so two intolerable situations are joined together: he increases the ambitious longing characteristic of a rich person without laying aside an attitude of begging. Hence divine Scripture teaches us how wretchedly he is in need and how abjectly he begs.

2.5. There was a king in Israel named Ahab and a poor man named Naboth. The former abounded in the wealth of a kingdom while the latter possessed a tiny plot of land. The poor man coveted none of the rich man's possessions, but the king seemed to himself to be lacking something because the poor man, who was his neighbor, had a vineyard. Who, then, seems to you to be the poor man? The one who is content with what is his or the one who covets another's property? Certainly the one seems to be poor in terms of goods, the other in terms of desire. A rich disposition knows not how to want, and abundant goods cannot satisfy an avaricious man's yearnings. Hence the rich man is covetous in his envy of [another's] property and complains of poverty.

2.6. But let us now consider the words of Scripture: 'And this came about,' it says, 'after these words: There was a vineyard belonging to Naboth the Jezreelite in Jezreel next to the house of Ahab, king of Samaria. And Ahab spoke to Naboth and said: Give me your vineyard and I shall make it a herb garden, because it is near my house, and I shall give you another vineyard in its place. But, if you prefer, I shall give you money for the vineyard, and I shall make it a herb garden. And Naboth said to Ahab: God forbid that I should give you my ancestral property. And his spirit was troubled, and he slept on his bed, covered his face and ate no bread' (1 Kgs. 21:1–3).

2.7. The divine Scripture had related beforehand that Elisha, although he was poor, left his oxen and ran after Elijah; he slew them, gave of them to the people, and clung to the prophet (cf. 1 Kgs. 19: 19–21). The previous words, then, were intended as a condemnation of the rich man whose story is told in the person of the king. For, although he possessed good things from God, as did

Ahab, to whom the Lord both gave a kingdom and at the prophet Elijah's prayer granted rain (cf. 1 Kgs. 17–18), he violated the divine commands.

2.8. Let us pay attention, then, to what he says. 'Give me,' he says. What else does someone say who is in need? What else does someone say who is asking for public assistance than 'Give me'? In other words: 'Give me because I am in need. Give me because I have no bread to eat, no money for something to drink, nothing to pay for a meal, no material for clothing. Give me because the Lord has given you, and not me, the means with which you should be generous. Give me because, if you do not, I shall have nothing. Give me because Scripture says "Give alms" (Luke 11:41).' How abject, how vile is all of this! There is no sense of humility here, but rather the fire of covetousness. And in this very degradation what impudence! 'Give me,' he says, 'your vineyard.' He confesses that it is another's in order to ask for what is not rightfully his.

2.9. 'And I shall give you,' he says, 'another vineyard in its place.' The rich person scorns what belongs to him as if it were vile, and he covets someone else's property as if it were the most precious of things.

2.10. 'But, if you prefer, I shall give you money.' Quickly he corrects his error by offering money for the vineyard. For he who desires to occupy everything with his own possessions wishes the other person to possess nothing.

3.11. 'And I shall make it a herb garden.' All this madness, all this uproar, then, was in order to find space for paltry herbs. It is not, therefore, that you desire to possess something useful for yourself so much as it is that you want to exclude others. Your concern is more to despoil the poor than to increase your own wealth. You consider it to your detriment if a poor person has anything that is thought worthy of a rich person's possession. You believe that whatever belongs to anyone else is your loss. Why does harm done to nature give you pleasure? The world was created for all, but you few rich try to keep it for yourselves. For not merely landed property but the heavens themselves, the air, the sea are claimed for the use of a few wealthy persons. This air, which you include in your widespread possessions – how many people can it provide for! Do the angels have portions allotted in the heavens to correspond with the divisions that you make on earth?

3.12. The prophet cries out: 'Woe to those who join house to house and field to field' (Isa. 5:8), and he reproaches them for their sterile avarice. For they flee the companionship of human beings and therefore exclude their neighbors. But they cannot flee because, when they have excluded some, others in turn take their place, and when they have driven out these, still others inevitably take up residence nearby. They cannot live by themselves on the earth. Birds associate with birds, and accordingly the skies are often darkened with the flight of a vast multitude; cattle are joined to cattle and fish to fish; it leads not to loss but to lively interaction when they strive for a large company, and they seek a kind of protection through the solace of great numbers. You alone, O man, exclude your fellow. You enclose wild animals and construct dwellings for beasts, but you destroy those of human beings. You allow the sea onto your estates so that its creatures may not be wanting [to you], but you extend the boundaries of your property so that you will have no neighbors.

3.13. We have heard the words of the rich man who sought what belonged to someone else. Now let us hear the words of the poor man who defended what belonged to him. 'God forbid that I should give you my ancestral property.' It is as if he thought that the rich man's money would somehow contaminate him. It is as if he had said: "'Let your money go with you to perdition'" (Acts. 8:20), but I cannot sell my ancestral property.' Here is something to emulate, O rich man, if you are wise: you should not sell your field for a night with a prostitute; you should not sell away your lawful rights to pay for revelry or to purchase luxuries; you should not put up your house for a wager at a game of dice, lest you lose the property acquired by your forebears.

3.14. When he heard this, the avaricious king was troubled in spirit, 'and he slept on his bed, covered his face and did not eat his bread.' The rich are in mourning if they have been unable to seize others' property. If a poor person has not been swayed by their wealth they cannot conceal the depths of their bitterness. They want to sleep, to cover their face, lest they see anything on earth that belongs to someone else, lest they notice anything in this world that is not theirs, lest they hear that a neighbor possesses something near them, lest they hear a poor person contradicting them. Such are the souls to whom the prophet says: 'Rich women, arise!' (Isa. 32:9).

4.15. 'And he did not eat his bread,' it says, because he sought someone else's. For the rich, who batten on plunder and meet their expenses with booty, prefer to eat someone else's bread rather than their own. Or at the very least he did not eat his bread since he wished to punish himself with death because something was being denied him.

4.16. Compare now the attitude of the poor person. He has nothing, and he cannot fast voluntarily except to God; he cannot fast except out of necessity. In fact you seize everything from the poor, you remove everything, you leave nothing; but it is you, O rich, who endure the suffering of the poor. They fast if they do not have – you, when you do have. You exact suffering from yourselves, therefore, before you inflict it on the poor. You undergo the distress of wretched poverty, therefore, as a result of your desire. The poor, to be sure, do not have what they could use, but you neither use it yourselves nor permit others to use it. You mine gold from the earth and conceal it again. How many lives do you bury in that gold!

4.17. For whom are those things kept, when you read of the avaricious rich person: 'He stores up treasures and knows not for whom he gathers them' (Ps. 39:6)? The idle heir looks forward to your death, while the disdainful heir complains that you will die too late; he hates increasing his inheritance and is eager to spend it. What, therefore, could be more wretched than losing the gratitude of the one for whom you are toiling? On his account you endure bitter hunger every day and fear daily losses to your table; on his account you provide for daily fasts.

4.18. I myself know of a rich man who, in setting out for the country, was in the habit of counting out the rather small loaves that he had brought from the city, so that from the number of loaves one could estimate how many days he was going to be in the country. He did not want to open his granary, which was sealed up, lest his stores be diminished. One loaf – hardly enough to feed the miser – was assigned for each day. I also found out from trustworthy evidence that, if an egg was added to this, he would complain that a chicken had been killed. I write this so that you may know that God's justice, which avenges the tears of the poor by your fasting, is vindicatory.

5.19. How religious your fasting would be if you assigned the costs of your banqueting to the poor! More acceptable was that rich man from whose table the poor man Lazarus, in his desire to fill himself, collected what had fallen (cf. Luke 16:21), but even his table was paid for by the blood of many poor people, and the cups that he drank dripped with the gore of the many whom he had driven to the gallows.

5.20. How many die so that pleasures may be prepared for you! Deadly is your greed, deadly your luxury. One man tumbled from a rooftop when he was readying large storerooms for your grain. Another fell from the top of a tall tree while searching for the sorts of grapes to bring down for the proper wines to be served at your banqueting. Another drowned in the sea in his anxiety that a fish or an oyster might be lacking to your table. Another froze to death in the winter as he made an effort to look for rabbits or to set snares for birds. Another was beaten to death before your eyes if he happened to do something displeasing, and he spattered your banquet with the blood that he shed. It was a rich man, finally, who commanded the head of a poor prophet to be brought to him at table, since he could find no other way of rewarding a dancer except by ordering the death of a poor man (cf. Matt. 14:6–11).

5.21. I myself have seen a poor man led away because he was obliged to pay what he could not, dragged to prison because there was no wine at the table of an influential man, bringing his sons to auction in order, if possible, to delay his punishment for a while; perhaps there would be someone who would help him in his hour of need. The poor man returned to his home with his sons and saw that everything was bare and that there was no food left for them. He wept over his sons' hunger, grieving that he had not instead sold them to someone who could feed them. Returning to his purpose, he makes the decision to sell them. But the damage inflicted by poverty and the obligations of a father's love for his family were in conflict, with hunger demanding the sale and nature urging its duties. Ready to die with his sons rather than be separated from them, he would take one step forward and then another back. But need and not desire conquered, and family feeling itself gave way to need.

5.22. Now let us consider the storms raging in the father's mind as to which of his sons he should give up first. 'Whom,' he says, 'should I sell first? For I know that the price of one is insufficient to feed the others.' (This alone would provide rich grounds for anxiety!) 'Whom should I offer? Whom will the grain auctioneer look upon with favor? I could offer my first-born. But he was the first to call me father. He occupies the first place among my sons, and him I rightly honor as the eldest. I shall give my youngest, then. But he is the one whom I love most tenderly. I am ashamed over the former and feel pity toward the latter; I groan over the former's position and over the latter's age. The one already senses anxiety, while the other knows nothing of it. The former's sorrow weighs me down, the latter's unawareness. I shall give thought to the others: one clings to me the more, another is more bashful; one is more like his father, another is more useful to him. In the one I would be selling my very image, in the other I would be betraying my hope. Woe is me! I have no idea what to do, no way of making a choice. Tragedy in all its shapes, a chorus of distress, surrounds me.

5.23. 'It is the madness of wild beasts to choose whom you must give up. The very beasts, when they sense danger threatening their offspring or themselves, are accustomed to choose which ones they will free from it, not which ones they will offer up to it. How, then, shall I set aside the affections of nature, how shall I strip myself of a father's mind? How shall I arrange to auction off a son, with what words shall I fix a price, into whose hands shall I deliver that son into slavery, with what eyes shall I look upon him as a slave, with what embraces shall I say farewell to him when he departs, with what words shall I excuse what I have done? "My son, I sold you for my food"? More fatal, then, is the poor man's table than that of the rich man: he sells off others, I sell what is mine; he obliges, I act voluntarily. In order to make my situation the more excusable I shall add: "My son, you shall serve in place of your brothers, so that food may be obtained for them. Even Joseph was sold into slavery by his brothers, and he fed both them and his father afterwards" (cf. Gen. 37: 2–36; 42ff.). He will respond: "But his father did not sell him but wept over his absence, and later even [Joseph] fell into the power of a rich man and could hardly be freed. Afterwards his posterity slaved many generations for the riches of Egypt. Sell me, then, father, on one condition – that the rich do not buy me."

5.24. 'I am at a standstill, I confess. What shall I do? I will sell no one. But as I reflect on the one, I see all of them perishing of hunger. If I give up one, with what eyes shall I look upon the others, who will be perturbed by my lack of family feeling and fearful lest I sell them also? With what shame shall I return home, how shall I go in, with what emotions shall I live there – I who denied myself a son whom disease did not carry off nor death remove? With what thoughts shall I look at my table, which so many sons, like olive vines, graced round about?' (cf. Ps. 128:3).

5.25. This is what the poor man laments in your presence, but in your avarice you stop up your ears, and your heart is not softened by the horror of the wretched situation. All the people groan, and you alone, O rich man, are unyielding. You do not heed the Scriptures, which say: 'Let your money go for the sake of a brother and a friend, and do not hide it under a stone to be lost' (Sir. 29:10). And, inasmuch as you pay no heed, Ecclesiastes exclaims in these words:

'There is an evil condition that I have seen under the sun – riches kept to the hurt of the one possessing them?' (Eccles. 5:13).

But perhaps you return home and talk with your wife, and she urges you to ransom the one who was sold.[53] On the contrary – she will urge you to buy feminine baubles for her out of what, however small, you would have been able to set a poor man free. She will emphasize to you the expenditures that will be necessary if she is to drink from a precious goblet, sleep on a purple bed, recline on a silver couch and burden her hands with gold and her neck with necklaces.

5.26. Women really enjoy fetters, so long as they are bound in gold. They do not think it burdensome, so long as they are precious; they do not consider them chains, so long as they are precious; they do not consider them chains, so long as a treasure glitters in them. They even enjoy wounds, so that gold may be inserted into their ears and pearls may hang down. Jewels are heavy too, and clothing is cold. They sweat in their jewels and freeze in their silks. Still, the costliness is gratifying, and what nature rejects avarice commends. With utter frenzy they are on the watch for emeralds and sapphires, beryl, agate, topaz, amethyst, jasper and carnelian. Even if half their inheritance is required they do not begrudge the expense, so long as they can indulge their covetousness. I do not deny that there is a certain pleasing luster to these stones, but they are still only stones. And they themselves, polished contrary to nature so that they may lose their rocky roughness, admonish us that it is, instead, the hardened soul that must be polished.

6.27. What craftsman has ever been able to add a single day to a person's life? Have riches ever ransomed anyone from hell? Whose sickness has money ever alleviated? 'A person's life,' it says, 'does not consist in abundance' (Luke 12:15). And elsewhere: 'Treasures are of no value to the unrighteous, but righteousness frees from death' (Prov. 10:2). Rightly does David cry out: 'If riches abound, do not set your heart on them' (Ps. 62:10). For of what value are they to me if they cannot free me from death? Of what value are they to me if they cannot be with me after death? Here they are acquired, and here they are left. We are speaking of a dream, then, and not of an inheritance. Hence the same prophet says well of the rich: 'They have slept their sleep, and all the men of wealth have found nothing in their hands' (Ps. 76:5). This means that the rich who have given nothing to the poor have found nothing in their own works. They have helped no one in need, they have been able to obtain nothing to contribute to their own well-being.

6.28. Reflect on the word itself.[54] The pagans refer to the rulers of hell and the judge of death as 'Dis'. They call a rich person 'dis' as well because a rich person can produce nothing but death, and his kingdom should be among the dead and his headquarters should be hell. For what is a rich person but a kind of bottomless pit as far as wealth is concerned, an insatiable hunger or thirst for gold? The more he devours, the more he burns. 'The one who loves silver,' it says, 'will not be satisfied with silver' (Eccles. 5:10). And further along: 'And this is indeed the greatest evil: just as he was, so has he gone, and his abundance labors for wind. And, indeed, all his days are in darkness and distress and much wrath and evil and anger' (Eccles. 5:16–17) – so much so that the condition of slaves is more tolerable, for they serve human beings, but he serves sin. 'For he who commits sin is the slave of sin' (John 8:34); he is always trapped, always fettered, never free of chains, because he is always in his sins. What a wretched slavery it is to serve sins!

6.29. Such a person cannot function according to nature, he cannot sleep when it is time to do so, nor does he enjoy the pleasures of food – even though none of this is foreign to a slave's condition. 'For sweet is the sleep of a slave, whether he eats a little or a lot, but for the one who is filled with riches there is no one who allows him to sleep' (Eccles. 5:12). Covetousness arouses him, a constant preoccupation with seizing others' property agitates him, envy torments him, delay vexes him, the unfruitful sterility of his crops disturbs him, abundance disquiets him.

Recall the rich man whose possessions gave him a copious harvest and who reflected within himself in these words: 'What shall I do, since I do not have a place to store my crops?' And he said: 'I will do this: I will tear down my granaries and build larger ones, and there I will gather everything that I have grown, and I will say to my soul: My soul, you have many good things laid aside for many years; relax, eat, drink, feast.' To him God responded: 'You fool! This night they are taking your soul from you. Who then will own what you have laid up?' (Luke 12:16–20.) Not even God himself allows him to sleep: he interrupts him as he thinks, disturbs him as he sleeps.

6.30. But neither does he permit himself to be at peace, since his abundance perturbs him and, in the midst of his copious harvest, he sounds like a beggar. 'What shall I do?' he asks. Is not this the voice of a poor man, of one who has no livelihood? In his need of everything he looks this way and that, searches through his home and finds nothing to eat. He considers nothing more wretched than to be consumed by hunger and to die from want of food. He seeks a quicker death and explores less tortuous ways of dying: he snatches a sword, suspends a noose, lights a fire, looks for poison. And, uncertain as to which of these he should choose, he asks: 'What shall I do?' Then the sweetness of this life makes him want to recall his decision, if only he could find the means to live. He sees everything bare and empty, and he asks: 'What shall I do? Where is there food and clothing for me? I want to live, if only I could find a way to sustain this life – but with what food, with what assistance? What shall I do,' he asks, 'since I do not have?'

6.31. The rich man cries out that he does not have. This is the way poverty talks. With his abundant harvest he complains of want! 'I do not have,' he says, 'a place to store my crops.' You would think that he was saying: 'I have no crops that I can live off.' Is he blessed who is put at risk by his abundance? On the contrary, with all his plenty he is more wretched than a poor person who is threatened by want. The latter has a reason for his anxiety; he suffers an injustice and he is without fault. The former has no one to reproach but himself.

6.32. And he says: 'I will do this: I will tear down my granaries.' You might think that he would say: 'I will open up my granaries. Let those come in who cannot endure hunger, let the needy come, let the poor enter, let them fill their satchels. I will tear down the walls that exclude the hungry. Why should I, whom God has provided abundantly with what I should give, hide anything away? Why should I shut up behind locked doors the grain with which God has filled the whole extent of my fields, and which grows and flourishes without anyone to oversee it?'

7.33. The hope of the avaricious man is borne out: the old granaries are bursting with the recent harvest. 'I had little and stored it in vain; now more has grown. For whom do I gather it? If I wait for the prices to go up, then I will have squandered a possibility of doing good. How many lives of the poor could I have saved with last year's harvest? Prices that are counted up in grace and not in money were the ones that should have given me pleasure. I will imitate the holy Joseph with his humane proclamation (cf. Gen. 41:56), and I will cry out with a loud voice: "Come, O poor, and eat my bread" (Prov. 9:5), open your bosoms, take my grain. The rich

127

man's plenty, the whole world's abundance, ought to be everyone's wealth.'

But this is not what you say. Instead you say: 'I will tear down my granaries.' Rightly do you tear down what no poor person ever leaves carrying anything. These granaries are the storehouses of iniquity and not the reserves of charity. Rightly does he tear them down because he knows not how to build wisely. The rich person tears down his property because he is oblivious of eternal things, he tears down his granaries because he knows not how to dispensé his grain but how to hoard it.

7.34. 'And I will build,' he says, 'larger ones.' Unhappy man, distribute to the poor what you spend on construction. In shunning the grace of generosity you are incurring the costs of construction.

7.35. And he added: 'I will gather everything that I have grown, and I will say to my soul: My soul, you have many good things.' The avaricious person is always concerned over an abundant harvest, for he calculates that food will be cheap. For abundance is advantageous to everyone, but a poor yield is so only to the avaricious person: he is pleased more by high prices than by abundant crops, and he prefers to have what he can sell by himself rather than with everyone else. Observe him as he worries lest the pile of grain be overflowing, lest in its copiousness it spill out of his granaries and in the direction of the poor, and the opportunity for doing some good be offered him. The produce of the earth he claims for himself alone, although he does not want to use it himself but deny it to others.

7.36. 'You have,' he says, 'many good things.' The avaricious person knows not how to enumerate anything except what is profitable. But I agree with him that what is pecuniary may be called good.[55] Why then, do you make evil things from good, when you ought to make good things from evil? For it is written: 'Make for yourselves friends from the mammon of iniquity' (Luke 16:9). For the one who knows how to use them, then, they are good; for the one who knows not how to use them rightly they are bad. 'He distributed, he gave to the poor; his righteousness endures forever' (Ps. 112:9). What is better than this? They are good if you give them to the poor, and when you do this you make God your debtor by a kind of charitable usury. They are good if you open up the granaries of your righteousness, so that you may be the bread of the poor, the life of the needy, the eye of the blind, the father of orphaned infants

7.37. You have the means to do this. Why are you afraid? I confront you with your own words: 'You have many good things laid aside for many years.' You can have plenty both for yourself and for others; you can have an abundance for everyone. Why tear down your granaries?

Let me show you a better place to store your grain, where you can keep it safe so that thieves will be unable to take it from you. Enclose it in the heart of the poor, where no worm will eat it, where it will not get stale with age. As storerooms you have the breasts of the needy, as storerooms you have the homes of widows, as storerooms you have the mouths of infants, so that it may be said of you: 'Out of the mouth of infants and sucklings you have perfected praise' (Ps. 8:1–2). Those are the storerooms that abide forever, those are the granaries that future abundance will not destroy. For what will you do a second time if you grow still more next year? If this happens a second time you will destroy what you are now building and build on a still larger scale. For God gives you abundance either to overcome or to condemn your avarice, so that you may not have any excuse. But you keep for yourself what he wished to grow for the many through you. More than that, you even deprive yourself of it, for you would save more for yourself if you distributed to others; the effects of good works revert to the very ones who have performed them, and the grace of generosity returns to its originator. Hence it is written: 'Sow for yourselves unto righteousness' (Hos. 10:12). Be a spiritual husbandman: sow what is profitable to you. Sowing is good in the hearts of widows. If the soil brings forth a richer yield than it received, how much more will be multiplied the recompense of the mercy[56] that you have shown!

8.38. Furthermore, O man, do you not know that the day of death overtakes the earth's begetting, but that mercy shuts out death's assault? Those who would demand your soul are already standing by, and do you still put off the fruits of your works, do you still calculate that you will live for a long time? 'You fool! This night they are taking your soul from you.' Rightly does he say 'night.' It is at night that the soul of the avaricious person is demanded. He starts off in darkness and abides in darkness. To the avaricious person it is always night, but to the righteous it is day, and to him it is said: 'Amen, amen I say to you: This day you will be with me in paradise' (Luke 23:43). 'But the fool is changed like the moon' (Sir. 27:43), 'whereas the righteous will shine like the sun in the kingdom of their Father' (Matt. 13:43). Rightly is that foolishness rebuked which sets its hope on eating and drinking. And therefore the time of death is pressed upon it, just as is said by those who pander to their gluttony: 'Let us eat and drink, for tomorrow we shall die' (Isa. 22:13). Rightly is that person called a fool who caters to the bodily aspects of his soul, because he knows not for whom he is preserving the things that he stores up.

8.39. Hence it is said to him: 'Who then will own what you have laid up?' To what purpose do you measure and count and seal every day? To what purpose do you weigh out gold and silver? How much better it is to be a generous distributor than an anxious custodian! How much it would profit you in terms of grace to be called the father of many orphans rather than to possess innumerable staters[57] sealed up in a sack! For our money is left behind here, but grace is transferred with us to the Judge for our merit.

8.40. But perhaps you will say what you are commonly in the habit of saying: 'We ought not to give to someone whom God has cursed by desiring him to be poor.' But the poor are not cursed, inasmuch as it is written 'Blessed are the poor, for theirs is the kingdom of heaven' (cf. Matt. 5:3 and Luke 6:20). It is not of the poor but of the rich that Scripture says: 'The one who controls the price of grain will be cursed' (Prov. 11:26). Furthermore, you should not look to what each person deserves. Mercy is not wont to judge on the basis of merit but to meet needs, not to examine as to uprightness but to help the poor. For it is written: 'Blessed is the one who is understanding concerning the needy and poor person' (Ps. 41:1). Who is it that understands? The one who is compassionate with him, who realizes that he is a companion given him by nature, who recognizes that the Lord made both the rich and the poor, who knows that he will hallow his income if he gives a small portion of it to the poor. Since you have the means to be gracious, then, do not delay and say: 'Tomorrow I will give' (Prov. 3:28), lest you lose the opportunity to give. Delay is dangerous when it touches upon another person's well-being; it could turn out that, while you hesitate, he will die. Better to make haste before death, lest perchance avarice hinder you tomorrow and your good intentions come to nothing.

9.41. But why do I say that you should not delay your generosity? It is more a matter of not hastening to robbery, it is more a matter of not extorting what you desire, it is more a matter of not seeking someone else's property, of ignoring what has been denied you, of patiently accepting what has been excused, of not listening to that Jezebel, avarice, when she appeals as it were to the diarrhetic discharge of your vanity: '"I myself will get for you" (1 Kgs. 21:7) the property that you desire. You are sad because you wish to consider the measure of justice, so that you do not snatch away another's property: I have my rights, I have my laws. I shall be calumniated, so that I may despoil him; and the life shall be beaten out of him, so that I may seize the poor man's possession.'

9.42. For what else is described in that narrative but the avarice of the rich, which is a vain and diarrhetic discharge that, like a river, carries everything away and brings to naught what might have been good?

This Jezebel does not exist alone; she is many. Nor does she belong to one age but to a multitude of ages. She says to all, as she said to her husband Ahab: 'Arise, eat bread and return to yourself. I myself will get for you the vineyard of Naboth the Jezreelite.'

9.43. 'And she wrote a letter in Ahab's name, sealed it with his ring and sent the letter to the elders and those freemen who were staying with Naboth. In the letter it was written: Fast a fast, set up Naboth at the head of the people and set up two men, sons of iniquity, against him, to bear false witness against him and to say: He has cursed God and the king. Then lead him out and stone him.' (1 Kgs. 21:7–10)

10.44. How clearly is the behavior of the rich expressed! They are grieved if they do not seize others' property; they refuse food, they fast – not to atone for a sin but to commit a crime. You may see them coming to church then, dutiful, humble, constant, in order to merit obtaining the successful outcome of their wickedness. But God says to them: 'This is not the fast that I have chosen, not even if you should bend your neck like a circle and spread out ashes and sackcloth. Not thus will you call an acceptable fast. Such is not the fast that I have chosen, says the Lord. But undo every tie of injustice, loose the bonds of contracts made under duress, set free the broken and break every unjust obligation. Break your bread for the hungry and bring the needy and homeless into your house. If you see someone who is naked, clothe him, and do not despise your own kin. Then will your morning light arise to you, and timely will your health arise, and righteousness will go before you, and the majesty of God will encompass you. Then will you cry out, and God will hear you. Even as you speak he will say: Behold, I am here.' (Isa. 58:5–9)

10.45. Do you hear, O rich man, what the Lord God is saying? And you come to church – not to give something to the poor person but to take it away. You fast – not so that what you would pay for your banqueting might profit the needy but in order to despoil the needy. What do you want for yourself with book and paper and seal and contract and legal obligation? Did you not hear: 'Undo every tie of injustice, loose the bonds of contracts made under duress, set free the broken and break every unjust obligation'? You offer me account books, but I rehearse to you the law of God. You write with ink, but I repeat to you the oracles of the prophets written by the Spirit of God. You compose false testimonies, but I demand the testimony of your conscience, which is your judge and which you will be unable to escape from or turn away from; its testimony you will be unable to reject on the day when God will reveal the secrets of men. You say: 'I will tear down my granaries,' but the Lord says: 'Allow instead whatever is in your granary to be assigned to the poor, allow these storerooms to benefit the needy.' You say: 'I will build larger ones, and there I will gather everything that I have grown,' but the Lord says: 'Break your bread for the hungry.' You say: 'I will take away the poor man's house,' but the Lord says that you should 'bring the needy and homeless into your house.' How, O rich man, can you wish for God to hear you when you think that God ought not to be heard? If the rich person's will is not respected, a pretext is established: it is considered an insult to God if the rich person's request is not granted.

11.46. 'He has cursed,' it says, 'God and the king.' Obviously the persons are equal, and so the affront is equal! 'He has cursed' it says, 'God and the king.' Lest the term 'curse' be offensive to the rich man and he be hurt by the very sound of the word, 'bless' is used in place of 'curse'.[58] Susanna was assailed by two witnesses (cf. Sus. 13:34), the Synagogue found two witnesses to hurl falsehoods at Christ (cf. Matt. 26: 60–61), and the poor man is slain on account of two witnesses.

'And so they led Naboth out and stoned him' (1 Kgs. 21:13). Would that he would even have been permitted to die among his own! The rich man even begrudges the poor man his grave.

11.47. 'And it happened,' it says, 'when Ahab had heard that Naboth was dead, that he rent his garments and covered himself with sackcloth. And after this it happened that Ahab arose and went down to the vineyard of Naboth the Jezreelite to take possession of it.' (1 Kgs. 21:16) The rich are enraged and bring false accusations in order to wreak harm if they do not get what they want. But when they have wrought harm with their false accusations they pretend to be downcast. Yet sad and grieving, as it were, not interiorly but exteriorly, they go out to the place where they have plundered property and make it their own by wicked means.

11.48. The divine righteousness is stirred by this and with appropriate severity condemns the avaricious man in these words: 'You have slain, and you have taken possession of the inheritance. Therefore, in the place where dogs licked up the blood of Naboth, dogs shall lick up your blood, and prostitutes shall bathe in your blood.' (1 Kgs. 21:19) How righteous, how severe a sentence – that he would be prevented, by the horror of his own death, from being separated from the harsh death that he inflicted on another! God sees the poor man unburied and therefore decrees that the rich man shall lie unentombed, so that, when dead, he may wash away the disgrace of his iniquity, although he thought that even the dead should not be spared. And so his corpse, moistened with the gore of his wound, manifested the cruelty of his life in the way that he died. When the poor man endured these things, the rich man was reproved; when the rich man followed after him, the poor man was vindicated.

11.49. But what does it mean that prostitutes bathed in his blood except perhaps that there appeared to be a certain meretricious wickedness[59] or bloody excess in the king's savageness, since he was so given to excess that he longed for herbs, so bloody that he would kill a man for herbs? A fitting punishment, fitting for his avarice, destroyed the avaricious man. And finally the dogs and the birds of the sky ate up Jezebel herself, in order to show that the plunder of the rich becomes the burial place of spiritual wickedness. Flee, then, O rich man, a death of this kind. But you will flee a death of that kind if you flee a crime of that kind. Do not be an Ahab, in that you desire your neighbor's property. Do not let that savage Jezebel, avarice, live in you. It is she who urges you on to bloody deeds, who does not restrain your desires but encourages them, who makes you sad even when you possess what you have desired, who strips you naked when you are rich.

12.50. For everyone who has an abundance considers himself the poorer when he thinks that he is lacking whatever others possess. The one whose desires the world does not contain is in need of the whole world, 'but the whole world of riches belongs to him who is faithful' (Prov. 17:6*). He flees from the whole world who, in consideration of his conscience, fears to be discovered. And therefore, although according to its symbolic value it is a rich person talking to a poor person, according to the narrative it is Ahab saying to Elijah: 'You have found me out, my enemy' (1 Kgs. 21:20). How wretched the conscience that was saddened when it was made manifest!

12.51. And Elijah said to him: 'I have found you out, for you did evil in the sight of the Lord' (1 Kgs. 21:20). Ahab was the very king of Samaria and Elijah was poor and in need of bread; he would have lacked sustenance if ravens had not provided him with food (cf. 1 Kgs.17:6). So downcast was the sinner's conscience that he was not uplifted even by his haughty royal power, and it is as if he were common and base when he says: '"You have found me out, my enemy," and have discovered in me what I believed was hidden. Nothing that is hidden in my mind is closed to you. "You have found me out," my wounds are clear to you, my captive condition is evident.' A sinner is found out when his wickedness is made manifest, but the righteous person says: 'You have tried me with fire, and no wickedness has been found in me' (Ps. 17:3). When Adam hid he was found out (cf. Gen. 3:8–9), but Moses' grave was never found (cf. Deut. 34:6). Ahab was found, Elijah has not been found (cf. 2 Kgs. 2:11?), and the wisdom of God has said: 'The wicked seek me and shall not find me' (Prov. 1:28). And so in the gospel, too, Jesus was sought and was not found (cf John 6:15, 8:21). Crime, therefore, makes manifest its author. Hence the Tishbite[60] also says: 'I have found you out, for you did evil in the sight of the Lord,' because the Lord hands over those who are guilty of crime, but the innocent he does not hand over to the power of their enemies. Finally, Saul sought the holy David and was unable to find him (cf. 1 Sam. 23:15, 24:4, 26:4), but the holy David found King Saul, for whom he was not searching, because the Lord handed him over to his power (cf. 1 Sam. 24:5). Wealth, then, is captive, but poverty is free.

12.52. O rich, you serve in a wretched slavery indeed when you serve error, when you serve covetousness, when you serve an avarice that cannot be satisfied. An insatiable whirlpool is the more violent when it swallows up things that have been thrown into it, and, like an overflowing well, it is polluted with mud and wastes away the ground, which will produce nothing. This very example is an appropriate warning for you. For if you draw nothing from a well, it is easily ruined by stagnant inactivity and base neglect, but movement clarifies its appearance and makes it sweet to drink. Likewise, a heap of riches that lies in a gritty pile is bright when it is used, but inactivity makes it useless. Draw something out from this well, then. 'Water puts out a burning fire, and alms will resist sins' (Sir. 3:30), but standing water quickly produces worms. Do not let your treasure stand and do not let your fire stand. It will stand in you unless you resist such a thing with your works of mercy. Consider, O rich man, how many blazes you are in. Yours is the voice of the one who says: 'Father Abraham, tell Lazarus to dip the tip of his finger in water and cool my tongue' (Luke 16:24).

12.53. Whatever you have contributed to the poor, therefore, is profitable to you; whatever you have diminished it by is gain to you. You feed yourself with the food that you have given to the poor, for the one who is merciful to the poor is fed himself, and there is fruit already in these things. Mercy is sown on the earth and germinates in heaven; it is planted in the poor and sprouts forth in God's presence.

'Do not say,' God declares, 'tomorrow I will give.' How does he who does not allow you to say: 'Tomorrow I will give' allow you to say: 'I will not give'? It is not anything of yours that you are bestowing on the poor; rather, you are giving back something of his. For you alone are usurping what was given in common for the use of all. The earth belongs to everyone, not to the rich, but there are fewer who do not use what is theirs than who do use it.[61] You are giving back something that is owed, then, and not bestowing something that is not owed. Hence Scripture says to you: 'Incline your soul to the poor, give back what is owed, and answer him with peaceable words in gentleness' (Sir. 4:8).

13.54. Why are you proud, O rich man? Why do you say to the poor man: 'Do not touch me'? Were you not conceived in the womb and born from the womb just as the poor man was born? Why do you boast of your noble heritage? You are accustomed to reckoning the pedigree of your hounds as if they were wealthy men, you are accustomed to talking up the nobility of your horses as if they were consuls: this one came from that sire and was born of that mare; this one boasts such and such a grandsire, that one is distinguished by reason of such and such great-grandsires. But none of that helps him to race; the prize is given not for nobility but for racing. Once defeated he is the more disgraceful, and his nobility is jeopardized as well. Beware, then, O rich man, lest the merits of your forebears be called into question on your account, lest perchance it also be said to them: 'Why did you designate such a person as your heir? Why did you choose him?' The standing of an heir has nothing to do with gold-fretted ceilings or porphyry decorations. The praiseworthy element there has to do not with men but with metal, for which men are punished. Gold is sought for by the needy and denied to the needy. They toil in search of it, they toil to find what they cannot possess.

13.55. Yet I marvel, O rich men, why you consider yourselves praiseworthy on its account, when gold is more a stumbling block than a mark of esteem, for 'gold is also a stumbling block, and woe to those who pursue it' (Sir. 31:7).

Blessed, therefore, is the rich person 'who has been found without blemish, who has not gone after gold and has not placed his hope in treasuries of money' (Sir. 31:8). But, as if he could not be known, he desires that such a person be shown him. 'Who is he?' he says, 'and we shall praise him' (Sir. 31:9). For he did something that we should admire as new rather than recognize as commonplace. And so he who can be approved with regard to riches – he it is who is truly perfect and worthy of glory, 'he who,' it says, could have transgressed and did not transgress, could have done evil and did not do it' (Sir. 31:10). Therefore he commends gold to you, in which there is so much inducement to sin, not as a thing favorable to human beings but as a punishment for them.

13.56. Or are you uplifted by spacious halls? They should instead arouse compunction because, although they might hold a crowd, they exclude the voice of the poor (although there is no point in hearing what has no effect once it has been heard). Furthermore, your palace itself does not serve to embarrass you, since in building it your aim is to overtop your wealth, and yet you do not overcome it. You clothe your walls and you strip human beings. A naked man cries out in front of your house and you ignore him; a naked man cries out and you are worried about what marbles you should use for your floor. A poor man looks for money and has none. A man begs for bread, and your horse champs on the gold [bit] under his teeth. Precious ornaments delight you, while others have no grain. What a judgement, O rich man, you are bringing on yourself! The people are starving, and you close up your granaries. The people are wailing, and you twist your jeweled ring. Unhappy man, in whose power it lies to save the lives of so many from death, and there is no will to do so! The stone in your ring could save the life of an entire people.

13.57. Listen closely to what kind of praise befits a rich person: 'I have freed,' it says, 'the poor from the hand of the mighty, and I have helped the orphan, who had no one to help him. The blessing of the one who was about to perish came upon me, the mouth of the widow blessed me. I was clothed in righteousness, I was the eye of the blind, the foot of the lame; I was the father of the weak.' (Job 29: 12–16) And further: 'Outside my gates no stranger has dwelled, but my door has been open to everyone who came. But even if I sinned by imprudence, I did not hide my fault; nor did I fear the multitude of the people, such that I would not tell of it in their presence if I had allowed a weak person to go out my door with empty bosom.' (Job 31:32–34) He also mentioned that he ripped up the debtor's pledge when [the debtor] returned it, without recovering what was owed him (cf. Job 31:35–37). But why should I repeat these things too – that he says that he wept over everyone who was sick and groaned when he saw a man in need while he was well off, and that they were evil days for him when he observed what he had and others lacked (cf. Job 30: 25–26)?

If he says this – he who never made a widow weep; who never ate his bread and did not give some to the orphan, whom from his youth up he fostered, fed and raised with the love of a parent; who never despised the naked; who covered the dead; who with the fleece of his sheep warmed the shoulders of the weak, did not oppress the orphan (cf. Job 31:16–21), never delighted in riches, never gloated over the downfall of his enemies (cf. Job 31:29): if he who did these things began, from the height of wealth, to be in need; if he kept nothing of his vast possessions but the fruit of mercy alone – then what shall become of you, who know not how to use your possessions, who at the pinnacle of wealth go through days of impoverishment because you give nothing to anyone and come to no one's help?

14.58. You are, then, the custodian of your riches and not their master. You who bury gold in the ground are, indeed, its servant and not its lord. 'Where your treasure is, there also is your heart' (Matt. 6:21). Hence in that gold you have buried your heart in the ground. Sell your gold, rather, and purchase salvation; sell your precious stone and purchase the kingdom of God; sell your field and buy back for yourself eternal life. What I say is true because I am adducing words of truth: 'If you wish to be perfect,' it says, 'sell all that you have and give to the poor, and you will have treasure in heaven' (Matt. 19:21). And do not be saddened when you hear this, lest it also be said to you: 'How difficult it is for those who have money to enter into the kingdom of God' (Mark 10:23). Rather, when you read this, reflect that death can snatch these things from you or one more powerful than you can take them away. Why then do you want little things instead of great things, empty things instead of eternal things, treasures of money instead of treasures of grace? The former are corruptible, the latter endure.

14.59. Reflect that you do not possess these things by yourself. The moth possesses them with you; rust, which consumes money, possesses them. Avarice has given these partners to you.

But see whom grace would place in your debt: 'The lips of the righteous shall bless the one who is prodigal with his bread, and there shall be a testimony of his goodness' (Sir. 31:23). It makes your debtor God the Father, who, like one in debt to a good creditor, pays the interest on the loan with which the poor person was helped. It makes your debtor the Son, who says: 'I was hungry and you gave me to eat, I was thirsty and you gave me to drink, and I was a stranger and you took me in, naked and you clothed me' (Matt. 25:35–36). For he says that whatever was given to any of the least ones was given to him (cf. Matt. 25:40).

14.60. You know not, O man, how to pile up wealth. If you wish to be rich, be poor to this world so that you might be rich to God. The one who is rich in faith is rich to God; the one who is rich in mercy is rich to God; the one who is rich in simplicity is rich to God; the one who is rich in wisdom, the one who is rich in knowledge – they are rich to God. There are those who possess an abundance in poverty and who are in need as far as wealth is concerned. The poor abound whose 'deep poverty has abounded in the riches of their simplicity' (2. Cor. 8:2), and 'the rich have been in need and have gone hungry' (Ps. 34:10). For not in vain does Scripture say: 'The poor shall be put over the rich, and their own slaves shall lend to their masters' (Prov. 22:7), because the rich and those who are masters sow what is useless and evil, from which they do not gather fruit but pluck off thorns. And therefore the rich shall be subject to the poor, and slaves shall lend spiritual things to their masters, just as the rich man asked that the poor Lazarus would lend him a drop of water. You also, O rich man, can fulfill these words: 'Give to the poor and you have lent to God.' For 'he who gives to the poor lends to God' (Prov. 19:17).

14.61. Here now is the holy David in the seventy-fifth Psalm, beautifully singing a hymn to God that addresses the Assyrian – that is to say, which is against the Assyrian of spiritual wickedness (cf. Eph. 6:12), the vain and foolish prince of this world (cf. John 12:31, 14:30, 16:11). It begins in this way: 'God is known in Judah' (Ps. 76:1) – that is to say, God is known not among the wealthy, nor among the noble and the powerful, but in the believing soul. 'And in

Israel,' it says, 'his name is great' (Ps. 76:1), not among princes and consuls, but in the one who sees God, for Israel is the one in whom a deep faith has been able to attain to the knowledge of God.

14.62. 'And his place,' it says, 'was established in peace' (Ps. 76:2), where a tranquil disposition is not agitated by the surges of the different desires, not disturbed by the tempests of avarice, not set ablaze by the fire of longing for riches. He it is who catches sight of eternal things and dwells in Zion (cf. Ps. 76:2), breaking all the instruments of spiritual warfare and destroying the bows (cf. Ps. 76:3) with which the devil is wont to aim fiery arrows (cf. Eph. 6:16) that burn grievous passions in the breasts of human beings. But those arrows can do no harm to the righteous person, whose light is God. So far removed is he from the horrible and gloomy darkness that the adversary can have no place in him, although he has been accustomed to find his way even into princes, as he found his way even into the traitor Judas (cf. Luke 22:3), cutting down the gates of his faith like trees in a forest (cf. Ps. 74:6) so that he would have access to his heart and lay hold of the tabernacle of the eternal name (cf. Ps. 74:7), consecrated by the office of apostle that had been conferred on him. Therefore he cut down the gates like a lawless usurper, so that he might enter in violence, but the Lord in his loving way casts light on his servants and illumines the darkness of this world with their shining merits and the brightness of their virtues. The peaceful and mild, who are settled in sober tranquility of mind, possess this grace before God, but those with foolish hearts are disturbed, and they themselves are responsible for their own agitation because they are tumbled about by their billowing desires and rise and fall as if they were on the open sea.

15.63. Who these might be he clearly said: 'All the men of wealth' (Ps. 76:5). He said 'all' and excluded no one. And well did he say 'the men of wealth,' not 'the wealth of men,' in order to show that they are not the possessors of their wealth but are possessed by their wealth, for the possession must belong to the possessor, not the possessor to the possession. Whoever, then, does not use his property as a possession and knows not how to give and dispense to the poor is the slave and not the master of his goods, for he watches over what belongs to others like a servant and does not use what is his like a master. When it comes to a disposition of this kind, then, we say that the man belongs to the wealth and not the wealth to the man.

'For there is a good understanding in those who use it' (Ps.

111:10), but the one who does not understand cannot claim for himself the grace of understanding and hence is lulled into a woozy torpor and falls asleep. Men of this sort, therefore, sleep their sleep (cf. Ps. 76:5) – that is, they sleep their own sleep, not Christ's. And those who do not sleep the sleep of Christ do not have the repose of Christ or rise in the resurrection of Christ, who says: 'I slept and rested and arose, because the Lord will support me' (Ps. 3:5).

15.64. In this world there also sleep those who are considered deserving of a rebuke from heaven (cf. Ps. 76:6), who have mounted horses that they were unable to rein in. We read elsewhere that either the Church or the soul says: 'He made me the chariots of Aminadab' (S. of S. 6:12). If, then, the soul is a chariot, see if the flesh is not a horse, whereas the strength of the mind is the driver, which rules over the flesh and restrains its urges with the reins of prudence as if they were some sort of horses.[62] They have fallen asleep, then, who have mounted the pleasures of the body but exercise no governance over them. For that reason they are called by preference riders rather than horses or drivers. For a driver uses his authority to drive his horses with discipline and skill, so that he may urge on the swift, restrain the unruly, recall the weary and transform the hesitant in accordance with his own desire. Hence, when Elijah was taken up and carried by chariot as if to heaven, Elisha cried out to him: 'Father, father, the driver of Israel and its horseman!' (2 Kgs. 2:12). This means: 'You who ruled over the Lord's people with good leadership have, thanks to your steadfastness, received these chariots and these horses racing toward the divine, because the Lord has approved you as a director of human minds, and therefore, like a good charioteer, you are crowned victor in the race with an eternal reward.' We also read in the prophet Habakkuk what was said to the Lord himself: 'You shall mount upon your horses, and your riding is salvation' (Hab. 3:8). For he drove his apostles, whom he directed to different places so that they might preach the gospel everywhere in the world. 'You shall mount': it says this as if to a driver rather than to a rider. For a horseman mounts, to be sure, but in order to control and not merely to sit down because he is lazy and sluggish in his weary mind and cannot keep up his pace.

15.65. Of the horseman one may read: 'And the horseman will fall backward, awaiting the salvation of the Lord' (Gen. 49:17–18). For, since no one is without fault, even if a horseman were to fall and be perverted by earthly vices, if he did not despair of rising again and were confident of the divine mercy, he would still attain to salvation. But, with regard to the rider, there is a clear indication that he is considered reprehensible when Moses himself says in the Canticle of Exodus: 'Horse and rider he has hurled into the sea' (Exod. 15:21). And in Zechariah the Lord spoke and said: 'I shall strike every horse with madness and its rider with foolishness' (Zech. 12:4). He did not speak of the horse alone but of the rider as well, just as you have it in Exodus too: 'Horse and rider.' For when there is a rider who cannot control his own horse, the horse itself rushes headlong and its fury carries it off to steep and dangerous places. Why then, O rich, do you trust in horses? 'Vain is the horse for safety?' (Ps. 33:17). Why do you applaud yourselves in chariots? 'These are in chariots and these are on horses, but we are exalted in the name of the Lord. They have been bound and have fallen, but we have arisen and been set upright' (Ps. 20:7–8). Do not love those that neigh after pleasure; do not, O rich, be aroused by the snorting of voluptuousness. Terrible is the Lord and no one, however powerful and rich, can resist him; from heaven he hurls his judgement.

16.66. It is good that you should be still, cease from your misdeeds and stand in awe of God's power. Therefore it was said to the parricide Cain: 'You have sinned, be still' (Gen. 4:7), so that he might put an end to his sinning. Let your thoughts be confessed to the Lord. Do not say: 'We have not sinned.' Paul said: 'Although I am conscious of nothing in myself,' yet he added: 'still I am not justified because of this' (1 Cor. 4:4). You too, although you are conscious of nothing, still confess to the Lord, lest there be anything that escapes you. For the one who confesses to the Lord and brings to confession his fragmentary thoughts 'will celebrate the festal day' in the sanctuary of his mind 'and will feast not with the leaven of malice and wickedness but with the unleavened bread of sincerity and truth' (1 Cor. 5:8).

16.67. And so in conclusion the prophet says, addressing you: 'Pray and make a return to the Lord your God' (Ps. 76:11). This means: Do not dissemble, O rich; the day is pressing on. Pray for your sins, return gifts for the good things that you have. You have received from [God] what you may offer; what you pay back to him is his. 'The gifts that I give,' he says, 'and the gifts that have been given to me – the gifts, in other words, that you offer me – are my gifts; I myself gave them to you and bestowed them upon you.' Hence the prophet says: 'You do not stand in want of my good things' (Ps. 16:2), and therefore I offer you what is yours, since I have nothing that you have not given me.

It is faith that makes gifts acceptable, and it is humility that commends offerings. 'Because of his faith Abel offered a greater sacrifice to God' (Heb. 11:4). The oblation of Abel was more pleasing than the oblations of his brother Cain (cf. Gen.4:3–5) because his faith was greater. How is it that the sacrifices of a poor man are more pleasing than those of a rich man? The poor man is richer in faith, wealthier in moderation. And although he is poor, he is of those of whom it is said: 'Kings shall offer you gifts' (Ps. 68:29). For the Lord Jesus takes delight not in those who make offerings, all clad in purple, but in those who rule over their own dispositions, who by the authority of their mind exercise dominion over bodily wantonness.

Pray, then, O rich! There is nothing that is pleasing in your works. Pray for your sins and misdeeds and return gifts to the Lord your God. Make a return in the poor person, pay back in the needy person, lend in that destitute person to whom, on account of your misdeeds, you cannot otherwise be reconciled. Make him your debtor whom you fear as an avenger. 'I shall not accept,' he says, 'calves from your home or goats from your flocks, for mine are all the beasts of the forest' (Ps. 50:9–10). 'Whatever you offer,' he says, 'is mine, because the whole world is mine. I do not demand what is mine, but from what is yours you can offer the zeal of your devotion and faith. I take no delight in the flattery of sacrifices; only, O man, "offer to God a sacrifice of praise and pay your vows to the Most High"' (Ps. 50:14).

16.68. Or at least it will be acceptable if we understand it in this way – that he said that the rich have slept their sleep, that he sent out in advance the Lord's rebukes against them, that he concocted something dreadful and that he proclaimed a power that the rich could not withstand.[63] Turning to all, he says: 'Let the rich sleep, let the rich be rebuked. "You pray and make return to the Lord your God. All who are round about him offer gifts"' (Ps. 76:11) – that is, give thanks, O poor – '"because God is not a respecter of persons"' (Acts. 10:34). Let them build up their wealth, let them hoard their money, let them heap up treasures of gold and silver. You pray, you who have nothing else; you pray, you who have this alone, which is more precious than gold and silver. You return gifts, you who are not far from the Lord, 'who are round about him,' for 'you who were distant have been brought close' (Eph. 2:13). But those who seem to themselves to be close on account of their riches and power have become distant because of their avarice. For no one is outside except the one whom wrongdoing has shut out, just as it cast out Adam from paradise and shut out Eve (cf. Gen. 3:23–24). No one is distant except the one whom his own misdeeds have banished.

16.69. Therefore you pray, you who are nearby, and return gifts 'to the one who is terrible, to him who cuts off the breath of princes, to him who is terrible among the kings of the earth' (Ps. 76: 11–12), because by no rich man's recompense will he be bought off, by no arrogance on the part of the powerful will he be moved, he who apportions the penalties for wrongdoing, who demands more from the one to whom he has given more (cf. Luke 12:48), who conferred a kingdom on Saul when he was a private citizen (cf. 1 Sam. 9–11), although he took away his kingdom and his life because he did not keep his commandment (cf. 1 Sam. 31), who on account of their faithlessness made many kings the captives of the Gentiles and took them from the people of their fathers (cf. 2 Kgs. 17:23–25) and, with reference now to the narrative at hand, who ordered that King Ahab, ungrateful for the good things that he had received from heaven, be slain in such a way that his wounds would be licked by dogs. For, because he who could not be sated by all the wealth of a kingdom had desired a poor man's vineyard, he was brought lower than utter destitution by the Lord. No one was found to wash his wounds, no one to cover his body. Human kindness failed in his regard, and canine savagery took its place. Clearly the avaricious man found worthy ministers for his obsequies.

17.70. At this point the question arises as to how to read what the Lord said to Elijah: 'Have you seen how Ahab has been shaken at my presence? I will not bring evils in his days, but I will bring evils in the days of his son' (1 Kgs. 21:29), or how to say that penance is efficacious before the Lord. 'Behold, the king was moved before the face of the Lord, he went away weeping, rent his garments, covered himself in haircloth and was clothed in sackcloth from the day when he killed Naboth the Jezreelite' (1 Kgs. 21:27). The result was that mercy moved God and changed his sentence. Therefore either his penance was inefficacious and did not bend a merciful Lord or the oracle was false, for Ahab was overcome and slain (cf. 1 Kgs. 22:34–37).

17.71. But consider that he had Jezebel for his wife, under whose influence he was inflamed, who turned his heart and made him accursed on account of his horrible sacrileges. She, then, recalled him from his penitential disposition. The Lord, however, cannot be considered fickle if he did not think that the promise which he had made when [Ahab] confessed [his guilt] should be kept when he was unmindful of his confession.

17.72. Listen to something else that is still truer. The Lord kept the terms of his sentence even though [Ahab] was unworthy, but [Ahab] was heedless of the divine benefits in his regard. The king of Syria had started a war. He was conquered and kept for pardon. Although a captive, he was set free and sent back to his kingdom (cf. 1 Kgs. 20:1, 29–34). In keeping with the divine sentence Ahab not only escaped but even triumphed, but through his own foolishness he armed against himself the enemy by whom he would be conquered. He had, to be sure, been warned by the prophet, who said: 'Give thought and see what you should do' (1 Kgs. 20:22). He had been warned, I say, because the help of heavenly grace was due in respect to the servants of the king of Syria, since he had said: 'The God of the mountains is the God of Israel and not the god Baal. Therefore, they have gotten the better of us. Hence, if we do not completely get the better of them, they will set up satraps in place of the king of Syria.' (1 Kgs. 20:23–24) In this way he would eliminate their strength and the king's power. And so in the first encounter he conquered, so that he put the enemy to flight (cf. 1 Kgs. 20:20); in the second he conquered, whereupon he sent his captive back to his own kingdom (cf. 1 Kgs. 20:29). It was on this account that there sprang up a clear oracle concerning his defeat, when one of the sons of the prophets said to his neighbor: '"Slay me." But the man refused to slay him. And he said: "Because you did not obey the word of the Lord, behold, when you leave me a lion will kill you." And he left him, and a lion found him and killed him.' (1 Kgs. 20:35–37) And after this another prophet stood before the king of Israel and said to him: 'The Lord says this: Since you let go from your own hand the man of destruction, behold, your life shall be in place of his life, and your people in place of his people' (1 Kgs. 20:42).

17.73. It is obvious from these oracles, then, that the Lord keeps his promises even with regard to the unworthy, but that the wicked are either overcome by their own stupidity or condemned for a second transgression even if they have escaped the snares of the first transgression. But it behoves us to act in such a way that we may be worthy by reason of our good works and may merit to receive what has been promised by the almighty God.

ON THE MYSTERIES

Introduction

This brief treatise, to which no date can be securely assigned (although a time in the early 390s is often suggested), was originally a series of sermons given by Ambrose during one Easter week to the newly baptized. Such sermons were commonly delivered at that time: they were the continuation and conclusion of the instructions that were provided for catechumens in the weeks preceding baptism, which usually occurred at Easter, and they explained the baptismal ceremonies, 'the mysteries,' which had not previously been divulged for reasons offered here in 1.2.

The ceremonies in question were dominated by three events, each of which is discussed by Ambrose. The first of these was what we today call baptism itself (although in Christian antiquity the entire process could be thus referred to), namely, a water bath. To this Ambrose devotes virtually the entire first half of his work. The second event, anointing, spoken of in 7.42 as 'a spiritual seal,' receives relatively little attention; it is identical with what we today call confirmation. The last few pages of the treatise are given over to the third and final aspect of the ceremonies, the eucharist, considered at length from the perspective of the transformation of the elements of ordinary bread and wine into the body and blood of Christ. In addition to these rituals there were others, such as a ceremony of footwashing and a vesting in white garments.

Central to Ambrose's presentation is his recourse to the Old Testament to justify and shed light on the various facets of baptism. The use of the Hebrew Scriptures in this way was a practice that went as far back as the New Testament, but in *On the Mysteries* it is particularly rich and elaborate. Of special interest is Ambrose's citation of passages from the Song of Songs in 6.29, 7.35–41 and 8.55–57. Since in Ambrose's day the Song of Songs was probably the pre-eminent mystical book of the Old Testament, seen as describing allegorically, in the language of human love, the possibilities of an intimate relationship with Christ, its use in this context implies that Ambrose viewed baptism not only as a sacrament, a 'mystery,' but also as a mystical event.

The present treatise, together with *On the Sacraments*, which is also by Ambrose, constitute the most detailed description of the ancient baptismal ceremonies that we possess in the Latin language, and for that reason it is of great importance. It must be noted, though, that Ambrose is speaking of baptism as it was carried out in Milan and that early baptismal practice was not uniform everywhere.

On the Mysteries has been translated here from Bernard Botte's critical edition of the text in SC bis, 156–93. Other editions of the original Latin are to be found in PL 16.405–26 and CSEL 73.13–116. There are a number of English translations, among them De Romestin 317–25 and FC 44.5–28.

1.1. Every day, after the deeds of the patriarchs or the precepts of the Book of Proverbs were read, we preached a sermon on virtuous behavior so that you might be educated and instructed by these things and grow accustomed to treading the paths of our forebears, cleaving to their way and obeying the divine oracles. Thus, having been renewed by baptism, you would hold fast to the style of life that befits those who have been washed clean.

1.2. Now the time has come to speak of the mysteries and to explain the very structure of the sacraments. If we had thought that mention should be made of this to you before your baptism, when you were not as yet initiated, we would have been considered betrayers rather than explainers. Moreover, it was better that the light itself of the mysteries be poured into you when you were without any previous knowledge than that discussion of some kind anticipate them.

1.3. Open your ears, then, and lay hold of the good odor of eternal life that was breathed upon you by the gift of the sacraments. This we signified to you when we celebrated the mystery of opening and said: 'Ephphatha – that is, open up' (Mark 7:34), so that each one who was advancing to grace would know what was being asked and would remember how to respond.

1.4. Christ celebrated this mystery in the gospel, as we read, when he healed the deaf mute (cf. Mark 7: 32–37). But, because the mute whom he healed was also a man, he touched his mouth. He did this, on the one hand, in order to open his mouth to the sound of his voice, which he poured into it, and, on the other hand, because a touch was appropriate for a man but would have been inappropriate for a woman.

2.5. After this the holy of holies was unclosed to you and you entered the sanctuary of rebirth. Look again at what you were asked, recall how you responded. You renounced the devil and his works, the world and its wantonness and pleasures. Your words are kept not in the tombs of the dead but in the book of the living (cf. Rev. 3:5).

2.6. You saw there the levite, you saw the priest, you saw the high priest.[64] Consider not their bodily forms but the grace of their ministries. You spoke in the presence of angels. As it is written: 'The lips of the priest safeguard knowledge, and from his mouth they search out the law, for he is the angel of the almighty Lord' (Mal. 2:7). There is no mistake, there is no gainsaying it: he is the angel who announces the reign of Christ, who announces eternal life. You must think of him in terms not of his outward appearance but of his office. Reflect on what he gave you, ponder his function and recognize his position.

2.7. Having entered, then, in order to look upon your adversary, who you deemed should be renounced to his face, you turned to the east. For the one who renounces the devil turns to Christ, and he looks upon him directly.[65]

3.8. What did you see? Water, to be sure, but not only that. The levites who were ministering there, and the high priest questioning and consecrating. The first thing that the Apostle taught you was that we must not contemplate 'what is visible but what is invisible, since what is visible is temporal, whereas what is invisible is eternal' (2 Cor. 4:18). And elsewhere you read that, 'since the creation of the world, the invisible things of God are understood by way of the things that have been made. His eternal power and also his divinity' (Rom. 1:20) are known through his works. Hence the Lord himself says as well: 'If you do not believe me, at least believe my works' (John 10:38). Believe, then, that the Deity is present there. Do you believe in his working but not in his presence? Where would his working come from were it not preceded beforehand by his presence?

3.9. Consider now how old this mystery is and that it is prefigured in the very origin of the world.[66] At the very beginning, when God made heaven and earth, 'the Spirit,' it says, 'hovered over the waters' (Gen. 1:2). Did he who was hovering over the waters not work upon the waters? But what shall I say? He was working. As far as his presence is concerned, he was hovering. Did he who was hovering not work? Know that he was working upon the construction of the world when the prophet tells you: 'By the word of the Lord the heavens were established and by the Spirit[67] of his mouth all their power' (Ps. 33:6). Both these things are supported by prophetic testimony – that he hovered and that he worked: Moses says that he was hovering and David testifies that he was working.

3.10. Here is another testimony. All flesh had been corrupted by reason of its sins. 'My Spirit,' it says, 'shall not remain in human beings because they are flesh' (Gen. 6:3). In this way God shows that by fleshly uncleanness and the stain of more serious sin spiritual grace is removed. Hence God, in his desire to restore what he had given, caused a flood and ordered Noah to get into the ark (cf. Gen. 6:17–18). When the flood was subsiding, he first sent out a raven, which did not return; then he sent out a dove, which we read returned with an olive branch (cf. Gen. 8:6–11). You see the water, you see the wood, you see the dove, and do you doubt the mystery?

3.11. Water is where the flesh is dipped so that every fleshly sin may be washed away; there every misdeed is buried. Wood is where the Lord Jesus was fastened when he suffered for us. The dove it is in whose appearance the Holy Spirit descended, as you learned in the New Testament (cf. Matt. 3:16); he breathes into you peace of soul and tranquility of mind. The raven is a symbol of the sin that departs and does not return if you too preserve the attentiveness and the demeanor of the just man.

3.12. There is a third testimony as well. As the Apostle teaches you: 'Our fathers were all under the cloud and all crossed the sea, and all were baptized into Moses in the cloud and in the sea' (1 Cor. 10:1–2). And then Moses himself says in his canticle: 'You sent your Spirit and the sea covered them' (Exod. 15:10). You notice that even then, in that crossing of the Hebrews, in which the Egyptian perished and the Hebrew escaped, holy baptism was prefigured. For what else are we taught every day with reference to this sacrament than that sinfulness is drowned and error abolished, whereas piety and innocence pass through unscathed?

3.13. You hear that our fathers were under the cloud, the good cloud that cooled the fires of the fleshly passions, the good cloud that overshadows those whom the Holy Spirit visits. He came upon the Virgin Mary and the power of the Most High overshadowed her when he begot redemption for the human race (cf. Luke 1:35). And that miracle was prefigured by Moses. If, therefore, the Spirit was present then in symbol, is he not present now in truth, when Scripture says to you that 'the law was given by Moses, but grace and truth came about through Jesus Christ' (John 1:17)?

3.14. Marah was a bitter spring. Moses placed wood in it and it became sweet (cf. Exod. 15:23–25). For water without the preaching of the Lord's cross is of no use for the salvation to come, but when it has been consecrated by the mystery of the saving cross it is ready to be used for the spiritual washing and the saving cup. Just as Moses the prophet, then, placed wood in that spring, so also the priest places the preaching of the Lord's cross in this spring and the water becomes sweet for grace.

3.15. You ought not, then, to believe solely with the eyes of your body. What is invisible is more completely seen, because the other is temporal, whereas this is eternal. What is not grasped by the eyes but perceived by the spirit and the mind is more completely viewed.

3.16. Let the passage from the Book of Kings that was read also teach you (2 Kgs. 5:1–14). Naaman was a Syrian and he had leprosy and could not be cleansed by anyone. Then a girl who was a captive said that there was a prophet in Israel who could cleanse him of the contamination of the leprosy. Taking gold and silver, it says, he went off to see the king of Israel. When he was apprised of the reason for his coming he rent his garments, declaring that he was being put to the test because what was being requested of him did not fall under his royal power. Elisha, however, told the king to send the Syrian to him so that he might know that there was a God in Israel. And when he came he ordered him to bathe seven times in the River Jordan.

3.17. Then [Naaman] began to think to himself that the rivers of his own homeland had better water and that he had often bathed in them without ever being washed of his leprosy; changing his mind on that account, he did not obey the prophet's orders. But, thanks to the admonition and persuasion of his attendants, he gave in and bathed, and when he was cleansed then and there he understood that it is not water but grace that cleanses a person.

3.18. Recognize now who that captive girl is. She is the younger assembly from among the Gentiles – that is, the Church of the Lord, once humiliated by the captivity of sin, when she did not as yet possess the freedom of grace. Thanks to her counsel that foolish people of the pagans listened to the prophetic word about which they had previously entertained doubts over a long period. Yet afterwards when they believed that it was to be obeyed, they were washed clean of every contamination of vice. [Naaman] doubted before he was healed; you have already been healed and therefore you must not doubt.

4.19. Hence you were told beforehand that you should not believe merely what you saw, lest perchance you yourself say: 'Is this that great mystery "that eye has not seen and ear has not heard, nor has it entered into the heart of man" (1 Cor. 2:9)? I see the water that I am accustomed to seeing every day. Is that water, which I have often gone into without ever having been cleansed, to cleanse me now?' Recognize from this that water does not cleanse without the Spirit.

4.20. And so you read that the three witnesses in baptism – namely, water, blood and the Spirit (cf. 1 John 5:6) are one because, if you remove one of them, the sacrament of baptism no longer exists. For, without the cross of Christ, what is water but an ordinary element without any sacramental effect? Neither, by the same token, is there a mystery of rebirth without water, for, 'unless one be born again of water and the Spirit, one cannot enter into the kingdom of God' (John 3:5). Of course the catechumen believes in the cross of the Lord Jesus, with which he himself is marked, but unless he has been baptized in the name of the Father and of the Son and of the Holy Spirit he cannot receive the remission of his sins or accept the gift of spiritual grace.

4.21. That Syrian, then, bathed seven times in the law, but you were baptized in the name of the Trinity. You confessed the Father (remember what you did!), you confessed the Son, you confessed the Spirit. Hold to this order of things. In this faith you died to the world and rose to God. Buried as it were in this element of the world,[68] and having died to sin, you rose to eternal life. Believe, then, that this water is not inefficacious.

4.22. Therefore it was said to you that 'the angel of the Lord would come down into the pool at a given moment and the water would be stirred, and the first one to go into the pool after the water had been stirred would be healed of any malady whatsoever that afflicted him' (John 5:4). This pool, in which one person a year was healed, was in Jerusalem, but no one was healed until the angel came down. The angel would come down, the water would be stirred. The water would be stirred for the sake of the incredulous. For them there was a sign, for you there is faith; for them an angel would come down, for you there is the Holy Spirit; for them a created thing was stirred, for you Christ the Lord himself is at work in a created thing.

4.23. Then one person was cured, now all are healed, or rather a single person who is the Christian people. For there is also among some 'a deceiving water' (Jer. 15:18). The baptism of the faithless does not heal or cleanse but pollutes. The Jews baptize pots and cups (cf. Mark 7:4), as if insensible things could receive either blame or grace. But you baptize this sensible cup of yours, in which your good works may shine and the splendor of your grace may sparkle.

That pool, too, is a symbol, so that you may believe that the divine power comes down into this font as well.

4.24. The paralytic was waiting for a man (cf. John 5:7). Who would that have been if not the Lord Jesus, who was born of a virgin? Thanks to his coming it was no longer a shadow that would heal single individuals but truth that would heal everyone. It is he, then, whose coming down was being waited for, and of him God the Father said to John the Baptist: 'The one on whom you see the Spirit come down and rest is the one who baptizes in the Holy Spirit' (John 1:33). Of him John testified and said: 'I saw the Spirit come down from heaven like a dove and rest upon him' (John 1:32). And why did this Spirit come down like a dove if not so that you might see, if not so that you might recognize that that dove also, which Noah, the righteous man, sent out from the ark, was a foreshadowing of this dove, so that you might acknowledge the symbol of the sacrament?

4.25. Perhaps you will say: 'Since that was a real dove that was sent out, whereas this came down like a dove, how can we say that the one was the foreshadowing and the other the reality inasmuch as, according to the [Greek text], it is written that the Spirit came down "in the appearance of a dove" (Luke 3:22)?' But what is as real as the Deity, who abides forever? A created thing cannot be real but is only an appearance, which is easily destroyed and changed. Likewise, the simplicity of those who are baptized must not be a mere appearance but must be real. Hence the Lord himself says: 'Be cunning as serpents and simple as doves' (Matt. 10:16). Rightly, then, does he come down like a dove in order to admonish us that we must have the simplicity of a dove. But we also read that appearance ought to be taken for reality in the case of Christ: 'In appearance he was found to be a man' (Phil. 2:7). And the same thing applies to God the Father: 'You have not seen his appearance' (John 5:37).

5.26. Is there anything else that you should doubt? For the Father cries out to you clearly when he says in the gospel: 'This is my Son in whom I take delight' (Matt 3:17). The Son, upon whom the Holy Spirit manifested himself, cries out. The Holy Spirit, who came down like a dove, also cries out. David cries out: 'The voice of the Lord upon the waters, the God of majesty has thundered, the Lord upon the many waters' (Ps. 29:3). Scripture testifies to you that at the prayer of Jerobaal fire came down from heaven (cf. Judg. 6:21) and, again, that when Elijah prayed fire was sent which consecrated the sacrifice (cf. 1 Kgs. 18:38).

5.27. Consider not the merits of the persons but the functions of the priests.[69] And if you should give thought to their merits, give thought to the merits of Peter and Paul just as you do Elijah. They handed down to us this mystery, which they received from the Lord Jesus (cf. 1 Cor. 11:23). A visible fire was sent to them that they might believe (cf. Acts 2:3), while an invisible one is at work in us who believe; for them it was a symbol, for us it is an admonition. I believe, then, that the Lord Jesus, who says: 'Wherever two or three are, there also am I' (Matt. 18:20), is present when he has been invoked by the prayers of the priests. How much more is it the case that, where the Church is and where the mysteries are, there he deigns to share his presence.

5.28. You went down, therefore. Remember how you responded, that you believe in the Father, that you believe in the Son, that you believe in the Holy Spirit. This is not to be understood as: I believe in a greater, a lesser and a least. Rather, with the same care that you exercise in your use of words you are constrained to believe in the Son just as you believe in the Father and to believe in the Spirit just as you believe in the Son. The sole difference consists in this – that you said that you must believe in the cross of Jesus, our only Lord.[70]

6.29. After this you came up to the priest. Consider what followed. Was it not what David says: 'Like ointment upon the head, which came down upon the beard, upon the beard of Aaron' (Ps. 133:2)? This is the ointment of which Solomon also says: 'Your name is ointment poured out; therefore the maidens have loved you and drawn you' (S. of S. 1:3). How many souls renewed today have loved you, Lord Jesus, saying: 'Draw us after you; let us run after the fragrance of your garments' (S. of S. 1:4), in order to possess the fragrance of the resurrection!

6.30. Understand why it is that 'the eyes of the wise man are in his head' (Eccles. 2:14). [The ointment] flows upon his beard (that is, upon the grace of youth), upon the beard of Aaron, so that you may become a race that is chosen, priestly and precious (cf. 1 Pet. 2:9). For we are all anointed with a spiritual grace for the kingdom of God and for the priesthood.

6.31. You came up out of the font. Recall the gospel reading: in the gospel, Jesus our Lord washed the feet of his disciples. When he came to Simon Peter and Peter said: 'You shall never wash my feet' (John 13:8), he was paying no heed to the mystery and therefore he refused the ministry, because he believed that, were he to accept patiently the Lord's service, it would be inappropriate to the humility of a servant. The Lord replied to him: 'If do not wash your feet, you shall have no part with me' (John 13:8). On hearing this, Peter said: 'Lord, not only my feet but also my hands and my head' (John 13:9). The Lord replied: 'He who has washed needs nothing but to wash his feet; but he is clean all over (John 13:10).

6.32. Peter was clean, but he had to wash his foot, for he had in his turn the sin of the first man, when the serpent tripped him up[71] and persuaded him to go astray (cf. Gen. 3:1–7). Therefore his foot is washed so that hereditary sins may be removed. Our own sins, on the other hand, are remitted by baptism.[72]

6.33. Recognize at the same time that the mystery itself consists in the ministry of humility. For he says: 'If I, your Lord and Master, have washed your feet, how much more ought you to wash one another's feet' (John 13:14). For inasmuch as the author of salvation himself has redeemed us by his obedience, how much more ought we, his servants, to perform the service of obedience ourselves.

7.34. After this you received white garments. As an indication that you were stripped of the covering of your sins you put on the chaste clothing of innocence, of which the prophet said: 'Sprinkle me with hyssop and I shall be cleansed, wash me and I shall be whiter than snow' (Ps. 51:7). For the one who is baptized according to the law and according to the gospel appears to be clean – according to the law because Moses sprinkled the blood of a lamb with a spray of hyssop (cf. Exod. 12:22); according to the gospel because the garments of Christ were white as snow when, in the gospel, he manifested the glory of his resurrection (cf. Matt. 17:2). He whose sin is forgiven is whiter than snow. Hence the Lord says through Isaiah: 'If your sins are like purple, I will make them white as snow' (Isa. 1:18).

7.35. After having received these garments 'through the bath of rebirth' (Titus 3:5) the Church says in the Canticles: 'I am black and beautiful, daughters of Jerusalem' (S. of S. 1:5). She is black because of the weakness of the human condition, beautiful because of grace, black because she has come from among sinners, beautiful because of the sacrament of faith. Seeing these garments, the daughters of Jerusalem are in amazement, and they say: '"Who is this coming up all white?" (S. of S. 8:5) She was black. How has she suddenly become white now?'

7.36. For the angels too were in doubt when Christ arose, the powers of heaven were in doubt when they saw flesh going up to heaven. And so they said: 'Who is this king of glory?' And while some said: 'Lift up your gates, you princes, and be lifted up, eternal gates, and the king of glory will enter in,' others were in doubt and said: 'Who is this king of glory?' (Ps. 24:9–10). In Isaiah as well you may read that the powers of heaven were in doubt and that they said: 'Who is this coming up from Edom? The red of his garments is from Bozrah; he is handsome in his white robe.' (Isa. 63:1)

7.37. But Christ, seeing his Church (for which he himself, as you may read the book of the prophet Zechariah, had worn filthy garments [cf. Zech. 3:3]) in white garments, or rather the soul cleansed and washed by the bath of rebirth, says: 'Behold, you are beautiful, my beloved, behold, you are beautiful; your eyes are like doves' (S. of S. 4:1), in the appearance of which the Holy Spirit came down from heaven. Her eyes are beautiful, as we said previously, because he came down like a dove.[73]

7.38. And further on: 'Your teeth are like a flock of shorn ewes that have come up from the washing. They all bear twins, and none of them is barren. Your lips are like a scarlet cord.' (S. of S. 4:2–3) This is no small praise – first of all by reason of the delightful comparison to the shorn ewes. For we know that she-goats pasture unthreatened upon the heights and that they feed safely in rugged places and, finally, that when they are shorn they are unburdened of what is superfluous. The Church is compared to a flock of these. She has in herself the many virtues of the souls that put off the superfluity of their sins by the washing, that bring to Christ their mystic faith and the grace of their conduct, and that proclaim the cross of the Lord Jesus.

7.39. In these [souls] the Church is beautiful. Hence God speaks this word to her: 'You are all beautiful, my beloved, and there is no fault in you' (S. of S. 4:7), because her sinfulness has been submerged. 'Come hither from Lebanon, my bride, come hither from Lebanon. From the beginning of faith you shall pass over and shall pass through' (S. of S. 4:8), because by renouncing the world she has passed over the world and passed through to Christ. And again God speaks a word to her: 'How beautiful and charming you have become! Love is among your pleasures. In stature you have become like a palm tree, and your breasts are like clusters of grapes.' (S. of S. 7:7–8)

7.40. The Church responds to him: 'Who will give you to me, my brother, who sucked at my mother's breasts? When I find you outside I will kiss you, and they shall not despise me. I will take you and

154

lead you into my mother's house and into the inner chamber of her who conceived me. You shall teach me.' (S. of S. 8:1–2) You see how she is allured by the gift of grace and yearns to have access to the mysteries of former times and to consecrate all her senses to Christ. Still she seeks, still she arouses love and begs that it be aroused for her by the daughters of Jerusalem (cf. S. of S. 5:8). By their grace – that is, by the grace of faithful souls – she desires to provoke her spouse to a more fruitful love for her.

7.41. Hence the Lord Jesus himself is attracted to this great eagerness for love and by such fair comeliness and grace, because in those who have been washed clean there are no longer any filthy stains, and he says to the Church: 'Set me as a seal on your heart, as a seal on your arm' (S. of S. 8:6). This means: You are comely, my beloved, you are all beautiful; nothing is lacking to you. Set me as a seal on your heart, so that your faith may shine forth in the fullness of the sacrament. Let your works, too, cast light, and let them display the image of God, in whose image you were created. Let no persecution diminish your love, which many waters will be unable to drive out and floods will be unable to quench (cf. S. of S. 8:7).

7.42. Recall, then, that you received a spiritual seal, 'the Spirit of wisdom and understanding, the Spirit of counsel and power, the Spirit of knowledge and piety, the Spirit of holy fear' (Isa. 11:2), and maintain what you received. God the Father sealed you and Christ the Lord confirmed you, placing the Spirit in your hearts as a pledge (cf. 2 Cor. 1:21–22), as you learned from the reading of the Apostle.

8.43. Washed clean in this way and rich with marks of distinction, the people now strain forward to the altar of Christ, saying: 'I will go to the altar of God, to the God who gladdens my youth' (Ps. 43:4). For, once they have sloughed off their long-standing error and renewed their youth like an eagle (cf. Ps. 103:5), they hasten to approach that heavenly banquet. They come, then, and upon seeing the most holy altar readied, they cry out and say: 'You have prepared a table in my sight' (Ps. 23:5). David introduces them speaking in this way when he says: 'The Lord pastures me, and nothing will be lacking to me. He has set me there in a place of pasture. He has led me forth to refreshing waters.' (Ps. 23:1–2) And further along: 'Even if I should walk in the midst of the shadow of death I shall fear no evils, for you are with me. Your rod and your staff: these have comforted me. You have prepared a table in my sight against those who trouble me. You have anointed my head with oil. And your inebriating cup – how excellent it is!' (Ps. 23:4–5)

8.44. Now let us consider this, lest perchance anyone, on seeing visible things (for invisible things are unseen and cannot be grasped by the human eye), say: 'God rained down manna for the Jews, he rained down quail (cf. Exod. 16:13–14). But for the Church that he loves he has prepared the sort of thing of which it is said: "What eye has not seen and ear has not heard, nor has it entered into the heart of man, what God has prepared for those who love him" (1 Cor. 2:9).' Therefore, lest anyone say this, we are particularly concerned to demonstrate that the sacraments of the Church are both more ancient than those of the Synagogue and more excellent than the manna is.

8.45. The passage from Genesis that was read teaches that they are more ancient. For the Synagogue had its start with the law of Moses. But Abraham lived long before him. When he had overcome his enemies and taken back his own nephew, when he had laid hold of victory, Melchizedek approached him and made him offerings that Abraham received with reverence (cf. Gen. 14:14–18). It was not Abraham who made the offering but Melchizedek, who is spoken of as being 'without father or mother, having neither beginning nor ending of his days, but like the Son of God' (Heb. 7:3). Of him Paul says to the Hebrews that 'his priesthood abides forever' (Heb. 7:3). In Latin his name means 'king of righteousness, king of peace' (Heb. 7:2).

8.46. Do you not recognize who this is? Can a man be king of righteousness if he is barely righteous? Can he be king of peace if he can barely be peaceable? He is without mother according to his divinity because he is begotten of God the Father and is of one substance with the Father;[74] he is without father according to his incarnation because he was born of a virgin. He has neither beginning nor end because he is himself the beginning and end of all things, 'the first and the last' (Rev. 1:17). What you have received, therefore, is a sacrament not of human but of divine provenance, offered by him who blessed Abraham, the father of our faith, whose grace and deeds you admire.

8.47. It has been demonstrated that the sacraments of the Church are the more ancient. Know now that they are better. It is marvelous indeed that God rained down manna for our fathers and that they were fed every day on food from heaven. Hence it is said: 'Man ate the bread of angels' (Ps. 78:25). Yet those who ate that bread in the desert all died. The food that you receive, however, 'the living bread that comes down from heaven' (John 6:49), provides the wherewithal for eternal life, and whoever eats it 'shall never die' (John 6:50), for it is the body of Christ.

8.48. Consider now whether the bread of angels or the flesh of Christ, which is in fact a life-giving body, is the more excellent. The one, the manna, was from heaven; the other is above heaven. The one was of heaven; the other is of the Lord of heaven. The one was liable to corruption if it was kept for more than a day (cf. Exod. 16: 19–20); the other is free of all corruption because whoever tastes of it devoutly will be unable to succumb to corruption. For them there flowed water from a rock (cf. Exod.17:6); for you there is the blood of Christ. Water satisfied them for a time; blood washes you forever. The Jew drinks and is thirsty; once you have drunk you will be unable to thirst. The one is a shadow; the other is a reality.

8.49. If what you marvel at is a shadow, how great is that whose shadow you marvel at! Listen to how what was accomplished for our fathers was a shadow: 'They drank,' it says, 'the rock that followed them, and the rock was Christ. But God was not pleased with many of them, for they were struck down in the desert. These things, however, happened as a symbol for us.' (1 Cor. 10:4–6) You have understood what is more excellent, for light is better than shadow, reality is better than symbol, the body of the Creator is better than the manna from heaven.

9.50. Perhaps you will say: 'I see something else. How can you assert to me that what I am receiving is the body of Christ?' This, then, still remains for us to demonstrate. How great the examples are that we shall use to prove that this is not what nature fashioned it to be but rather what the blessing consecrated, and that there is a greater force in the blessing than there is in nature, because nature itself is altered by the blessing!

9.51. Moses took his staff, threw it down, and it became a serpent. Then, when he seized the serpent's tail, it reverted to the staff that it had been by nature. (Cf. Exod. 4:3–4) You see, then, that by a prophet's grace the nature of a serpent and of a staff was twice altered. The rivers of Egypt flowed with pure water, when suddenly from out of their sources blood began to pour forth; there was nothing drinkable in the rivers (cf. Exod. 7:19–21). Then, at the prophet's prayer, the bloody water subsided and natural water resumed its flow. The Hebrew people were surrounded on all sides; on one side they were hemmed in by the Egyptians, on the other they were closed in by the sea. Moses lifted his staff, the water was divided and became hardened like walls, and in the midst of the waves a footpath appeared. (Cf. Exod. 14:9–22) The Jordan, contrary to its nature, turned back and returned to its source (cf. Josh. 3:16). Does this not show that the nature of the sea's movement and the rivers' courses was altered? The people of the fathers was thirsty; Moses touched a rock and water flowed from the rock (cf. Exod. 17:1–7). Was not a grace beyond nature at work so that the rock would burst forth with the water that it did not possess by nature? Marah was such a bitter spring that the thirsty people could not drink from it. Moses placed wood in the water and the nature of the water laid aside its own bitterness, which a sudden inpouring of grace sweetened. (Cf. Exod. 15:23–25) When the prophet Elisha was alive, one of the sons of the prophets knocked the iron head off his axe, and at once it sank into the water. The one who lost the axehead called to Elisha, Elisha also placed wood in the water, and the axehead floated to the top. (Cf. 2 Kgs. 6:5–6) We recognize that this as well was most certainly accomplished apart from nature, for iron is heavier than water, which is liquid.

9.52. We see, then, that grace has a wider scope than nature, and even so we place a limit on the grace of the prophetic blessing. If a human blessing was so powerful that it could alter nature, what shall we say of that divine consecration in which the very words of the Lord, the Savior, are at work? For the sacrament that you receive is brought about by the word of Christ. If the word of Elijah was so powerful that it could bring down fire from heaven (cf. 1 Kgs. 18:38), will the word of Christ not be able to alter the appearances of the elements? You have read of the whole world's works that 'he spoke and they were made, he commanded and they were created' (Ps. 33:9). Since the word of Christ, then, was able to make out of nothing what had not existed, can it not change what already exists into what it had not been? For it is not a lesser matter to give new natures to things than to change natures.

9.53. But why do we make use of arguments? Let us use [Christ's] own examples and establish the truth of this mystery by the mysteries of his incarnation. Had nature prepared the way when the Lord Jesus was born of Mary? In the normal course of events, generation occurs after a woman has had relations with a man. It is obvious, then, that the Virgin conceived outside the normal course of nature. And this body that we bring into being is from the Virgin. Why do you look for the normal course of nature in the case of Christ's body when the Lord Jesus himself was born of a virgin and apart from nature? Most certainly, therefore, the true flesh of Christ, which was crucified and which was buried, is truly the sacrament of his flesh.

9.54. The Lord Jesus himself declares: 'This is my body' (Matt. 26: 26). Before the blessing with heavenly words occurs it is a different thing that is referred to, but after the consecration it is called a body. He himself says that it is his blood (cf. Matt. 26:28). Before the consecration it has another name, but after the consecration it is designated blood. And you say: 'Amen,' which means: 'It is true.' What the mouth speaks, let the mind confess within; what the word says, let love acknowledge.

9.55. With these sacraments, then (the same by which the stuff of the soul is strengthened), Christ feeds his Church. Seeing her make uninterrupted progress in his grace, rightly does he say to her: 'How beautiful have your breasts been made, my sister and my bride, how beautiful have they been made by wine, and the fragrance of your garments surpasses every spice. Your lips drip honey, O my bride. Honey and milk are under your tongue, and the fragrance of your garments is like the fragrance of Lebanon. You are an enclosed garden, my sister and my bride, an enclosed garden, a sealed fountain.' (S. of S. 4:10–12) What this means is that you must keep the mystery sealed, lest it be violated by the works of an evil life and by the adulteration of chastity, lest it be publicized to those for whom it would not be fitting, lest by chatter and talkativeness it be disseminated to unbelievers. The guardian of your faith must be good, then, so that the integrity of your life and of your silence may remain unspoiled.

9.56. It is for this reason as well that the Church, protective of the loftiness of the heavenly mysteries, rejects violent winds and storms and summons forth the sweetness of springlike grace and, knowing that her garden cannot displease Christ, calls to him as her bridegroom and says: 'Rise up, north wind, and come, south wind: blow through my garden, and let my ointments flow. Let my brother come down into his garden and eat the produce of his fruit trees.' (S. of S. 4:16) For he has good fruit-bearing trees that have soaked their roots in the moisture of the holy font and have sprouted forth good fruit thanks to their new and fertile origin. Hence they are no longer chopped down by the prophetic axe (cf. Matt. 3:10) but are well established in gospel productiveness.

9.57. And so the Lord himself is delighted by their fertility, and he responds: 'I have entered into my garden, my sister and my bride, I have gathered my myrrh with my ointments, I have eaten my food with my honey, I have drunk my drink with my milk' (S. of S. 5:1). You who are faithful should understand why I have spoken of food and drink. There is no doubt that he eats and drinks in us, just as you read that he says that he is in prison with us (cf. Matt. 25:36).

9.58. Hence the Church herself, seeing such great grace, exhorts her sons, exhorts her friends, to run to the sacraments, saying: 'Eat, my friends, and drink and be inebriated, my brothers' (S. of S. 5:1). What you are to eat and what you are to drink the Holy Spirit explains to you elsewhere when he says through the prophet: 'Taste and see how sweet the Lord is; blessed is the man who trusts in him' (Ps. 34:8). Christ is that sacrament, because it is the body of Christ. It is not, therefore, a bodily food but one that is spiritual. Hence also the Apostle says in regard to its symbol that 'your fathers ate spiritual food and drank spiritual drink' (1 Cor. 10:3). For the body of God is a spiritual body. The body of Christ is the body of a divine Spirit, because the Spirit is Christ, as we read: 'The Spirit before our face is Christ the Lord' (Lam. 4:20*). And in the Epistle of Peter we read: 'Christ died for you' (1 Pet. 2:21). And so this food strengthens our heart and this drink 'rejoices the human heart' (Ps. 104:15), as the prophet has declared.

9.59. Hence we who have received all these things should know that we have been reborn, and we should not say: 'How have we been reborn? Did we enter into our mother's womb and were we reborn (cf. John 3:4)? I do not recognize here the common usage of nature.' But there is no normal course of nature here, where grace is found to be so excellent. Finally, it is not always the usual course of nature that is responsible for generation: we profess that Christ the Lord was begotten of a virgin and we deny that nature took its normal course. For Mary did not conceive of a man but was impregnated by the Holy Spirit, as Matthew says: 'She was found to be pregnant by the Holy Spirit' (Matt. 1:18). If, then, the Holy Spirit came upon the Virgin, brought about conception and carried out the function of generation, there must be no doubt at all that, when the Spirit comes upon the font and upon those who are to be baptized, he is bringing about a true rebirth.

THE PROLOGUE FROM THE *COMMENTARY ON THE GOSPEL ACCORDING TO LUKE*

Introduction

The *Commentary on Luke*, which consists of ten books, is preceded by the prologue that is translated here. In his discussion of the three kinds of wisdom – natural, moral and rational – Ambrose prepares his readers for the three senses of Scripture that he will disclose to them in the *Commentary* itself – the historical, the moral and the mystical, or allegorical. The prologue is a demonstration of Ambrose's proficiency (some of it borrowed, to be sure) in mystical exegesis, as shown by his ability to discover the mystical meanings of such things as Isaac's three wells and the quaternity of the gospels and the living beings. It also provides an example of how artificial such exegesis could be: Ambrose's attempts to make the four gospels and the three persons of the Trinity fit into the scheme of threefold wisdom are clearly forced.

The prologue is translated from CCSL 14.1–6. Cf. also pp. 59–60.

1. As we are about to begin writing on the book of the gospel that Saint Luke composed when he arranged the Lord's deeds in a certain fuller way, we think that its style should be commented on first: it is historical. Although, to be sure, divine Scripture rejects worldly learning and wisdom, because that is embellished with a great parade of words instead of relying on the real nature of things, none the less, if anyone seeks in the divine Scriptures those matters that [worldly people] consider admirable, he will find them.[75]

2. For there are three most excellent things that the philosophers of this world have considered to constitute a threefold wisdom – the natural and the moral and the rational.[76] These three things are already evident even in the Old Testament. For what else do those three wells signify – one being 'vision', the second 'abundance' and the third 'oath' – if not that that threefold quality existed in the patriarchs (cf. Gen. 26:19–22, 33)? The rational well is 'vision' because reason sharpens the mind's vision and cleanses the eye of the soul. The moral well is 'abundance' because, once the foreigners had departed (whose appearance symbolizes the vices of the body), Isaac discovered the limpidity of the living mind, for good morals flow forth pure, and native goodness itself abounds for others when it is more disciplined in its own regard. The third well is 'oath' (that is, natural wisdom, which includes things that are above nature and things that are of nature), for what it asserts and swears – with God as its witness, so to say – also embraces divine things, when the Lord of nature is cited as a witness to one's credibility.

Likewise, what do the three books of Solomon show us – the first being that of Proverbs, the second Ecclesiastes and the third that of the Song of Songs – if not that the holy Solomon was skilled in this threefold wisdom? It was he who wrote of rational and moral matters in Proverbs; of natural matters in Ecclesiastes, because what exists in this world is 'vanity of vanities, and all of it is vanity' (Eccles. 1:2), for 'creation has been subjected to vanity' (Rom. 8:20); and of marvelous and rational matters in the Song of Songs, because, when love of the heavenly Word is poured into our soul and a holy mind is by some link joined to Reason,[77] wondrous mysteries are revealed.[78]

3. Do you think that this wisdom was wanting to the evangelists? Although they are filled with various kinds [of wisdom], none the less each excels in his own kind. For in fact there is natural wisdom in the book of the gospel that was written by John. For no one else, I venture to say, has seen God's majesty and preserved it for us in his own words with such sublime wisdom. He went beyond the clouds, he went beyond the powers of heaven, he went beyond the angels and discovered the Word 'in the beginning' and saw the Word 'with God' (John 1:1). And who pursued particular things with greater morality, for the sake of human beings, than Saint Matthew, who published for us the precepts of life? What is more rational than Saint Mark's idea that right at the beginning [of his gospel] there should be placed, in that marvellous conjunction: 'Behold, I am sending my messenger' (Mark 1:2) and: 'The voice of one crying in the desert' (Mark 1:3)? In this way he evoked our admiration and taught man that he must be pleasing by humility, abstinence and faith, just as the great Saint John the Baptist mounted to immortality by these steps – by his garb, his food and his message (cf. Mark 1:6–8).

4. But Saint Luke maintained as it were a certain historical order and revealed to us more of the Lord's wondrous deeds – yet in such a way that the history in this gospel embraces the qualities of wisdom in its entirety. For what is more excellent, as far as natural wisdom is concerned, than his disclosure that the Holy Spirit was also the creator of the Lord's incarnation (cf. Luke 1:35)? That the Holy Spirit creates, then, is a teaching about natural things. Hence

162

David, too, is teaching natural wisdom when he says: 'Send forth your Spirit, and they shall be created' (Ps.104:30). He teaches moral things in the same book when he teaches morality to me in the beatitudes[79] – how I must love my enemy (cf. Luke 6:27), how I must not repay the one who has struck me by striking him back (cf. Luke 6:29), and how I must do good and make a loan without hope of repayment and with [an eternal] reward as my recompense (cf. Luke 6:34–35), for [such a] reward is more likely to go to the one who is not looking for it. He also taught rational things when I read that 'he who is trustworthy in a small matter is also trustworthy in a greater one' (Luke 16:10). What else should I say about natural things – that he taught that the powers of heaven were moved (cf. Luke 21:26) and that the Lord alone was the only-begotten Son of God, during whose suffering night fell in the daytime, the earth was darkened and the sun vanished (cf. Luke 23:44)?

5. Therefore spiritual wisdom truly possesses every domain that worldly knowledge falsely claims for itself, particularly inasmuch as, to express ourselves rather boldly, our faith itself, the very mystery of the Trinity, cannot exist apart from this threefold wisdom. We must believe in that Father who of his nature begot for us the Redeemer; and in that moral [son] who redeemed us, being obedient to his Father until death (cf. Phil. 2:8) according to his manhood; and in that rational Spirit who instills in human hearts the rationale for worshiping the Deity and governing our lives. Nor should anyone think that we have divided their power or virtue, when one could even slander Paul in this way. He certainly did not divide when he said: 'There are different graces, but the same Spirit; and there are different ministries, but the same Lord; and there are different works, but it is the same God who works all in all' (1 Cor. 12:4–6). For the Son also works all in all; as you read elsewhere: 'Christ is all things and is in all things' (Col. 3:11). The Holy Spirit also works, because 'one and the same Spirit works all things, distributing to each person as he wills' (1 Cor. 12:11). There is no division, no separation in works, then, when in none [of them], either Father or Son or Holy Spirit, is there a second fullness of virtue.[80]

6. We should consider these things diligently, therefore, when we read, so that in these very passages we may be more enlightened. 'For the one who seeks finds, and to the one who knocks it shall be opened' (Matt. 7:8). Diligence opens for itself the door of truth, and therefore we should comply with the heavenly precepts. For not in vain is there said to man what is said to no other living being: 'In the

sweat of your face you shall eat your bread' (Gen. 3:19). For by
God's order the earth has been commanded to provide sustenance
for those animals that are by nature irrational (cf. Gen. 1:11, 30),
while for man alone is it prescribed that the course of his life is to be
toilsome, so that he may exercise the rational faculty which he has
received. For he who is not content with the other animals' sustenance and for whom the fruit tree that was given to all in common for
food (cf. Gen. 2:16) is insufficient, but who seeks out for himself
different kinds of dainty food, who looks for dainties for himself
from lands beyond the sea, who dredges the waters for dainties and
who obtains his provisions with toil – he must not reject a little toil
if he is to make progress toward eternal life.

And so if a person who is entering these contests of sacred
disputations strips himself of worry concerning this life, which is
exposed to error, and, bare of wickedness, after having been anointed like a wrestler for piety with spiritual oil on certain limbs of his
soul, so to speak, undertakes to fight for the truth, there is no doubt
that he will merit the perpetual prizes of sacred crowns.[81] 'For the
fruit of good labors is noble' (Wisd. 3:15), and the more contests
there are the more excellent the crown of virtues will be.

7. But let us return to our main thought. We have said that this
gospel book was composed in a historical style. In comparison with
the other [gospels] we notice that considerably more attention was
given to describing things than to imposing precepts. The evangelist
himself starts out in historical fashion with a narrative: 'In the days
of Herod, king of Judaea, there was,' he says, 'a certain priest by the
name of Zechariah' (Luke 1:5), and he continues with that story in
the most orderly way. Hence, also, those who think that the four
books of the gospel are to be seen in the forms of the four living
beings revealed in the Apocalypse (cf. Rev. 4:6–7) want this book to
be represented by the likeness of the calf, for a calf is a priestly
sacrificial offering. And a calf is quite appropriate for this gospel
book, because it begins with priests and concludes with the calf that
took on the sins of all and was sacrificed for the life of the whole
world (cf. 1 John 2:2), for that calf is priestly too. Indeed, he is both
calf and priest. He is a priest because he is our propitiator – for 'we
have him as our advocate with the Father' (1 John 2:1) – and a calf
because he has redeemed us with his blood (cf. Heb. 9:12). Inasmuch as we have said that the gospel book according to Matthew
has to do with morality, it is well that such an opinion not be passed
over, for morality is properly called human.

8. Yet there are many who think that our Lord himself is depicted in the four gospel books by the forms of the four living beings – that he is at one and the same time a man, a lion, a calf and an eagle: a man because he was born of Mary, a lion because he is strong (cf. Judg. 14:18; Luke 3:16), a calf because he is a sacrificial victim and an eagle because he is the resurrection (cf. Ps. 103:5). And thus in the individual books the form of the living beings is depicted so that each book in turn might correspond to the nature and virtue and grace and wondrous quality of the living beings that we have spoken of. Although all [of them] are in each [book], none the less there is a certain fullness of particular qualities in a particular book. One describes the origin of the man [Christ] in greater detail and instructs human morality with more copious precepts; another begins with an expression of divine power since, being king from a king, strength from strength and truth from truth, he would with vitality disdain death; the third commences with a priestly sacrifice and describes the immolation itself of the calf with a certain greater detail; the fourth sets out more fully than the others the wonders of the divine resurrection. There is one, therefore, who 'is all things,' and who 'is in all things,' as has been read – not different in the individual [gospels] but true in all [of them].[82]

But now let us approach the very words of the gospel.

HYMNS

Introduction

Of the many hymns attributed to Ambrose, these four seem to have the most right to be considered authentic; all of them are attested to by Augustine. For the most part the meaning of the first and third hymns, which were destined to be sung in the morning and the evening respectively, is quite clear, but a few words should be said about the second and the fourth.

The second hymn would have been used at midmorning, at the 'third hour,' which corresponds roughly to nine o'clock. This traditional time for prayer offers Ambrose the opportunity to reflect on the crucifixion which, according to the evangelist Mark, occurred then. Ambrose, however, sees Christ's suffering in terms not of pain and woe but of glory and victory and the cross itself as 'the lofty summit of his triumph.' In this respect the poet reflects his age, which tended not to dwell on the sufferings of the God–man. The last two stanzas rebuke the Jews for their unbelief and, as it were by contrast, make a statement of faith in the humanity and divinity of Christ.

The fourth hymn was written for the celebration of Christ's nativity, and it begins with a paraphrase of Ps. 80:1–2. From the second until midway through the fifth stanza Ambrose concentrates on the marvelous fact of Christ's chaste conception, accomplished 'not by a man's seed but by a mystical inbreathing.' Mary's womb, then, is rightly called 'the royal hall of chastity.' But it can also, in an oxymoron, be spoken of as a bridal chamber, because in it divinity has been joined to humanity. From the mid-fifth until the seventh stanza the emphasis is on the mystery of Christ's two natures, the human and the divine, and, with regard to the latter, his co-equality with the Father. His incarnation is placed in tandem with his ascension, and his whole 'journey' from heaven to earth, and even to the depths of hell, and then back again to heaven is compared with the course that the hero (or 'giant,' as Ambrose's Latin version had it) of Ps.19:5 is eager to run. The final stanza features the light imagery that is typical of the feast of Christmas, when the days are just beginning to get longer again after the winter solstice – a phenomenon that corresponds neatly with the birth of the light of the world.

The Latin text of these four hymns is found in August Steier (1903: 651–53), and Jacques Fontaine *et al.* (1992: 149–51, 211–13, 237–39 and 273–75). The present translation has been made from

Fontaine's edition, which has also provided the Latin that is reproduced here. Cf. also pp. 65–66 of this volume.

I AETERNE RERUM CONDITOR

1 Eternal author of creation,
who rule both night and day
and give us varying moments and times
to relieve our tedium:

2 The herald of the day now sounds,
ever watchful in darkest night,
a nocturnal light to travelers,
who separates night from night.

3 At his cry the morning star, aroused,
frees the heavens of their duskiness;
at his cry the whole choir of stars
abandons their harmful courses.

4 At his cry the sailor takes heart
and the waters of the sea grow calm;
at his cry, and as he crows,
he himself, the Church's rock, washes away his sin
(cf. Matt. 16:18, 26:75).

5 Let us, then, be quick to rise:
the cock rouses us from our beds
and reproaches us for our drowsiness;
the cock rebukes us for our sluggishness.

6 As the cock crows, hope returns,
health is restored to the sick,
the bandit sheathes his weapon,
and faith returns to the doubting.

7 Jesus, we are tottering; look upon us
and by your gaze set us to rights.
Should you look, our sins will founder,
and tears will dissolve our guilt.

8 Light that you are, illumine our senses
and shake sleep from our minds;
may our first words be of you
and may your praise open our mouths.

> 1 Aeterne rerum conditor,
> noctem diemque qui regis
> et temporum das tempora
> ut alleves fastidium,

2 praeco diei iam sonat,
noctis profundae pervigil,
nocturna lux viantibus
a nocte noctem segregans.

3 Hoc excitatus Lucifer
solvit polum caligine,
hoc omnis errorum chorus
vias nocendi deserit.

4 Hoc nauta vires colligit
pontique mitescunt freta;
hoc ipse petra ecclesiae
canente culpam diluit.

5 Surgamus ergo strenue;
gallus iacentes excitat
et somnolentos increpat;
gallus negantes arguit.

6 Gallo canente, spes redit,
aegris salus refunditur,
mucro latronis conditur,
lapsis fides revertitur.

7 Iesu, labantes respice
et nos videndo corrige;
si respicis, lapsus cadunt
fletuque culpa solvitur.

8 Tu lux refulge sensibus
mentisque somnum discute,
te nostra vox primum sonet
et vota solvamus tibi.

II   IAM SURGIT HORA TERTIA

1 It is now the third hour,
when Christ mounted the cross (cf. Mark 15:25).
May our minds ponder nothing unseemly
but incline to sentiments of prayer.

2 Whoever receives Christ into his heart
has a disposition free from blame,
and by his earnest prayers he strives
to merit the Holy Spirit.

3 This is the hour when Christ checked
the ancient, dreadful crime,
overthrew death's reign
and took the age-old sin upon himself (cf. 2 Cor. 5:21).

4 Henceforth, now, by the grace of Christ,
days of blessedness have begun:
the true faith has filled
the churches throughout the earth.

5 From the lofty summit of his triumph
he spoke to his mother:
'Mother, behold your son;
apostle, behold your mother' (cf. John 19:27),

6 Teaching that the vows of a married woman
concealed a high mystery,
that the virgin's holy bringing forth
would not harm the mother's chastity.

7 The impious folk to whom Jesus offered faith
through heavenly miracles
did not believe;
the one who has believed will be saved.

8 We believe the God who was born,
the offspring of the holy virgin,
who, seated at the Father's right,
has taken away the sins of the world (cf. John 1:29).

1 Iam surgit hora tertia,
qua Christus ascendit crucem;
nil insolens mens cogitet,
intendat affectum precis.

2 Qui corde Christum suscipit,
innoxium sensum gerit,
votisque praestat sedulis
Sanctum mereri Spiritum.

3 Haec hora, quae finem dedit
diri veterno criminis,
mortisque regnum diruit
culpamque ab aevo sustulit.

4 Hinc iam beata tempora
Christi coepere gratia:
fide replevit veritas
totum per orbem ecclesias.

5 Celsus triumphi vertice
matri loquebatur suae:
'en filius, mater, tuus;
apostole, en mater tua,'

6 praetenta nuptae foedera
  alto docens mysterio,
  ne virginis partus sacer
  matris pudorem laederet.

7 Cui fidem caelestibus
  Iesus dedit miraculis;
  nec credidit plebs impia,
  qui credidit salvus erit.

8 Nos credimus natum Deum
  . partumque virginis sacrae,
  peccata qui mundi tulit
  ad dexteram sedens Patris.

III   DEUS CREATOR OMNIUM

1 God, creator of all things
  and ruler of the heavens, fitting
  the day with beauteous light
  and the night with the grace of sleep:

2 May rest restore our slackened limbs
  to the exercise of toil,
  lighten our wearied minds,
  and relieve our anxious preoccupations.

3 Now that the day is over and night has begun,
  we, your devotees, sing our hymn,
  offering thanks and begging
  that you would help us in our sinfulness.

4 May the depths of our hearts magnify you,
  may our harmonious voices sound you,
  may our chaste affections love you,
  may our sober minds adore you.

5 Thus, when the deep gloom of night
  closes in upon the day,
  our faith may not know darkness
  and the night may shine with faith.

6 Do not permit our minds to slumber;
  it is sinfulness that knows slumber.
  May faith, which refreshes the chaste,
  temper sleep's embrace.

7 When the depths of our hearts have been stripped of
      unclean thoughts,
  let them dream of you,

nor let worry, the stratagem of the envious foe,
disturb us as we rest.
8 We beseech Christ and the Father,
and the Spirit of Christ and the Father,
who are one and omnipotent.
O Trinity, assist us who pray to you!

1 Deus creator omnium
polique rector, vestiens
diem decoro lumine,
noctem soporis gratia,
2 artus solutos ut quies
reddat laboris usui,
mentesque fessas allevet,
luctusque solvat anxios,
3 grates peracto iam die
et noctis exortu preces,
voti reos ut adiuves,
hymnum canentes solvimus.
4 Te cordis ima concinant,
te vox canora concrepet,
te diligat castus amor,
te mens adoret sobria,
5 ut, cum profunda clauserit
diem caligo noctium,
fides tenebras nesciat,
et nox fide reluceat.
6 Dormire mentem ne sinas,
dormire culpa noverit,
castis fides refrigerans
somni vaporem temperet.
7 Exuta sensu lubrico,
te cordis alta somnient,
nec hostis invidi dolo
pavor quietos suscitet.
8 Christum rogamus et Patrem,
Christi Patrisque Spiritum,
unum potens per omnia;
fove precantes, Trinitas.

IV   INTENDE QUI REGIS ISRAEL

1 Hearken, you who rule Israel,
   you who sit upon the cherubim.
   Appear before Ephraim; rouse up
   your power and come! (Cf. Ps. 80:1–2)

2 Come, redeemer of the nations,
   show forth the virgin's begetting.
   Let the whole world marvel:
   such a birth befits God.

3 Not by a man's seed
   but by a mystical inbreathing
   did the Word of God become flesh
   and the fruit of the womb flourish.

4 The virgin's womb swells
   but the door of chastity remains shut.
   The banners of virtue are radiant:
   God dwells in his temple.

5 Let him come out from his bridal chamber,
   the royal hall of chastity,
   a giant of twofold nature,
   eager to run his course (cf. Ps. 19:5).

6 His going out is from the Father,
   his coming back is to the Father,
   his journey is as far as hell,
   his return is to the throne of God.

7 The equal of the eternal Father,
   he girds on the trophy of our flesh,
   fortifying the frailty of our body
   with his enduring strength.

8 May your crib now shine forth
   and the night produce a new light.
   May no night destroy it,
   and may it beam with constant faith.

1 Intende, qui regis Israel,
   super Cherubim qui sedes,
   appare Ephraem coram, excita
   potentiam tuam et veni.

2 Veni, redemptor gentium,
   ostende partum virginis,
   miretur omne saeculum,
   talis decet partus Deo.

172

3 Non ex virili semine,
   sed mystico spiramine
   verbum Dei factum est caro
   fructusque ventris floruit.

4 Alvus tumescit virginis,
   claustrum pudoris permanet,
   vexilla virtutum micant,
   versatur in templo Deus.

5 Procedat e thalamo suo,
   pudoris aula regia,
   geminae gigas substantiae
   alacris ut currat viam.

6 Egressus eius a Patre,
   regressus eius ad Patrem;
   excursus usque ad inferos,
   recursus ad sedem Dei.

7 Aequalis aeterno Patri,
   carnis trophaeo cingere,
   infirma nostri corporis
   virtute firmans perpeti.

8 Praesepe iam fulget tuum
   lumenque nox spirat novum
   quod nulla nox interpolet
   fideque iugi luceat.

THE LETTERS PERTAINING TO THE ALTAR OF VICTORY CONTROVERSY

Introduction

Some of the background to the following documentation has been discussed on pp. 29–31. Two of Ambrose's most famous letters (17 and 18) flank the *relatio* of the great pagan senator Quintus Aurelius Symmachus. *Relatio* is translated here as 'appeal,' although it can also be rendered as 'memorial' or 'memorandum.' Readers of these three writings have typically been impressed by the breadth and tolerant tone of Symmachus, in contrast to the harsh and sometimes threatening and even sarcastic approach of Ambrose. The difference between the two can be partially explained by the fact that Symmachus knew he was pleading from a position of relative weakness, where a call to tolerance makes the most sense. Ambrose, on the other hand, seems never to have entertained any doubts about the ultimate triumph of his cause.

Ambrose's two letters and Symmachus' appeal are translated from the critical text in CSEL 82.3.11–53. The Latin text can also be found in PL 16.1001–1024. There are English translations in De Romestin 411–22 and FC 26.31–51 (excluding the *relatio*).

Letter 17

Bishop Ambrose to the most blessed prince and most Christian Emperor Valentinian.

1. While all the people who are under Roman rule do battle on behalf of you, O emperors and princes of the earth, you yourselves do battle on behalf of almighty God and the sacred faith. For salvation cannot be assured unless each person truly worships the true God – namely, the God of the Christians, by whom all things are governed. For he alone is the true God who is to be venerated in the inmost recesses of the mind, 'for,' as Scripture says, 'the gods of the pagans are demons' (Ps. 96:5).

2. Whoever, therefore, does battle on behalf of this God, and understands that he must be worshiped deeply within, does not act heedlessly or connive at wrongdoing but engages in the pursuit of faith and devotion. In any event, if he does not do that, he should at least not display any sympathy for idol worship and for the impious cults and their ceremonies. For no one deceives God, to whom all things, even the hidden things of the heart, have been made manifest (cf. Ps. 44:21).

3. Hence when you, most Christian emperor, are to display your faith to the true God, and your zeal, attentiveness and devotion with regard to that faith, I am astonished at how some people have seized upon the hope that, at your command, you will bind yourself to restore the altars to the gods of the pagans and meet the expenses connected with impious sacrifices. For what has long since been assigned either to the treasury or the public coffers you would seem to be giving from what is yours rather than to be repaying from what belongs to it.

4. And the ones who are looking for financial assistance are those who have never spared our blood, who demolished the very church buildings. They are also asking you to grant them privileges – they who, under Julian's recent law, denied our co-religionists the commonplace right to speak and to teach.[83] These are privileges by which even Christians have often been led astray, for by these privileges they sought to ensnare a number of people – some through heedlessness and others anxious to avoid the burdens of public responsibilities. And, inasmuch as not everyone is strong, many fell even under Christian princes.[84]

5. But, if these [privileges] had not already been done away with, I would demonstrate that they ought to be abolished at your command. However, since some time ago they were nullified and removed nearly everywhere in the world by many princes and were, by Your Clemency's brother, Gratian of august memory, done away with at Rome and canceled by public rescripts for the sake of the true faith, I entreat you not to overturn what was prescribed in faith or rescind your brother's orders. If something has been prescribed with respect to civil affairs, no one thinks that it should be violated, and yet a precept concerning religion is treated with disdain!

6. Let no one take advantage of your youthful age. Should that pagan[85] be pleading for these things, he should not bind your soul with the chains of his superstition; rather, by his own zeal he should teach and admonish you how zealous you should be for the true faith, when with such spirit he defends a travesty of the truth. I myself am in favor of deferring to the merits of men of rank, but I say that the true God is to be preferred to anything else.

7. When some military matter is under discussion, the opinion of a man experienced in war should be sought out and his advice heeded. When it is a question of religion, think of God. No person is insulted when almighty God is given precedence over him. He may hold to his own views. You do not oblige someone who is unwilling to worship what he does not want to. Let the same thing be allowed you, O emperor, and let everyone patiently endure what, if he could not extort it from the emperor, he would endure with difficulty if the emperor wished to extort it from him. A shilly-shallying attitude is offensive even to the pagans, for each person should willingly stand up for and faithfully adhere to the resolutions of his own mind.

8. If some people who are nominally Christians think that such a thing should be decreed, let not mere words capture your mind or empty pretexts deceive it. Whoever is in favor of this and whoever has decided upon it is welcome to sacrifice. Yet the sacrifice of one person is more tolerable than the fall of all. The whole Christian membership of the Senate is endangered here.

9. Suppose that today some pagan emperor – which God forbid! – had erected an altar to his idols and was making Christians gather at it in order to be among those sacrificing, so that the ashes of the altar, the cinders of the sacrilegious act and the smoke of the embers were filling the nostrils and mouths of the faithful. Suppose that he had issued a ruling at that Senate, where those who had been sworn at the idol's altar were bound to the ruling, for they believe that the altar is there so that, as they think, each session may deliberate under its sacred influence, although the Senate is now filled with a majority of Christians. In such circumstances a Christian who was obliged to come to the Senate (which is frequently the case, for they are even obliged under violence to assemble) would consider it a persecution. Shall Christians be made to swear at the altar, then, while you are emperor? What is swearing but acknowledging the divine power of him whom you invoke as the patron of your trust? While you are emperor the petition and request are being made of you to order an altar to be set up and the expenses of the impious sacrifices to be met!

10. But this cannot be decreed without sacrilege. Hence I entreat you not to decree this and not to impose or subscribe to any decrees of this sort. As Christ's bishop I appeal to your faith. All of us bishops would have made this appeal had the fact that such a thing was brought up in your privy council and petitioned by the Senate not come to our notice as something unbelievable and unexpected. But let no one say that the Senate has petitioned this when there are only a few pagans who are usurping its name. For when they wanted this about two years ago as well, the holy Damasus, chosen bishop of the Roman Church by God's decision,[86] sent me a pamphlet that the Christian senators published (and indeed they were innumerable), in which they complained that they had not requested such a thing, that they were not in accord with petitions of this sort on the part of the pagans, that they did not give their approval, and that the complainants would not even attend the Senate, whether publicly or privately, if such a thing were decreed. Is it worthy, then, of your times – which are Christian times – that the dignity of Christian senators should be jeopardized so that the fruits of an impious decision may be offered to pagan senators? I forwarded this pamphlet to Your Clemency's brother.[87] It is evident from it that the Senate made no request concerning payment of the expenses of superstition.

11. But perhaps it will be said that some time ago, when these things were being petitioned, they were not in attendance at the Senate. Those who were not in attendance are saying clearly enough what they want; those who have spoken to the emperor have spoken clearly enough. And yet we are amazed that those who do not want you to be at liberty not to order what you do not approve of or to do what you think best are snatching away from private persons at Rome the liberty to resist!

12. Therefore, mindful of the commission that was so recently entrusted to me,[88] I once again appeal to your faith, I appeal to your conscience: do not resolve to respond favorably to a petition of this kind made by the pagans; do not, by a response of that kind, add the sacrilege of your approval. Think at least of Your Piety's parent, the prince Theodosius,[89] whom you have been in the habit of consulting before almost anyone else in important matters. Nothing is more important than religion, nothing loftier than faith.

13. If this were a civil case, a response would be conceded to the opposing party. Since this is a case of religion, I call upon you as a bishop. Let a copy of the appeal that was sent be given to me so that I too might respond more fully, and then, when Your Clemency's parent has been consulted in all aspects, let him deign to respond. Certainly, if something else is prescribed, we bishops will be unable to endure it with equanimity or to let the matter pass unnoticed. You may well come to the church, but there you shall either find no bishop or one who resists you.

14. What will you reply to the bishop when he says to you: 'The Church does not seek your gifts because you have adorned the temples of the pagans with gifts. Christ's altar refuses your gifts because you set up an altar to idols. For yours is the voice, yours the hand, yours the approval, yours the deed. The Lord Jesus rejects and refuses your service because you offered service to idols; for he said to you: "You cannot serve two masters" (Matt. 6:24). The virgins consecrated to God do not enjoy your privileges but the virgins consecrated to Vesta[90] lay claim to them. Why are you looking for the bishops of God when you preferred the impious petitions of the pagans to them? We cannot associate ourselves with alien error.'

15. What will you reply to these words? That you are a boy who made a mistake? Every age is perfect as far as Christ is concerned, every age is mature as far as God is concerned. It is not a boyish faith that is approved. Even children have with fearless words confessed Christ before their persecutors.

What will you reply to your brother?[91] Will he not say to you: 'I did not believe that I was defeated since I left you as emperor. I did not regret dying since I had you as my successor. I did not lament leaving imperial rule since I believed that my mandates, especially concerning divine religion, would remain forever. I had set up these monuments of pious virtue; I made offerings of this booty from the world, of these spoils from the devil, of this loot from the enemy of all, in which there is eternal victory. What more could my foe have taken from me? You abrogated my decrees, which even he who took up arms against me did not do.[92] Now I receive a more deadly blow in my body, because my own precepts are being overturned by my brother. I am imperiled by you in the better part of myself, for then it was a body that died, but now it is virtue. Now my ruling is abrogated and – what is worse – it is being abrogated by your people, it is being abrogated by my people, and what is being abrogated is that which even my adversaries extolled in me. If you have acquiesced willingly you have destroyed my credibility; if you have given in unwillingly you have surrendered your own. Therefore – what is worse – I too am imperiled in you.'

16. And what will you reply to your father,[93] who will approach you with still greater sorrow and say: 'My son, you have very badly misjudged me in thinking that I would connive with the pagans. No one reported to me that there was an altar in the Roman Senate. Never did I believe that such a wicked deed was possible – that in that council, common to both Christians and pagans, the pagans would offer sacrifice; that, in other words, the pagans would perform an insulting act in the presence of the Christians; and that Christians would be compelled against their will to attend the sacrifices. Many different crimes were committed during my rule, and I punished whichever ones I detected. If someone concealed one from me, does it therefore follow that I approved what no one had reported to me? You have very badly misjudged me in supposing that an alien superstition and not my faith preserved my rule.'

17. Hence, O emperor, since you realize that you will be doing injury to God first and then to your father and brother if you decree such a thing, I entreat you to do what you know will profit your salvation before God.

The appeal of Symmachus, prefect of the city of Rome

1. When first the most honorable Senate, ever faithful to you, heard that criminal behavior had been subjected to law and saw that the ill fame of recent times was being changed for the better by the pious princes, following the precedent of a good age, it spewed out the grief that had long burdened it and once more ordered me to be the emissary of its complaints. [But] an audience with the divine prince was denied me by the wicked because, my lords, Emperors Valentinian, Theodosius and Arcadius,[94] renowned victors and ever august triumphant ones, justice would not have been wanting.

2. I carry out, then, a double function: as your prefect I manage public affairs, and as an emissary I promote the concerns of the citizens. There is no conflict of interest here because people have now ceased to believe that they excel in the zeal of courtiers if they happen to disagree. It is more important, in terms of imperial rule, to be loved, to be cherished, to be esteemed. Who could bear to have private struggles do harm to the common weal? Rightly does the Senate censure those who have placed their own person before the reputation of the prince. But our task is to be watchful on behalf of Your Clemency. For to what is it more appropriate that we defend the teachings of our forebears, the laws and oracles of the homeland, than to the glory of the times? This is all the more important when you understand that nothing is permitted you contrary to the custom of your ancestors.

3. We demand once more, then, the religious situation that has for so long benefited the common weal. Let there be taken into account, to be sure, the princes of both persuasions, of both opinions: the earlier part of them practiced the ceremonies of their forefathers, the latter did not do away with them. If the religious devotion of the ancients does not serve as an example, then let the neglect of those who were more recent serve as such. Who is so friendly with the barbarians as not to need the Altar of Victory? We are being heedful about the future and are avoiding catastrophe in this respect. Yet at least let the name be given the honor that has been denied to the divinity.[95] Your Eternity owes much to Victory and shall owe still more. Let those reject this power whom it has profited nothing, but do not abandon the patronage that has favored your triumphs. This power is longed for by all. Let no one deny that what he professes to be desirable should be fostered.

4. But if abandoning this solemn practice was not just, at least it was proper that the ornaments of the Senate be spared. Vouchsafe, I beseech you, that what we received as boys we may as old men leave to those who come after us. The love of custom is great. Rightly did the deed of the divine Constantius not long endure. You must avoid all precedents that you have learned were soon annulled. We are attentive to the immortality of your reputation and your name, so that no future age may find anything there that should be corrected.

5. Where shall we swear to your laws and words? By what religious dread will the false mind be terrified so that he will not lie when he is giving testimony? Everything is full of God, to be sure, and no place is safe for the dishonest, but to be impelled in the very presence of religion is particularly conducive to fear of wrongdoing. That altar maintains the peace of all, that altar arouses the trust of each, nor does anything else provide more authority for our decisions than the fact that everything is decreed, as it were, in an orderly fashion and after an oath has been taken. Shall, then, a place of impiousness be offered to perjury, and, my illustrious princes, will those who have been given assurance by public oath consider this credible?

6. But the divine Constantius is said to have done the same thing. Let us rather emulate other deeds of that prince, who would not have undertaken such a thing if someone else before him had not gone down the wrong path. For an earlier person's mistake serves to correct the one who follows him, and, in finding fault with what has gone before, a bad precedent is altered. It was allowable for the ancestor of Your Clemency to be unaware of impropriety in a situation that was still new.[96] Could we invoke the same defense if we imitate what we remember was blameworthy?

7. Let Your Eternity embrace other deeds of the same prince that you might more worthily translate into common usage. He removed none of the privileges of the sacred virgins; he filled the priestly ranks with nobles; he did not refuse to pay for the Roman ceremonies; and, following the rejoicing Senate, he gazed with placid mien upon the shrines on every street of the eternal city, read the names of the gods inscribed at the tops of buildings, inquired about the origins of the temples, admired their founders and, although he himself followed another religion, preserved this one for the empire.[97]

8.[98] Each person has his own customs, each person his own religious observance. The divine mind has distributed various forms of worship to different cities as their protection; just as souls are apportioned to the newborn so are the destined tutelar deities to whole peoples. Hence there accrues an advantage that in particular claims the gods for man. For, since all of reason lies in obscurity, whence more rightly does awareness of the divinities come than from the memory and from instances of favorable events? Now, if it is long duration that gives religions their authority, we should keep faith with so many centuries and follow our parents, who happily followed their own.

9. Let us imagine for a moment that Rome is present and that she is addressing you in these words: 'Most excellent princes, fathers of your country, have respect for the years to which pious observance has brought me. Let me perform the ancestral cere- monies, for they are inoffensive. Let me live by my customs, because I am free. This form of worship brought the whole world under my sway; these rites kept back Hannibal from the walls and the Senones from the Capitol.[99] Have I, then, been spared up till this point so that at a great old age I might be cast aside?

10. 'I shall see what sort of thing is under consideration to be instituted, but tardy and abusive is the reformation of old age.'

We ask, then, for peace for the gods of the homeland, for the divine heroes. It is equitable that whatever all worship be considered one. We gaze upon the same stars, the sky is common to all, the same world envelops us. What difference does it make by what judgement a person searches out the truth? So great a mystery can- not be arrived at by one path. But this is a dispute for the idle: now let us come forward with prayers, not arguments.

11. How much was your sacred treasury benefited when the privilege of the Vestal Virgins was withdrawn? Under the most bountiful emperors is there denied what the most niggardly guaran- teed? There is nothing but honor in that stipend – as it is called – for chastity. As fillets adorn their heads so is leisure for the functions of the priesthood accounted their distinction. They look to a certain degree for the mere title of immunity, because on account of their poverty they are spared expenditures. And so those who withdraw any of [their subsidy] contribute that much more to their praiseworthiness, since in fact the virginity that is dedicated to the public weal increases in merit when it lacks a reward.

12. Far be such things as these from the integrity of your treasury! The revenues of good princes are increased not by the losses of the priests but by the spoils of enemies. Can any profit make up for ill will? Avarice is in any event not part of your character. Those to whom the old payments have been allotted are all the more unfortunate inasmuch as, under emperors who respect others' property and who refrain from covetousness, what does not provoke the desire of the robber is taken away solely for the sake of hurting the one who has been robbed.

13. The treasury also holds lands deeded to virgins and ministers by the will of dying persons. I entreat you, priests of justice, to see to it that the inheritance of which they have been deprived be restored to the sacred personages of your city. Once they are secure let them compose wills, and let them know that what they have written is immutable under princes who are not avaricious. Let this contentment on the part of humankind be delightful to you. The precedent established in this regard has begun to worry those who are dying. Does Roman religion, then, have no bearing on Roman law? What name would one give to the alienation of property that no law and no misfortune have rendered uninheritable?

14. Freedmen receive inheritances, and just awards made to slaves in wills are not denied them. Only noble virgins and ministers of ordained rites are excluded from landed property acquired by inheritance. What use is it to consecrate one's chaste body for the sake of the public weal and sustain the eternity of the empire with celestial defenses, to attach friendly powers to your arms and your standards, to make vows that are beneficial to all and yet not to enjoy the same benefits of the law that everyone else does? Better, then, is the servitude that is exercised on behalf of men. We are grieving the republic, to whose advantage it never is to be ungrateful.

15. Let no one think that I am defending the cause of religion alone. From evil deeds of this sort have arisen all the misfortunes of the Roman race. The law of our forefathers had honored the Vestal Virgins and the ministers of the gods with adequate sustenance and with just privileges. This subsidy remained untouched until the days of the degenerate money-changers, who turned the upkeep of sacred chastity into wages for common day-laborers. Widespread famine followed upon this deed, and a poor harvest gave all the provinces a sense of hopelessness.

16. This was not the failure of the earth. We lay no blame on the winds from the south; blight caused no injury to the crops nor did darnel ruin the growth. The year was dry on account of sacrilege, for it was inevitable that what was denied to religion would perish for all. Certainly, if there were any precedent for an evil like this, we would blame so great a famine on the alternation of the years. A serious cause lay at the origin of this barrenness. Life is sustained in sylvan groves, and rustic folk have once more betaken themselves in their need to the trees of Dodona.[100]

17. Did the provinces ever endure anything like this when public esteem made provision for the ministers of religion? When was the oak ever shaken for human usage, when were the roots of weeds ever pulled up, when did fruitfulness on all sides desert the land, despite its failures from year to year, when provisions were shared by both the people and the sacred virgins? For the care that was taken of the priests (which was more a matter of equity than of liberality) served to promote the abundance of the earth. Is there any doubt, now that everyone's need has proved it true, that what was bestowed was always for the benefit of everyone?

18. Suppose someone should say that public funds have not been allowed to subsidize foreign religions. Far be it from good princes to think that what was once bestowed upon some from the common funds should now seem to be at the disposal of the treasury. For since the republic is composed of individuals, whatever originates from it becomes once again the property of individuals. You govern all things, but you protect for each person what belongs to him, and with you justice prevails over license. Consult with your own munificence as to whether what you have transferred to others should not be considered public. Benefits once granted for the sake of honoring a city cease to belong to those who have bestowed them, and through custom and over time what began as a gift becomes a right.

19. If anyone asserts that you are of the same mind as the donors unless you submit to the odium of those who withdraw [their donations], he is trying to instil a senseless fear in your divine soul. Let the hidden guardians of all the sects be well disposed to Your Clemency, and especially those which of old assisted your forebears. Let them defend you, and let them be worshiped by us.

We petition for that religious situation which preserved the empire for the divine father of Your Highness and which furnished legitimate heirs to that fortunate prince.

20. That divine elder looks from the starry height upon the tears of the priests and blames himself when the custom is violated that he himself willingly preserved. Provide as well for your divine brother the correction of inappropriate counsel; cover over the deed that he did not know was displeasing to the Senate. For it is clear that the delegation was kept from him lest he be informed of public opinion.[101] For the sake of the honor of times past you should not hesitate to abolish what it is proved did not originate with that prince.

Letter 18

Bishop Ambrose to the most blessed prince and most clement emperor, the Augustus Valentinian.

1. When the most noble man Symmachus, prefect of the city, had appealed to Your Clemency to return to its place the altar that had been removed from the Senate of the city of Rome, and you, O emperor, although still fresh by reason of years and the inexperience of youth, but a veteran none the less in terms of the virtue of faith, did not approve the entreaties of the pagans, I wrote a letter as soon as I heard about the matter, in which, although I included what seemed necessary for my petition, I still asked for a copy of the appeal to be given to me.

2. And so, not doubtful as to your faith but mindful of being cautious, and confident of a just hearing, I am responding by this note to the statements in the appeal. I ask one thing – that you count as desirable not fine words but persuasive facts. For, as divine Scripture teaches, the tongue of wise and learned men is golden (cf. Prov. 15:2). Adorned with ornate words and flashing with a kind of gleaming and eloquent sheen, like the lustre of some precious object, it allures the eyes of the soul with its lovely shape and draws them by its appearance. Yet gold, if you go over it quite carefully with your hand, is precious on the outside but only metal within. Reflect on and examine the sect of the pagans, I pray you: they utter precious and grand things but defend what does not conform to the truth; they speak of God but adore an idol.

3. The most noble man, the prefect of the city, made three points in his appeal, then, that he thought were of importance – Rome, he said, asks for its ancient cults; subsidies should be granted to their priests and to the Vestal Virgins; and widespread famine resulted when the subsidies of the priests were denied.

4. In the first point, as he says, with tearful and plaintive voice Rome weeps over and asks for her ancient cults and ceremonies. These rites, she declares, kept back Hannibal from the walls and the Senones from the Capitol. And so, while the power of the rites is extolled, their weakness is betrayed. Hannibal for a long time mocked the Roman rites and, although the gods were contending against him, came as a conqueror up to the very walls of the city. Why did they on whose behalf their gods were fighting in arms allow themselves to be besieged?

5. And what shall I say of the Senones? The remnants of the Roman troops would have been unable to resist them as they were penetrating the recesses of the Capitol had not a goose's alarmed honking betrayed them. Look at the kind of protectors that the Roman temples have! Where was Jupiter then? Was he speaking in the goose?

6. But why should I deny that the rites and ceremonies soldiered on behalf of the Romans? Hannibal himself worshiped the same gods. Which do they want? Let them choose! If the rites conquered for the Romans, then they were defeated in the Carthaginians; if they were triumphant in the Carthaginians, then they were certainly of no benefit to the Romans.

7. Let that odious complaint of the Roman people cease, then. Rome did not order these things. She accosts them in other words: 'Why do you bloody me every day with the worthless gore of a harmless herd? The trophies of victory are found not in the entrails of cattle but in the strength of warriors. I subdued the world by other techniques. Camillus fought, who cut down those who had triumphed at the Tarpeian Rock and brought back the standards that had been carried off from the Capitol; force overthrew those whom religion did not drive away. What shall I say of Atilius, who soldiered even to his death? Africanus discovered victory not among the altars of the Capitol but among the troops of Hannibal.[102] Why do you offer me the examples of the ancients? I hate the rites of the Neros. What should I call the two-month emperors and reigns joined in quick succession? Or is it perhaps something new for the barbarians to go beyond their boundaries? Were they Christians too in that wretched and unheard-of case in which one captive emperor, and a world held captive under another,[103] proved that the ceremonies which promised victory were deceptive? Was the Altar of Victory not there at the time? My fall grieves me. My hoary years are embarrassed with bloodshed. I am not ashamed to be converted along with the whole world in my old age. But certain it is that it is not too late at any age to learn. Let that old age be ashamed which cannot change itself for the better. It is not great age but great virtue that is praiseworthy (cf. Wisd. 4:8–9). There is nothing to blush at in going on to better things. This alone I had in common with the barbarians – that I used not to know God. Your sacrifice is a rite of being sprinkled with the blood of beasts.[104] Why do you search for the judgements of God in dead cattle? Come and learn on earth the heavenly warfare. Here we live and there we fight. Let God himself, who created them, teach me the mystery of the heavens – not man, who did not even know himself. Whom should I believe more than God about God? How can I believe you when you confess that you are ignorant of what you worship (cf. Acts 1 7:23)?'

8. 'So great a mystery,' he says, 'cannot be arrived at by one path.' What you are ignorant of we have known by the word of God, and what you seek through hints we have ascertained from the very wisdom and truth of God. What you have, then, is not in accord with us. You beg peace for your gods from the emperors; we ask for peace for the emperors themselves from Christ. You adore the works of your own hands (cf. Wisd. 13:10); we consider it an insult that anything that can be made be thought of as a god. God does not want to be worshiped in stones. Even your own philosophers have mocked these things.

9. But if you deny that Christ is God because you do not believe that he died (for you do not know that that death of the flesh was not a death of the Deity, who brought it to pass that no believer would die from then on), what is more foolish than you, who worship with affront and disparage with honor? For you think that your god is a piece of wood: O affronting reverence! And you do not believe that Christ could have died: O honoring obstinacy!

10. And, he says, the old altars must be restored to the idols and the ornaments to the shrines. Let them ask for these things back from a partner in superstition; a Christian emperor has learned to honor the altar of Christ alone. Why do they compel pious hands and faithful mouths to minister to their sacrileges? Let the voice of our emperor ring out, and let him speak only of him whom he knows, for 'the heart of the king is in the hand of God' (Prov. 21:1). Has a pagan emperor ever erected an altar to Christ? In asking back

186

for what used to be, they call to mind by their own example how much reverence Christian emperors ought to show to the religion that they follow, when the pagans have given their all to their own superstitions.

11. We began some time ago, and they follow those whom they excluded. We glory in blood, but subsidies move them. We put these things on the level of victory, but they consider them an outrage. Never did they bestow on us more than when they ordered Christians to be beaten and proscribed and slain. What faithlessness considered to be torture, religion turned into profit. Look at them in their magnanimity! We thrived through insult, through want and through torture, but they do not believe that their ceremonies can survive without cash.

Let the Vestal Virgins, he says, have their immunity. Let those say such a thing who cannot believe that a gratuitous virginity is possible. Let those who have no trust in virtue stimulate it with money. Yet how many virgins have been produced as a result of the advantages promised to them? Just seven young women are taken as Vestals. This is the total number that has been assembled by the adornment of fillets for the head, purple-dyed garments, the ostentation of a litter surrounded by a crowd of attendants, huge privileges, vast sums of money and, finally, prescribed times for chastity.

12. Let them lift up the eyes of their mind and their body, let them look upon the community of purity, the people of chastity, the assembly of virginity. No fillet adorns their head but rather a veil ignoble for wear but noble for chastity. The allurements of beauty they have not sought out but renounced. Not for them the tokens of dignity; no opulent dishes but the practice of fasting; no privileges, no money: all such things you might consider as advantages to be renounced while exercising a public office, but the desire for them is stimulated as the office is being exercised. Chastity is increased at its own cost. Virginity cannot be purchased at a price nor be possessed except by the pursuit of virtue. Purity cannot be bid for as it were at an auction for a sum of money and on a temporary basis. Chastity's first victory is to overcome the desire for possessions, because a yearning for money represents a trial for purity. Let us suppose, none the less, that generous grants should be made to virgins. What gifts will abound for Christians! What treasury will suffice for such riches? Or, if they are of the opinion that this should be conferred only on Vestals, is it not unfitting that the very persons who claimed everything for themselves under the pagan emperors do not think that they should share with us under the Christian emperors?

13. They also complain that public support is not being provided to their priests and ministers. What a wordy uproar has broken out in this regard! But on the other hand the income from an individual inheritance is even denied us under recent laws and no one is complaining about it, for we do not consider it a slight because we do not regret the loss.[105] If a priest seeks a privilege in order to avoid the burdens imposed on a town councilor, it is to be granted at the cost of all his possessions, ancestral and paternal. If this was true in the case of the pagans, why did they complain all the more that a priest had to purchase free time for his obligations by giving up his entire inheritance and had to buy the exercise of his public service by renouncing any gain from the private sector? Alleging vigilance for the common weal, he takes comfort in the reward of his domestic indigence, because he has not sold a service but obtained a favor.[106]

14. Compare the issues. You want to excuse a decurion[107] when it is not permitted the Church to excuse a priest. Wills are written for ministers of the temples; no impious person, no person of the most base condition, no person of easy virtue is excluded. Of all people, this universal right is denied to the cleric alone, by whom alone the universal prayer is raised on behalf of all and upon whom alone a universal office is conferred; not even grave widows can give him any bequests or a single donation. And although no crime is detected in his behavior, a penalty is none the less imposed on his office. What a Christian widow may have willed to the priests of a pagan shrine is licit, but not what she may have willed to the ministers of God. I have not made mention of this in a tone of complaint but rather so that they may know why I am not complaining, for I prefer that we lack money rather than grace.

15. But they assert that what has been given or left to the Church has not been violated. Let them also say who has removed gifts from the temples – which has been done in the case of the Christians. If this had been done to the pagans it would be a matter of repaying abuse rather than inflicting it. Is justice now at last being alleged and fairness being asked for? Where was that attitude when, after having plundered the possessions of all the Christians, they begrudged them their very life's breath and prevented their access to a final resting place, which had never been denied to the dead? The sea restored those whom the pagans threw into it. This is the victory of the faith – that now they themselves revile the deeds of their forebears. But what sense does it make to ask for the benefits of those evil people whose acts they condemn?

16. But no one has forbidden offerings to the shrines and bequests to the soothsayers. The only thing that has been taken away is their landed property, because they did not use in a religious way what they claimed by right of religion. If they are using us as an example, why did they not have our sense of morality? The Church possesses nothing of its own apart from faith. It exhibits these returns, this yield. The possession of the Church is the upkeep of the needy. Let the temples enumerate which captives they have redeemed, what sustenance they have provided for the poor, to which exiles they have given support. Their landed property has been removed, then, but not their rights.

17. This is what happened: a widespread famine, which was to atone for the horrid crime, as they say, wreaked vengeance because what had previously served to benefit the priests now began to be of benefit to everyone. On this account, as they say, the tongues of the faint licked the bare trees after their bark had been stripped off, all for the sake of the wretched sap. On this account they shook down the oak tree and, exchanging grain for the Chaonian fruit,[108] they alleviated their extreme hunger in the woods, having been reduced to the fodder of cattle and a miserable sustenance. These were clearly new prodigies on earth, which had never occurred before, when pagan superstition raged throughout the world! Indeed, when before did the harvest mock the prayers of the greedy farmer with its empty straw and the green crop sought in the furrow disappoint the expectations of rustic folk?

18. And whence did the Greeks get the oracles of the oaks that they had if not from the fact that they thought that relief in the form of food from a tree was the gift of a heavenly religion? For such, they believe, are the gifts of their gods. Which people adored the trees of Dodona but that of the pagans, when they offered the pitiable food of their fields in honor of the groves?[109] It is unlikely that their gods in their indignation would have inflicted as a punishment that which they were in the habit of bestowing as a gift when they were pleased. But what justice is there in lamenting that sustenance is denied to a few priests while they themselves would refuse it to everyone, when the punishment would be harsher than the misdeed? It is inappropriate, then, to have so intensified the misery of a world in decline as to allow the high expectations for the season to perish suddenly as the crops were flourishing.

19. And in fact the rights of the temples were done away with everywhere many years ago. Have the gods of the pagans only now begun to think of avenging their injuries? Has the Nile risen higher than usual in order to avenge the losses of the civic priests, when they did not avenge themselves?

20. But let the point be conceded. If they think that the injuries to their gods were avenged last year, why have they been overlooked this year? For no longer do rustic folk eat the roots of weeds that they have pulled up or look for relief from the fruits of trees or snatch food from briers. Instead, joyful in their labors and amazed at their harvests, they have brought their fasting to an end through the fulfillment of their wishes. The earth has provided us with an overabundant yield.

21. Who, then, is so new to human ways as to be stunned at the changes that each year brings? And yet we know that even last year many provinces overflowed with crops. What shall I say of the Gauls, which were richer than usual? The Pannonias sold grain that they had not sown, and Raetia Secunda suffered from envy by reason of its fruitfulness, for it was wont to be safer in lean times but attracted the enemy to itself on account of its abundance. The autumn harvests fed Liguria and the Venetias.[110] That year did not dry up, then, because of sacrilege, and this year has flourished with the fruits of the earth. Would they also deny that the vines have been weighed down with a huge yield? And so we have both gathered an overabundant harvest and now enjoy the good results of a more bountiful vintage.

22. The last and most important matter that remains is whether, O emperors, you should restore the subsidies that are supposed to benefit you. For he says: 'Let them defend you, and let them be worshiped by us.' It is this, most faithful princes, which we cannot bear – that they throw it in our faces that they are supplicating their gods in your name and that, in the absence of a command from you, they are committing a monstrous sacrilege and interpreting your neglect as consent. Let them have their own guardians, and let them defend their devotees if they can. For if they can be of no help to those by whom they are worshiped, how can they defend you, by whom they are not worshiped?

23. But, he says, the ceremonies of the ancients should be maintained. What about the fact that all things have eventually progressed to something better? Did not the world itself, which first took shape in the likeness of a fragile disk by compressing particles of the elements from throughout the void, and which existed in the darkness of the dreadful disorder of the as yet chaotic undertaking, eventually receive the forms of things through the clear separation of sky and sea and land, thanks to which its appearance is beautiful? The land, freed of mists and darkness, was astounded by the newness of the sun.

At its start the day is not clear, but as time goes on it is bright with an increase of light and grows warm with an increase of heat.

24. The moon itself, by which in prophetic oracles the beauty of the Church is alluded to,[111] is hidden by the dark of night when first it makes its reappearance and is renewed in its monthly cycle, but gradually it grows fuller, departs from the region of the sun and shines with a clear and splendid brightness.

25. The earth in former times knew nothing of agriculture. Later, when the diligent husbandman began to exercise control over his fields and to clothe the rude soil with vines, it laid aside its wild disposition, having been softened by homely cultivation.

26. The first season of the year itself, which corresponds to the way we are, is bare in its beginnings but, as it advances, blooms with the flowers that appear imperceptibly, and in the end it is ripe with fruits.

27. We too have the uninstructed perceptions of the age of infancy, but over the course of the years we lay aside the raw beginnings of our natures.

28. Let them say, then, that everything should have stayed as it was in the beginning, and that the world once covered in darkness is now displeasing because it has grown luminous with the brightness of the sun. And how much better is it to have driven away the darkness of the soul than that of the body, and for the radiance of faith to have shone forth than that of the sun? Hence too the youthful beginnings of the world, as of all things, have given way so that the venerable old age of mature faith might follow. Let those whom this disturbs reject the harvest because its fruitfulness is late in coming, let them reject the vintage because it occurs at the decline of the year, let them reject the olive because it is the last of the crops.

29. Hence too the faith of souls is our harvest; the grace of the Church is our vintage of merits, which from the foundation of the world flourished in the saints but in this last age has been spread out among the peoples, so that all might realize that the faith of Christ has not come into uninstructed souls (for without an adversary[112] there is no crown of victory). Rather, what is true rightfully carried the day after the opinion that previously prevailed had been rejected.

30. If the old rites were pleasing, why did the same Rome give way to foreign rites? I make no mention of the ground covered at great cost and shepherds' cottages glittering ignobly with gold.[113] Why (so as to respond to the very thing that they are complaining of) did they emulously accept the idols of captured cities, the vanquished gods and the foreign rites and ceremonies of an alien superstition? What provided the example for Cybele to go through the motion of washing her chariots in the River Almo?[114] Whence come the Phrygian seers and the divinities of unfriendly Carthage, which have always been hostile to the Romans.[115] She whom the Africans worship as the Heavenly One, the Persians as Mithra and the multitude as Venus has a variety of names but is not a different divinity.[116] Likewise, they believed that victory was a goddess. In fact it is a gift and not a power; thanks to the army and not by the power of religion it is bestowed, but it does not rule. Is the goddess great, then, whom a multitude of soldiers claims for itself or whom the outcome of battles bestows?

31. They ask that her altar be set up in the Senate of the city of Rome – that is, where the majority who gather are Christians. There are altars in all the temples; there is an altar in the Temple of Victories as well. Since they take pleasure in numbers, they celebrate the sacrifices everywhere. What is it but an insult to the faith to demand this one altar for sacrifice? Must this be endured so that pagans may sacrifice and Christians be in attendance? Let them take, he says, let them take the smoke into their eyes, the music into their ears, the ashes into their throats and the incense into their nostrils, and let the ashes stirred up from our hearths besprinkle the faces even of those who are repulsed. Do they not have enough baths, enough arcades, enough streets sufficiently filled with idols? Shall there not be a common state of affairs even in that common council chamber? Shall the devout portion of the Senate be annoyed by the voices of suppliants and the solemn formulas of oath-takers? Should it resist this it will be looked upon as betraying the fiction; should it acquiesce it will be looked upon as concurring in sacrilege.

32. 'Where,' he says, 'shall we swear to your laws and words?' Do your decisions, then, which are bound by the laws, obtain approbation and compel credence through the ceremonies of the pagans? Now the faith not only of those present but also of the absent and, what is more, O emperors, of you yourselves is being defamed, for you compel if you command. Constantius of august memory, when he was not yet initiated into the sacred mysteries, considered that he would be contaminated if he happened to see that altar. He ordered it to be removed; he did not order it to be replaced.[117] The removal has a *de facto* authority; the replacement would not have a *de jure* authority.

33. Let no one be pleased with himself because of his absence. One who joins himself to our souls is more present than one who appears before our eyes, for to be linked by the mind is more than to be joined in body. The Senate has you as its overseers, who can compel the assembly; it comes together for your sake; it offers its conscience to you and not to the gods of the pagans; it places you above its own children, although not above its faith. This is the desirable charity, this is the charity that is greater than an empire – that the faith which preserves the empire should be secure.

34. But perhaps it will trouble someone that a most faithful prince has been abandoned in this way,[118] in the same manner that a reward for merits might fluctuate in value according to the fashion of the day. For what wise person does not know that human affairs are arranged in a kind of recurring cycle, because they do not always have the same successes but vary in condition and undergo changes?

35. Who was more fortunate than Gnaeus Pompeius, whom the Roman temples sent out? But, when he had girded the earth with three triumphs, he was struck down in an engagement, fled the battle and, exiled from his own empire, died at the hand of a eunuch of Canopus.[119]

36. What nobler king than Cyrus of the Persians have all the lands of the East produced? When he had conquered some very powerful princes who were his adversaries and spared them once they were conquered, he himself perished, having been overcome by the arms of a woman. And that king, who even used to confer the honor of sitting with him on those whom he had vanquished, was made sport of at a woman's orders, when his head had been cut off and put into a sack full of gore. To such an extent in the course of his life was he not repaid in kind but far differently.[120]

37. Whom, too, do we find more devoted to the sacrifices than Hamilcar, the leader of the Carthaginians? During the whole time of battle he was in the midst of his soldiers, offering sacrifice while they fought. But, when he learned that a part of his troops had been defeated, he threw himself into the very fire that he had lit for worship, so that he might at least extinguish with his body what he realized had been of no use to him.[121]

38. And what shall I say of Julian? When he was foolishly credulous of the answers of the soothsayers he deprived himself of his means of retreat.[122]

Hence in like cases there is not a like offense, for our promises have fooled no one.[123]

39. I have responded to those who are provoking me without being provocative myself, for my concern was to rebut the appeal and not to expose the superstition. But, O emperor, let that very appeal of theirs make you all the more cautious. For when it related of former princes that 'the earlier part of them practiced the ceremonies of their forefathers, the latter did not do away with them,' and also added that, 'if the religious devotion of the ancients does not serve as an example, then let the neglect of the more recent serve as such,' it clearly pointed out what you owe to your faith – that you should not accept the example of pagan worship; and what you owe to familial devotion – that you should not violate your brother's decisions. For if only for their own faction they have praised the neglect of those princes who, although they were Christians, did not do away with the decrees of the pagans, how much more ought you to defer to brotherly love, in order that you who were supposed to practice neglect, even if perhaps you did not approve, might not dishonor your brother's decisions, and now you should hold to what you judge to be consistent both with your faith and with the bond of brotherhood.

4

PAULINUS OF MILAN, *THE LIFE OF SAINT AMBROSE*

INTRODUCTION

The author of this *Life*, the deacon Paulinus, asserts at the very beginning of his work that he wrote it at the urging of Augustine, who owed his conversion at least in part to Ambrose's preaching and who regarded the Bishop of Milan with the profoundest respect. Paulinus knew Ambrose personally, as we learn from various passages in the *Life*, and he probably became acquainted with Augustine when he moved to Africa after Ambrose's death. Scholars differ as to whether the text should be dated to 412–13 or to 422, based on certain internal evidence, although the earlier date seems convincing at present. For all its faults, it still provides useful information, and it also allows us some experience of Ambrose's posthumous reputation; the very fact that Ambrose had a biographer at all is telling in itself.

Paulinus insists in §2 that what he has written is true, but such an insistence was a commonplace and must be taken with a grain of salt. In fact the *Life* includes several unlikely events, ranging from the episode of the bees in §3 to that of the resurrection of a dead boy in §28. Still Paulinus' account of Ambrose's life commands some respect when it is compared, for example, with the *Lives* that our author mentions in §1, particularly those of Paul and Martin of Tours, which are full of fantastical improbabilities. With Paulinus one has a real sense of historical rootedness because of (among other reasons) his use of documentation from Ambrose's own hand. None the less Paulinus does not always maintain the chronological order of events, nor does he attempt to establish a connection between them; the result is a feeling that things are jumbled together.

Of our author we know very little. He surfaces only in the *Life* and then again in connection with the Pelagian controversy, when he wrote a pamphlet against Coelestius, who was associated with Pelagius. It is thanks to Augustine that we are told of Paulinus' diaconate which he received after having left Milan (cf. *On Original Sin* 3.8; *Against Two Letters of the Pelagians* 2.4.6). Apart from that there is largely silence.

This translation is made from the critical text in Michele Pellegrino (1961: 50–129). The Latin text is also in PL 14.29–50 and Mary S. Kaniecka (1928). Kaniecka's work includes an English translation, and there is another one in FL 15.33–66.

1. Venerable Father Augustine, you urge me to set in writing the life of the most blessed Ambrose, bishop of the church of Milan, just as the blessed men Athanasius the bishop and Jerome the priest set in writing the lives of the holy Paul and Anthony, who lived in the desert, and just as the servant of God Severus put into words the life of the venerable Martin, bishop of the church of Tours.[1] But I know that I am unequal to the talents of those great men, who are bulwarks of the churches and fountains of eloquence, just as I am to wordcraft. Yet, because I consider it improper to refuse what you command, aided by the prayers and merits of this great man, and heedless of my unskilled language, I shall describe the things that I learned from the very trustworthy men who attended him before I did, and especially from his own sister, the venerable Marcellina, that I saw myself when I attended him, that I came to know from those who said that they saw him in different provinces after his death, and that were written to him when people were still unaware that he had died. And in so doing I shall be brief and succinct. Thus, even if my language is offensive to my reader's intelligence, my brevity will spur him to read on. Nor will I drape the truth in fancy words. Otherwise the writer will satisfy himself with pompous elegance but the reader, whom it behoves to gaze upon virtuous deeds and the grace of the Holy Spirit rather than the pompous trappings of words, may lose sight of the man's great virtues. For we know that travelers are more thankful for water dripping from a narrow channel, particularly when they are thirsty, than for streams gushing from a source, from which they are unable to collect enough in time of thirst. And barley bread tastes good even to those who are accustomed to belch up the richness of their daily banquet with its hundreds of courses in succession. Plants in the wild, too, are likely to please those who admire pleasant gardens.

2. For this reason I beg all of you into whose hands this book will fall to believe that what we have written is true; let no one think that, out of an overweening love, I have put anything in it that is unreliable. Indeed, it would be better to say nothing at all than to put forward something false, since we know that we are to give an account of all our words (cf. Matt 12:36). Nor should I doubt that, even if everything is not known by everyone, none the less different things are known by different people, and there are things known to some people that I myself was unable to hear and see. Hence I shall start this narrative with the day of [Ambrose's] birth, so that the man's grace, which was present from the cradle, may be recognized.

3. And so, when his father Ambrose was administering the prefecture of the Gauls, Ambrose was born.[2] The infant was placed in a cradle in the courtyard of the praetorium.[3] All at once, as he slept with his mouth open, a swarm of bees came and covered his face and mouth in such a way that they would go in and out [of his mouth]. His father, who was taking a walk nearby with [Ambrose's] mother and his daughter, prevented the nurse, who was responsible for feeding the infant, from driving them away, for she was concerned that they might hurt the infant, and he waited with fatherly affection to see how this marvel would conclude. But after a short time passed they flew out and were lifted so high into the air that they could not be seen by the human eye. When this happened his father was shaken, and he said: 'If this little baby lives, he will become something great.' Even then, in his infancy, the Lord was at work in his servant, so that what had been said might be fulfilled: 'Good words are a honeycomb' (Prov. 16:24). For that swarm of bees produced for us the honeycombs of his writings, which would tell of heavenly gifts and raise the minds of human beings from earthly things to heaven.

4. Afterwards, in fact, when he had grown up and was living in Rome with his widowed mother and his sister (who had already professed her virginity and had another virgin as her companion, which virgin's sister was Candida, who had made the same profession and is now already an old woman living in Carthage),[4] and he would see his sister and his mother's servant girl kissing the hands of bishops, he would jokingly offer his own hand and say that she should do this to him as well, since he thought that he was going to be a bishop. It was the Spirit of the Lord, who was preparing him for the episcopacy, that was speaking in him. She, however, used to dismiss it as the utterance of a young man who did not know what he was talking about.

5. After he had been trained in the liberal arts he left Rome and, having been accepted to practice law before the prefecture of the praetorium, he argued cases so brilliantly that he was chosen by the illustrious man Probus, then praetorian prefect, to serve as his counsel. After this he was invested as consularis, to rule the provinces of Liguria and Aemilia, and he came to Milan.

6. Around the same time, with the death of Auxentius, the bishop of the Arian perfidy (who burdened the church after the confessor Dionysius, of blessed memory, had been condemned to exile),[5] the people were in a state of unrest over the search for a bishop.[6] It was [Ambrose's] responsibility to quell the unrest. Lest the people of the city be endangered, he went to the church, and there, as he was speaking to the throng, the voice of a small child all at once made itself heard among the people: 'Ambrose for bishop!' At the sound of this voice the whole tone of the gathering changed, and they acclaimed Ambrose as their bishop. So it was that those who had previously been violently divided, because the Catholics and the Arians each wanted to best the other and to have a bishop ordained for themselves, suddenly agreed, with remarkable and unbelievable harmony, on this one man.

7. When he realized this, he left the church and had a tribunal set up for himself. He who was in fact soon to be bishop mounted it, and then, contrary to his own custom, ordered that individuals be put to torture. But even when he did this the people cried out: 'Your sin be upon us!' These people, however, did not shout as did the people of the Jews, for the ones shed the Lord's blood with their voices when they said: 'His blood be upon us' (Matt. 27:25), while the others, knowing that [Ambrose] was a catechumen, were assuring him with words of faith that all his sins would be forgiven through the grace of baptism. With that, returning to his house in anguish, he determined to become a philosopher. But he was to be Christ's true philosopher who, having disdained worldly display, would follow in the footsteps of those fishermen who gathered together peoples for Christ not with fancy words but with simple speech and the doctrine of the true faith, who were sent out without a satchel or a staff (cf. Matt. 10:10) and even converted philosophers themselves. When he was prevented from doing this, he had prostitutes come to him in the open, for no other reason than that the people might see them and change their minds. But the people cried out all the more: 'Your sin be upon us!'

8. When, however, he saw that he could not accomplish his plan, he decided to flee. He left the city in the middle of the night, with Pavia as his destination, but in the morning he found himself at the so-called Roman Gate of the city of Milan. For God, who was setting up the bulwark of his Catholic Church against his enemies and establishing David as a tower in the face of Damascus (cf. 2 Sam. 8:5–6) – that is, against the perfidy of the heretics – prevented his flight. When he was found and taken into custody by the people, a report was sent to the most clement emperor, who at the time was Valentinian. He was exceedingly glad when judges whom he had selected were sought for the episcopate. Probus the prefect rejoiced as well, because his words were being fulfilled in Ambrose; for, as the custom is, he had said to him as he was departing, when he was being given his orders: 'Go, and act not as a judge but as a bishop.'

9. And so, while the report was pending, he decided to flee again, and for a while he hid on the property of a certain Leontius, who had the title of 'clarissimus.'[7] But when the answer to the report came, he was handed over by this same Leontius, for the vicar had been commanded to see that the matter was settled.[8] Since he wished to carry out what had been enjoined upon him by the edict in question, it was best for everyone to hand over the man if they wanted to safeguard both themselves and their property. And so he was handed over and brought to Milan and, when he understood God's will in his regard and that he could no longer resist it, he asked to be baptized by no one but a Catholic bishop, for he was wary of the perfidy of the Arians. Once he was baptized he is said to have fulfilled all the ecclesiastical offices, and on the eighth day, with great grace and to the joy of everyone, he was ordained a bishop.

A few years after his ordination he went to the city of Rome – in other words, to his own home – and there in his own house he found the holy servant girl, whom we previously mentioned, to whom he used to offer his hand, along with his sister, just as he had left them. (His mother had died meanwhile.) And as she was kissing his hand he said to her with a smile: 'See, just as I told you: you are kissing the hand of a bishop.'

10. Around the same time, when he had been invited across the Tiber to the home of a woman with the title of 'clarissima' and was offering the sacrifice[9] in her house, a certain bathkeeper, a woman, who was paralyzed and was confined to bed, learned that the Lord's bishop was in the same place. She had herself carried by litter to the very house where he had come by invitation, and she touched his garments while he prayed and placed his hands on her. As she was eagerly kissing them, all at once she recovered her health and began to walk, so that what the Lord had said to the apostles was fulfilled: 'Those who believe in my name will do even greater things than these' (John 14:12). Just as this sign of health was miraculous, so also it did not go undisclosed, for after many years, when I was living in Rome, I heard of it in the same region from the accounts of holy men.

11. When he came to Sirmium to ordain Anemius bishop,[10] however, he was nearly driven out of the church there by the power of Justina, who was empress at the time, and by a large mob, so that not he but the heretics might ordain an Arian bishop for that church. When he was in the sanctuary, paying no heed to those who had been stirred up by the woman, one of the Arian virgins who was more impudent than the others came up into the sanctuary and got hold of the bishop's clothing, intending to drag him to the women's section so that they could knock him down and drive him out of the church. But she heard [him say], as he himself used to relate: 'Even if I myself am unworthy of the lofty office of a bishop, still it is improper for you or for one of your profession to lay your hands on any bishop whatsoever. You ought to fear God's judgement, therefore, lest something befall you.' What he said came to pass, for the next day she died and he brought her to her grave, thus repaying insolence with kindness. This event aroused considerable fear among his adversaries and obtained great peace for the Catholic Church for the bishop's ordination.

12. Once a Catholic bishop was ordained, then, [Ambrose] returned to Milan, and there he endured the countless plots of the aforementioned woman Justina who, with offers of gifts and honors, was wont to stir up the people against the holy man. The minds of the weak were ensnared by promises of this sort, for she used to promise the tribuneship and other kinds of dignities to people if they would seize him from out of the church and drag him off to exile. Many attempted this but were unable to accomplish it, thanks to God's protection. But a certain man by the name of Euthymius, more wretched than the others, was incited to such a fury that he acquired a house for himself near the church and readied a wagon in it; with this he would be able to seize him more easily, put him in the cart and take him off into exile. 'But his iniquity came down upon his own head' (Ps. 7:17), for, a year after the very day that he planned to seize him, he himself was put in the same cart and sent into exile from the same house, reflecting to himself all the while that it was by God's just judgement that the tables had turned and that he was being exiled in the very cart that he had readied for the bishop. But the bishop offered him much relief by supplying him with money and other necessities.

13. But the man's confession put an end to neither the woman's fury nor the insane Arians' madness. Inflamed by still greater madness, they endeavored to break into the Portian Basilica. Even an armed force was stationed to guard the doors of the church so that no one would dare to enter the Catholic church. But the Lord, who regularly bestowed triumphs on his Church in the face of her enemies, turned the hearts of the soldiers to the defense of his Church, so that with shields reversed they protected the entrances of the church, not allowing the Catholic people to leave but not preventing them from going into the church. Yet this was not enough for the soldiers who had been assigned: they even acclaimed the Catholic faith along with the people. It was at this time that antiphons, hymns and vigils first came into use in the Milanese church. Their devout usage continues to this day not only in that church but in almost all the provinces of the West.[11]

14. Around the same time the holy martyrs Protasius and Gervasius revealed themselves to the bishop. As a matter of fact they were located in the basilica where the bodies of the martyrs Nabor and Felix are today.[12] The holy martyrs Nabor and Felix, however, were very popular, whereas neither the names nor the graves of the martyrs Protasius and Gervasius were known – so much so that everyone who wanted to go to the enclosure where the graves of the holy martyrs Nabor and Felix were protected from harm used to walk on top of the graves [of Protasius and Gervasius]. But when the bodies of the holy martyrs were exhumed and placed on biers, the illnesses of many were seen to have been cured there. There was even a blind man by the name of Severus, who up to this day serves devotedly in the same basilica, called the Ambrosian, where the bodies of the martyrs were brought: when he touched the martyrs' garments he at once received his sight. Likewise, bodies possessed by unclean spirits were healed and returned home with the deepest gratitude. Thanks to the martyrs' good works the faith of the Catholic Church increased to the same extent that the perfidy of the Arians decreased.

15. It was during this period that the persecution, which had been inflamed by Justina's fury and which was aimed at driving the bishop from the church, began to subside. Still, within the palace there was a multitude of Arians who, along with Justina, mocked the great grace of God that the Lord Jesus had deigned to confer on the Catholic Church through the merits of his martyrs. They used to spread the story that the venerable man Ambrose was bribing people to lie about being troubled by unclean spirits and to say that they were being tormented just as much by him as by the martyrs.[13] But the Arians, being like them, were speaking in a Jewish way. For [the Jews] said of the Lord that 'he casts out demons by Beelzebub, the prince of demons' (Luke 11:15), whereas the others were saying of the martyrs and of the Lord's bishop that it was not by the grace of God, which was at work through them, that unclean spirits were being driven out, but that people would lie about being tormented after they had been bribed. For the demons would cry out: 'We know that you are martyrs,' and the Arians would say: 'We do not know that they are martyrs.' Now we read the same thing in the gospel, when the demons said to the Lord Jesus: 'We know you, that you are the Son of God' (Mark 1:24), while the Jews said: 'Where this man comes from we do not know' (John 9:29). What is being taken here, however, is not the demons' testimony but their confession. Hence the Arians and the Jews are all the more wretched for denying what the demons confess.

16. But God, who is accustomed to adding to the grace of his Church, did not long allow his holy ones to be abused by the perfidious. And so, one of that very multitude was suddenly seized by an unclean spirit, and he began to cry out that, just as he was being tormented, so also would they be tormented who denied the martyrs and did not believe in the unity of the Trinity, which Ambrose taught. But those who were disturbed by these words and should have been converted and performed a penance worthy of such a confession killed the man by drowning him in a pool, thus joining murder to their perfidy; there was a fitting inevitability in their having been led to this extreme. The holy Ambrose, however, having become a man of greater humility, maintained the grace that the Lord had given him, and daily he grew in faith and love before God and men (cf. Luke 2:52).

17. About the same time there was a certain man of the heresy of the Arians who was a very sharp debater, hard and obdurate with regard to the Catholic faith. He was in church when the bishop was preaching and, as he himself said afterwards, saw an angel speaking into the bishop's ear while he was preaching, so that the bishop seemed to be proclaiming the angel's words to the people. When he saw this he was converted, and he began to defend the faith that he had been resisting.

18. There were also at that time two chamberlains of the Emperor Gratian, of the heresy of the Arians, who, while he was preaching, posed a question to the bishop for him to respond to. They promised to be present to hear the answer on the following day in the Portian Basilica, for it was a question about the Lord's incarnation. But on the following day the pitiable men – bloated with a swelling pride and forgetful of their promise, disdaining God in his bishop and heedless of the inconvenience to the people who were waiting, forgetful also of the Lord's words that 'whoever is an obstacle to one of these little ones should have a millstone fastened to his neck and be sunk in the depths of the sea' (Matt. 18:6) – got into a carriage and rode off, leaving the city, while the bishop and the people were waiting in the church. But the outcome of this arrogance I shudder to relate, for all of a sudden they were hurled out of the carriage and breathed their last, and their bodies were brought to be buried. But the holy Ambrose, unaware of what had happened, could not keep the people any longer. Mounting the tribunal, he took up the very question that had been posed, and he said: 'Brothers, I wish to pay my debt, but I do not see my creditors from yesterday,' and he went on with what has been written in the book entitled *On the Incarnation of the Lord.*[14]

19. When the Emperor Gratian was slain, [Ambrose] undertook a second mission to Maximus in order to obtain his body. Whoever wishes to know how firmly he acted in his regard will approve when he reads the letter that his delegation delivered to Valentinian the Younger.[15] For it seemed to us that to insert it here would not be to keep our promise [of brevity and succinctness] and that the length of the letter, were it to be added, would induce tedium in the reader. In any event, he cut Maximus off from the fellowship of communion, warning him that if he wished to be in good standing before God he would have to do penance for the blood of his master, an innocent man (that being still more serious), which was shed. But when with proud spirit he refused to do penance, he forfeited not only his future but also his present well-being, and the kingdom that he had wickedly usurped he gave up with a kind of womanly fear, declaring that he had been not the emperor of the republic but its procurator.

20. When Justina died, a certain soothsayer named Innocent (although he was not such in deed) began to confess something else than what he was being interrogated about when he was being tortured by a judge for his crimes. For he cried out that he was suffering still greater torments from the angel who was guarding Ambrose because, in the days of Justina, he had climbed to the top of the roof of the church to incite the people's hatred against the bishop and there, at midnight, had performed a sacrifice. But the more urgently and carefully he carried out his evil deeds, the stronger grew the people's love for the Catholic faith and the Lord's bishop. He confessed that he had even sent demons to kill him, but that the demons had declared that they could not only not get near him but that they could not even get near the entrance of the house where he was staying, because an impassable fire was protecting the entire building, so that even those who were far away would be set ablaze, and that therefore he put an end to the machinations by which he thought that he could accomplish something against the Lord's bishop. Another man who was carrying a sword penetrated as far as his bedroom in order to slay the bishop but, when he lifted his hand and stretched out his sword, he became immobile, with his hand extended stiffly in the air. When he confessed later that he had been sent by Justina, the arm that had stiffened when it was wickedly extended was healed by the confession.

21. Around the same time, when the illustrious man Probus had sent a servant, his secretary, who was seriously troubled by an unclean spirit, to the bishop, the devil abandoned him as he left Rome, fearing to be brought to the holy man. And so, as long as the servant was in Milan with the bishop, the devil appeared to exercise no power over him. But, when he left Milan and came near Rome, the same spirit that had possessed him before began to trouble him [again]. When he was asked by exorcists why he had not appeared in the man as long as he was in Milan, the devil confessed that he was afraid of Ambrose and had therefore withdrawn for a while and waited in the spot where he had left the man until he returned, and that when he returned he sought out once more the vessel that he had forsaken.

22. When Maximus had been destroyed and Theodosius was at Milan as emperor, while Bishop Ambrose was in Aquileia, in the regions of the Orient,[16] in a certain fortified town,[17] a synagogue of the Jews and a grove sacred to the Valentinians[18] were burned down by Christian men because the Jews and the Valentinians had reviled some Christian monks. (The heresy of the Valentinians worships thirty gods.) The Count of the Orient sent a report to the emperor about the deed. When he received it, the emperor ordered that the synagogue be rebuilt by the bishop of the place and that the monks be punished. When the contents of this order reached the ears of the venerable man, Bishop Ambrose, he sent a letter to the emperor[19] because he himself was unable to reach him in time. In it he demanded that he revoke what he had commanded and that an audience be granted him, because if he were not worthy to be heard by him then he was also not worthy to be heard by the Lord on his behalf, nor was there any worthy person to whom he might address his prayers and promises. Moreover, he was ready to die on this account, lest by his own dissimulation he make a sinner of the emperor, who had ordered such unjust things against the Church.

23. Later, when he returned to Milan, he preached to the people about the same matter while the emperor was in the church. In his sermon he had the Lord speak to the emperor: 'From the least I made you emperor; I handed over to you your enemy's army; I gave you the troops that he had readied from his army to use against you; I brought your enemy into your power; I set you up from your seed upon a royal throne; I made you triumphant without any effort of your own: and you let my enemies triumph over me!' When he was leaving the apse of the basilica the emperor said: 'You have spoken against us today, bishop.' [Ambrose] replied, however, that he had spoken not against him but for him. Then the emperor said: 'It is true that I issued a harsh order against the bishop about rebuilding the synagogue, but the monks must be punished.' The counts who were there at the time said the same thing as well. To them the bishop said: 'My business now is with the emperor; with you I will deal later in another way.' And thus he obtained the revocation of what had been commanded, nor was it his wish to approach the altar until the emperor had first given him his word that he should do so. The bishop said: 'Am I acting, then, on your word?' The emperor replied: 'Act on my word.' When this pledge had been repeated, the bishop, now reassured, carried out the divine mysteries. But all of this has been written down in the letter that he sent to his sister.[20] In it he included the sermon that he delivered on the same day about the staff of the nut tree that is said to have been seen by the prophet Jeremiah (cf. Jer. 1:11).

24. Around the same time, great distress overtook the bishop concerning the city of Thessalonika, when he found out that the city was nearly destroyed. For the emperor had promised him that he was going to pardon the citizens of the aforesaid city, but the counts acted secretly with the emperor, unbeknownst to the bishop, and the city was given over to the sword until the third hour,[21] and many innocent people were slaughtered. When the bishop became aware of the deed, he did not allow the emperor to enter the church, and he judged him unworthy of the assembly of the Church and of participation in the sacraments until he did public penance. The emperor defended himself to him by observing that David had committed both adultery and murder (cf. 2 Sam. 11). But the immediate response was: 'If you have followed him in his sin, then follow him in his amendment.' When the most clement emperor heard this, he was so moved that he did not shrink from public penance, and the improvement that resulted from his amendment won for him a second victory.

25. Around the same time, two very powerful and wise Persian men came to Milan because of the reputation of the bishop, bringing with them numerous questions in order thereby to try the wisdom of the man. From the first hour of the day until the third hour of the night[22] they discussed them with him through an interpreter, and when they left him it was in wonderment. And in order to prove that they had come for no other reason than to know better the man whose reputation they had heard of, they bade farewell to the emperor on the following day and set out for the city of Rome. They were eager to acquaint themselves there with the power of the illustrious man Probus, and when they had acquainted themselves with it they returned home.

26. But when Theodosius had left Italy and established himself in Constantinople, a mission was sent to the Augustus Valentinian, who was in Gaul, by Symmachus, then prefect of Rome, in the name of the Senate. It concerned the return of the Altar of Victory and the expenses of the ceremonies. But when the bishop heard of this, he sent a letter to the emperor[23] and requested that he receive copies of the report, so that by using it he might be able to respond on his side. When he received the report he composed a most remarkable letter to which Symmachus, a most eloquent man, would never dare to respond. After this, however, Valentinian, of august memory, ended his life in the city of Vienne, which is a city of Gaul, and Eugenius entered upon the imperial rule. Not long after he began to rule, at the request of Flavian, who was then the prefect, and Count Arbogast, [Eugenius] assented, heedless of his faith, to the Altar of

Victory and to the expenses of the ceremonies, which Valentinian, of august memory, had denied to his petitioners while still a young man.

27. When the bishop learned of this he left the city of Milan, to which he had hastily come, went to the city of Bologna, and traveled from there to Faenza. When he had stayed there a few days he was invited by the Florentines and went down to Tuscany, refusing to look at the sacrilegious man and not fearing the emperor's wrath. For he had sent him a letter in which he addressed his conscience, from which I quote a small portion of all that he wrote: 'Even if the imperial power is great, O emperor, yet consider how great God is. He sees the hearts of all, he probes the conscience within, he knows all things before they transpire, he knows the depths of your heart. You do not allow yourself to be deceived, and do you wish to conceal things from God? Did it not occur to you that, if they were acting so insistently, it was your responsibility, O emperor, to resist them still more insistently, out of reverence for the most high, true and living God, and to forbid what was injurious to the sacred law?' And again: 'Since, therefore, I am held to my words before God and before men, I see that nothing else is permitted me, nor is anything else appropriate for me, than to rely on myself, since I have not been able to rely on you.'[24]

28. In the aforesaid city of the Florentines he stayed at the home of the late Decens, who had the title of 'clarissimus' and – what is more – was a Christian.[25] He had a son named Pansophius who, while a small child, was troubled by an unclean spirit, but he was cured by the bishop's frequent prayers and by the imposition of his hands. A few days later, however, the little boy was seized by a sudden illness and breathed his last. His mother, a deeply religious woman, full of faith and the fear of God, removed him from the upper part of the house, brought him downstairs and, in the bishop's absence, placed him in his bed. When the bishop returned and found him in his bed (for he had been out of the house at the time), he took pity on the mother and, seeing her faith, placed himself on top of the child's body, like Elisha (cf. 2 Kgs. 4:34–35), and by his prayers merited to return alive to his mother him whom he had found dead. He also wrote a letter to the little boy, so that he might learn by reading what he had not been able to know as a small child. He did not, it is true, mention this deed in his writings, but it is not for us to judge what he had in mind when he failed to mention it.

29. In the same city he also erected a basilica in which he placed the remains of the martyrs Vitalis and Agricola,[26] whose bodies he had exhumed in the city of Bologna. For the bodies of the martyrs had been put among the bodies of the Jews, and none of this would have been known to the Christian people had not the holy martyrs revealed themselves to the bishop of that very church. When they had been placed beneath the altar which was set up in that basilica, great was the rejoicing and exultation of all the holy people there, but the merits of the martyrs who had confessed their faith were a source of distress to the demons.

30. Around the same time Count Arbogast was waging war against his own people, the Franks, and in the battle overcame no small number with his own hand; with those who were left, however, he made peace. During a banquet he was asked by the kings of his people whether he knew Ambrose, and he replied that he knew the man and was his friend, and that he was in the habit of dining frequently with him. With this he was told: 'You are victorious, count, because you are that man's friend. He says to the sun: "Stand still," and it stands still' (cf. Josh 10:12–13). I have put this in writing so that my readers may see how famous the holy man was even among the barbarians. We also know of this from a certain very religious young man in the service of Arbogast who was present then; for, at the time we are speaking of, he was a cupbearer.

31. When the bishop left the region of Tuscany and returned to Milan, Eugenius had already gone out from there against Theodosius. There [Ambrose] awaited the arrival of the Christian emperor, confident that God in his power would not hand over the one who believed in him to unrighteous persons 'nor leave the rod of sinners over the lot of the righteous, lest the righteous stretch out their hands to wickedness' (Ps. 125:3). For Arbogast, who was count at the time, and Flavian the prefect had promised, as they were leaving Milan, that when they returned victorious they would set up a stable in the basilica of the church of Milan and would draft clerics into the army. But wretched are the men who are wickedly confident of their demons and who open their mouth to blaspheme God (cf. Rev. 13:6): they have deprived themselves of victory. This was the cause of their discomfiture: the gifts of the emperor who had involved himself in sacrilege were spurned by the Church, nor was fellowship in prayer with the Church granted him. But the Lord, who always protects his Church, 'cast down his judgement from heaven' (Ps. 76:8) and gave total victory to the devout emperor Theodosius.

And so, when Eugenius and his minions had been destroyed and [Ambrose] had received the emperor's letters, he had no greater concern than to intervene on behalf of those whom [the emperor] had found culpable. He first sent a deacon to the emperor with a letter of entreaty.[27] After he had sent John, who was a tribune and secretary at the time but is now a prefect,[28] to look after those who had fled to the church, he himself went to Aquileia to plead on their behalf. Pardon was easy to obtain for them, for the Christian emperor prostrated himself at the feet of the bishop and declared that he had been saved thanks to [Ambrose's] merits and prayers.

32. He returned, then, from the city of Aquileia, preceding the emperor by one day. Nor did the Emperor Theodosius, of most clement memory, remain in the land of the living for very long after his sons had been received into the Church and given over to the bishop. [Ambrose] survived his death by barely three years.

About this time the body of the holy martyr Nazarius,[29] which had been in a garden outside the city, was exhumed and brought to the Basilica of the Apostles, which is in [the area of Milan called] Romana. But, at the tomb where the martyr's body lay (when he suffered nobody knows to this day), we have seen the martyr's blood as fresh as if it had just been shed. His head, too, which had been cut off by the ungodly, was whole and incorrupt, with its hair and its beard, so that, when it was exhumed, it appeared to us as if it had been washed and arranged in the grave. But what is so astonishing about that, inasmuch as the Lord had promised beforehand in the gospel that not a hair of their head would perish (cf. Luke 21:18)? We have also been filled with an odor whose delightfulness surpasses that of every spice.

33. When the body of the martyr had been exhumed and placed on a bier, we at once went over to pray, along with the holy bishop, near the holy martyr Celsus, who was located in the same garden. We know, however, that he had never prayed before in that spot, but this was the sign that a martyr's body had been revealed – if the holy bishop went to pray in a spot where he had never been before. We know from the guardians of the place, though, that they had been told by their parents never, from one generation to the next, to leave that place because great treasures were buried there. And indeed these were great treasures, which neither rust nor moth could destroy nor thieves dig up and steal (cf. Matt. 6:19), for, to those to whom 'to live was Christ and to die was gain' (Phil. 1:21), their guardian is Christ and their place is the heavenly court.

When the body of the martyr, then, had been brought to the Basilica of the Apostles where the relics of the holy apostles had previously been placed with the greatest devotion on the part of all, and as the bishop was preaching, one of the crowd, who was possessed by an unclean spirit, began to cry out that he was being tormented by Ambrose. But [Ambrose] turned to him and said: 'Be still, devil, because it is not Ambrose who is tormenting you but the faith of the saints and your envy, for you see human beings mounting to the place from which you were cast down; you cannot puff up Ambrose.' When this had been said, the one who was crying out became still; he threw himself on the ground and no longer made disturbing noises.

34. Around the same time, when the Emperor Honorius was consul and was putting on a show of wild animals from Libya in the city of Milan and the people were gathering there, leave was given to some soldiers, who had been sent by Stilicho, who was then a count, with the encouragement of the prefect Eusebius, to seize a certain Cresconius from the church.[30] As he sought refuge at the altar of the Lord, the holy bishop, along with the clerics who were there at the time, surrounded him to protect him. But the many soldiers, whose commanders came from the perfidy of the Arians, prevailed over the few. They carried off Cresconius and returned to the amphitheater in an exultant mood, leaving the Church in a state of no little lamentation, for the bishop lay prostrate before the Lord's altar and wept over the deed for a long time. But when the soldiers returned and reported to those who had sent them, some leopards that had been released bounded up to the place where those who had triumphed over the Church were sitting, and they left them savagely mangled. When Count Stilicho saw this he was moved to penance, such that for many days he made reparation to the bishop and even released unharmed the man who had been seized. But because [Cresconius] was guilty of very grave crimes and could not otherwise atone for them, [Stilicho] sent him into exile, although he was pardoned not long after.

35. Around the same time, [Ambrose] happened to be going to the palace and we were accompanying him by reason of our office. Theodore, who was his secretary then and later ruled the church of Modena with great grace,[31] laughed when someone accidentally tripped and fell down on the ground. Ambrose turned to him and said: 'You who are standing, see that you do not fall' (cf. 1 Cor.

10:12). When he said this, the one who had laughed at another's fall immediately mourned his own.

36. Around the same time a certain Frigitil, queen of the Marcomanni, having heard about [Ambrose's] reputation from a certain Christian man who had probably come from the region of Italy, believed in Christ, whose servant she recognized that he was. She sent gifts to the church at Milan and asked through her envoys if he would explain in writing how she should believe. He sent her a marvelous letter in the form of a catechism, in which he also advised her to persuade her husband to keep peace with the Romans. When she received the letter, the wife persuaded her husband to surrender himself and his people to the Romans. When she came to Milan she was deeply sorry that she did not meet the holy bishop, whom she had hastened to see, for he had already departed this life.

37. But in the days of Gratian (to retrace my steps), when [Ambrose] had gone to the headquarters of Macedonius, who was master of offices at the time,[32] in order to intercede on someone's behalf, and had found the doors closed on the order of the aforesaid man and could not get in, he said: 'You too will come to the church and will not find a way to enter, because the doors will be closed.' That is what happened, for, when Gratian died, Macedonius sought refuge in the church, but he was unable to get in, although the doors were open.

38. The venerable bishop was a man of great abstinence and of many vigils and labors. Every day he would afflict his body with fasting. It was his custom never to take breakfast except on Saturday and Sunday, or when it was the birthday[33] of some very important martyrs. He was also most assiduous in prayer day and night. He did not shun the task of writing books with his own hand, except when his body was troubled by some infirmity. There was also in him a 'solicitude for all the churches' (2 Cor. 11:28), and a great diligence and firmness in his interventions. He was very vigorous, too, in attending to divine matters, to the extent that what five bishops could hardly accomplish after his death he had been accustomed to accomplish by himself in the case of those about to be baptized. He was also exceedingly solicitous for the poor and for captives, for at the time when he was ordained bishop he gave all the gold and silver that lay at his disposal to the Church and to the poor. The estates, too, that he had he bequeathed to the Church, after having secured the income from them for his sister. He left nothing behind for him to call his own, so that, as his stripped and unencumbered soldier, he might follow the Lord Christ, 'who, although he was rich, became poor for our sake, so that we might be enriched by his poverty' (2 Cor. 8:9).

39. He was joyful with those who rejoiced and wept with those who wept (cf. Rom. 12:15). Indeed, whenever someone confessed his faults to him in order to obtain pardon, he so wept as to compel the other person to weep as well, for he seemed to himself to be cast down along with anyone else who was cast down. But the crimes that he confessed to him, [Ambrose] spoke of to no one but to God alone, to whom he made intercession, thus leaving behind a good example to later bishops – that it was better for them to be intercessors before God than to be accusers before men. For, according to the Apostle too, love ought to be confirmed in a person of this sort (cf. 2 Cor. 2:8) because he is his own accuser, and he does not await his accuser but anticipates him. Thus by confessing he himself mitigates his misdeed, so that his adversary may have nothing to reproach him with. Therefore Scripture says: 'The righteous man is his own accuser in the beginning of his speech' (Prov. 18:17). For he snatches the words from his adversary and by the confession of his sins, as it were, breaks the teeth that were ready to prey upon him with a hostile accusation. In this way he gives honor to God, 'to whom all things lie uncovered' (cf. Heb. 4:13) and who desires the life of the sinner rather than his death (cf. Ezek.18:23). But confession alone is not enough for the penitent unless correction of the deed follows. So that the penitent may not do things to repent of, let him also humiliate his soul as did the holy David who, after he heard from the prophet: 'Your sin has been forgiven' (2 Kgs. 12–13), so humbled himself in correcting his sin that he ate ashes like bread and mingled tears in his drink (cf. Ps. 102:9).

40. [Ambrose] also used to weep very bitterly whenever he happened to be told of the death of a holy bishop – to the extent that we would try to cheer him up, unaware of the loving feelings of the man and not understanding why he wept so much. When we did this he would respond to the effect that he was not weeping because the one whose death had been announced had departed but because he had preceded him, and because it would be difficult to find a man who might be considered worthy of the high priesthood. He himself foretold beforehand, with respect to his own death, that he would be with us up until Easter. This in fact he merited by beseeching the Lord that he might be freed earlier from this place.

41. He used to groan deeply when he saw avarice, the root of all evils (cf. 1 Tim. 6:10), sprouting up. This can be diminished neither by abundance nor by want and is constantly increasing in human beings, especially in the powerful, such that it was a very burdensome task for him to confront them, because everything could be had for a price. It was this thing that introduced every evil into Italy, and with it came a general deterioration. And what is left to say when this wreaks such havoc in persons of this sort that they allege the needs of their children and their kinsfolk, 'making excuses in sin' (Ps. 141:4), seeing that it seizes upon many, even celibate bishops and levites[34] whose portion is the Lord (cf. Deut. 18:2), so that they too pant after it? And woe to me in my misery, for not even at the end of the world[35] are we moved to wish to be freed of a yoke of slavery so heavy that it drags us down to the depths of hell (cf. Isa. 7:11), or to make for ourselves 'friends of wicked mammon, who will receive us into the eternal dwellings' (Luke 16:9). But blessed is the one who, once having been converted and having broken his fetters and cast off the yoke of this kind of domination, 'shall seize and shall dash his little ones against a rock' (Ps. 137:9) – that is, shall dash all his yearnings against Christ, who according to the Apostle is a rock (cf. 1 Cor. 10:4), which destroys all who are dashed against it while it itself remains imperishable. Nor does it make him guilty, but innocent, who has dashed against it the bad offspring of a wicked womb, so that thus he can say with confidence: 'My portion is the Lord' (Ps. 119:57), for, to him who has nothing in the world, his portion is truly Christ, and he who has disdained few things will receive many things, and in addition he will possess eternal life (cf. Matt. 19:29).

42. A few days before he was confined to his bed, as he was dictating his commentary on the forty-third psalm and as I was recording it and looking about, a small flame in the shape of a shield suddenly came down over his head and slowly entered his mouth like a tenant entering his home. After this his face became like snow, but then his features regained their appearance. When this happened I was transfixed and could not write down the things that he was saying until after the vision had passed away, for at the time he was giving a testimony concerning sacred Scripture, which I used to retain very well. That very day he put an end to the writing and the dictation, since he was unable to finish the psalm. But I at once reported what I had seen to the deacon Castus, a good man under whose care I was living, and he, filled with the grace of God, showed me through a reading of the Acts of the Apostles (cf. Acts. 2:3) that I had seen the coming of the Holy Spirit in him.[36]

43. A few days before, a servant of Stilicho (who was then count), who had been possessed by a demon but was now healed, was staying in the Ambrosian Basilica, after having been placed there by his master.[37] For it was being reported, as the general consensus concerning him, that he had counterfeited letters of the tribuneship, so that persons who were on their way to work were being detained. But when Count Stilicho came to know of his servant's reputation he did not want to punish the servant. With the bishop as his intermediary he even dismissed the persons who had been victimized, but about the servant himself he complained to the bishop. When the holy man left the Ambrosian Basilica he had him summoned and brought to him. When [Ambrose] questioned him and discovered that he was responsible for such a great crime he said that he ought to be handed over to Satan for the destruction of his flesh (cf. 1 Cor. 5:5) lest anyone in the future dare to commit a similar act. At the very moment when these words were still on the bishop's lips an unclean spirit seized him and began to tear him into pieces. When we saw this, we were filled with no little fear and astonishment. In those days we saw many others purged of unclean spirits when he imposed his hands and commanded [them to depart].

44. Around the same time there was a certain Nicentius,[38] a former tribune and secretary, who suffered such pain in his feet that he was rarely seen in public. As he was going to the altar to receive the sacraments, he cried out when the bishop accidentally kicked him, and he heard: 'Go, and henceforth you are healed.' When the holy bishop departed this life he bore tearful witness that his feet no longer pained him.

45. But after these days, having ordained a bishop for the church of Pavia, [Ambrose] fell sick. When this had confined him to his bed for many days, Count Stilicho is reported to have said that, when it came time for so great a man to leave his body, Italy would be menaced with ruin. Hence he convoked the distinguished men of that city, who he knew were friends of the holy bishop, and partly threatened and partly flattered them into approaching the holy bishop in order to persuade him to beseech the Lord to prolong his life. When he heard this from them he responded: 'I have not lived among you in such a way as to be ashamed to live, nor do I fear to die, for we have a good Lord.'

46. Around the same time, while [Ambrose] was lying at the very end of the portico, Castus, Polemius, Venerius and Felix,[39] who were then deacons, were there and, in a voice so low that they could barely hear one another, were discussing among themselves who should be ordained bishop after [Ambrose's] death. Although he lay at a distance from them, when they brought up the name of the holy Simplicianus, he cried out approvingly three times, as if he were involved in the discussion: 'He is an old man, but a good one.' For Simplicianus was of a ripe age. When they heard his voice they fled in terror. Yet when he had died, no one else succeeded him in the episcopacy but him whom he had thrice called a good man. Venerius, whom we mentioned previously, was Simplicianus' successor, whereas Felix rules the church of Bologna to this day. And Castus and Polemius, brought up by Ambrose, the good fruits of a good tree (cf. Matt. 7:17), are exercising the office of deacon in the church of Milan.

47. In the same place where he was lying, as we learned from the holy Bassianus, bishop of the church of Lodi[40] (who had heard it from [Ambrose himself]), as he was praying with the aforementioned bishop, he saw the Lord Jesus come to him and smile upon him. Not many days later he was taken from us. But at the very time that he left us for the Lord, from about the eleventh hour of the day[41] until the hour when he breathed his last, he prayed with his hands stretched out in the form of a cross. We saw his lips moving but did not hear his voice. As he was getting ready to go to bed upstairs in the house, Honoratus, the bishop of the church of Vercelli,[42] heard a voice calling him three times and saying to him: 'Arise, hasten, because just now he is about to depart.' Going downstairs, he offered the Lord's body to the holy man, and when he took it and swallowed it he breathed out his spirit, bringing with him good provisions for the journey. Thus his soul, refreshed by the power of that food, rejoices now in the company of the angels, whose life he lived on earth, and in the fellowship of Elijah, because, just as Elijah, thanks to his fear of God, never hesitated to speak to kings or to any powerful people, neither did he.

48. At the hour of dawn, when he died, his body was brought from there to the major church.[43] This was the same night when we were keeping vigil there for Easter. When many of the baptized children were returning from the font they saw him: some said that he was sitting in his chair in the tribunal, while others pointed him out, walking, to their parents, but these latter were unable to see him when they looked because their eyes were not purified; many related that they saw a star above his body. As Sunday dawned, his body was removed from the church after the divine sacraments had been celebrated, in order to be taken to the Ambrosian Basilica, where it was laid out. There a crowd of demons made such a clamor that they were being tormented by him that their wailing could not be borne. This grace of the bishop is evident to this very day not only in that place but even in a number of the provinces. Crowds of men and women also laid down their handkerchiefs and aprons so that they might come into some contact with the holy man's body. There was a vast crowd at the obsequies from every rank, of each sex and of almost every age, not only of Christians but also of Jews and pagans, yet because of their greater grace the ranks of those who had been baptized were in front.

49. On the very day that he died he appeared to certain holy men, and he prayed with them and imposed hands on them. This is what the text of the letter indicates which was received by his successor, the venerable man Simplicianus, from the regions of the Orient; it was sent to [Ambrose himself] as if he were still alive in our midst, and to this day it is kept at the monastery in Milan. For the letter mentions the day that it was sent, and when we read it we discovered that it was the day on which he died.[44]

50. In Tuscany, too, in the city of Florence, where now the holy man Zenobius is,[45] we learned from the holy man himself, Bishop Zenobius, that [Ambrose] was frequently seen praying at the altar which is in the Ambrosian Basilica, which had been built by him, because he had promised his petitioners that he would often visit them. In the same house, too, where he stayed when he repudiated Eugenius, at the time when Radagaisus was besieging the afore-mentioned city and the men of that city had given up all hope for themselves, he appeared to a certain person in a vision and promised that they would be saved on the following day. When this was made public, the spirits of the townspeople were strengthened, and on the following day Stilicho, who was then count, arrived with his army and exacted victory from the foe.[46] This we know from the report of Pansophia, a devout woman and the mother of the boy Pansophius.[47]

51. He also appeared in a vision of the night, staff in hand, to Mascezel, who despaired of his own safety and that of his army, which he was leading against Gildo. When Mascezel prostrated himself at the feet of the holy man, the old man struck the ground three times with the staff that he used for walking (for that was how he had appeared to him) and said: 'Here, here, here,' indicating a particular spot. And he made the man whom he had thought worthy of his visitation understand that, in the very spot where he had seen the Lord's holy bishop, he would achieve victory on the third day, and thus reassured he began and ended the war.[48] We learned of this from Mascezel himself when we were in Milan. In this province, too, where we are now living and writing these things,[49] he reported this to many bishops. Since they reported it as well, we felt all the more confident about putting these things, which are known to us, into this book.

52. When we were receiving the remains of the martyrs Sisinnius, Martyrius and Alexander (who attained the crown of martyrdom in our time – namely, after the death of the holy Ambrose – in the region of Anaunia, after having suffered under pagan men)[50] with deepest devotion at Milan, a certain blind man approached who touched the coffin in which the remains of the holy men were being carried, and on that same day he obtained his sight. We know from a report of his that, in a vision of the night, he saw a ship nearing the shore, in which there were a great number of men clothed in white. As they got out onto the land, he asked one of the crowd who the men were, and he heard that they were Ambrose and his companions. Having heard that name, he begged to obtain his sight, and he heard from him: 'Go to Milan and meet my brothers who are on their way there' – indicating the day – 'and you shall obtain your sight.' For, as he himself asserted, he was a man from the Dalmatian coast, and he asserted that he had never been to the city until, still blind, he made the journey safely and came upon the remains of the holy men, and that when he touched their coffin he began to see.

53. Having gone through these facts, I do not consider it a serious matter if we disregard somewhat the constraints that we promised to observe, so that we may show that the Lord's word, which he spoke by the mouth of his holy prophets (cf. Luke 1:70), has been accomplished: 'I will persecute the man who encamps against his brother and secretly slanders him' (Ps. 101:5). And elsewhere: 'Do not love to slander, lest you be rooted out' (Prov. 20:13). Thus, whoever may have been caught up in this sort of behavior will himself find amendment in the person of others when he reads how vengeance was taken against those who dared to slander the holy man.

54. Accordingly, a certain Donatus, an African by birth but a priest of the church of Milan,[51] slandered the reputation of the bishop when he was at a banquet attended by a number of devout military men. As they were repudiating and rejecting his wicked tongue, he was suddenly smitten with a grave wound, and from the spot where he lay he was borne off by the hands of strangers and put in a bed, from which he was taken to his grave. Likewise, in the city of Carthage, when I had been invited to the home of the deacon Fortunatus, the brother of the venerable man Bishop Aurelius, along with Bishop Vincent of Colossitanum, Bishop Muranus of Bolita[52] and other bishops and deacons, I told the story of the death of the aforementioned priest to Bishop Muranus when he was slandering the holy man. These words about someone else turned out to be a prophecy of his own speedy death. For he was suddenly smitten with a terrible wound, and from the spot where he lay he was borne off by the hands of strangers to a bed; from there he was taken to the house where he was staying, and there he met his end. That was the fate of the men who slandered [Ambrose], and those who were present at the time and saw it were amazed at it.

55. Hence I exhort and beg each person who reads this book to imitate the life of the holy man, to praise the grace of God and to shun the tongues of slanderers if he wishes to have fellowship with Ambrose in the resurrection of life rather than, with those slanderers, to undergo a punishment that no one who is wise does not avoid.

56. I also beseech your blessedness, Father,[53] to deign to pray for me, the most lowly and sinful Paulinus, along with all the holy ones who, with you, call upon the name of our Lord Jesus Christ in truth, that, inasmuch as I am unworthy to join so great a man in the acquisition of grace, I might acquire pardon for my sins and, as my reward, escape punishment.

NOTES

INTRODUCTION

1 Neil B. McLynn (1994: 1–13) suggests that Ambrose was in fact not neutral but pro-orthodox (as his personal background would imply) and made his presence felt during the uproar in order to lend support to the orthodox, without being prepared for the result.

2 For December 1, 373 cf., e.g., F. Homes Dudden (1935), vol. 1, p. 68, n. 5. For December 7, 373 cf., e.g., Hans von Campenhausen (1929: 26, 90–2). For December 7, 374 cf., e.g., Angelo Paredi (1964: 124, 393, n. 2).

3 For different dates for Ambrose's birth cf. Emilien Lamirande (1983: 45, n. 2).

4 The real function of Ambrose's father has been questioned since there is no testimony to his prefecture independent of Paulinus. Cf. ibid.

5 Cf., e.g., Amato Amati (1897: 313); Dudden, op. cit., vol. 1, p. 2., n. 3.

6 Cf. Pierre Courcelle (1973: 9–16).

7 Cf. Balthasar Fischer (1970: 527–31). A relatively unknown work, recently translated from Coptic, indicates, however, that it was not totally unusual to make a candidate pass very quickly – in this instance in a single day! – through all the stages from layman to bishop: cf. Paphnutius (1993: 112).

8 On all of this cf. Richard Krautheimer (1983: 68–92). Regarding the construction of the Church of the Holy Apostles in Constantinople, not every scholar is agreed that it was built by Constantine himself and that he was buried in it. Concerning the similarity between that church and the Basilica of the Apostles in Milan, it would have been a more obvious and effective anti-Arian symbol had Ambrose modeled one of his churches on Saint Irene, in which the anti-Arian Council of Constantinople had actually been held.

9 Cf. Daniel H. Williams (1995: 119–21). While rightly observing that Letter 197.2 is inadequate evidence upon which to base an argument that Ambrose was anti-Arian from the beginning of his episcopate, Williams fails to mention that the first half of the same letter offers the reasonable inference that he was not neutral *vis-à-vis* Arianism.

10 This is suggested by Williams, ibid., pp. 139–40.

11 Cf. McLynn, op. cit., pp. 173–76.

12 Von Campenhausen, op cit., p. 216, finds nothing suspicious in Ambrose's discovery of the relics or in the events surrounding it. On the other hand, McLynn, pp. 215–17, argues for something very like a staged discovery in connection with a strong element of spontaneity.

13 Augustine treats him as such some two decades later in *The City of God* 5.26.

14 Thomas Aquinas is reported to have undergone something similar shortly before his death on 7 March 1274. The previous December 6th, while celebrating Mass, he had an undefined experience that immediately resulted in his being unable to write any more. In addition, between that day and his death two visitors to his cell witnessed a star come in through the window and remain for a while over his head. Cf. James A. Weisheipl (1974: 320–33).

15 Aloys Grillmeier (1975: 405). R.P.C. Hanson (1988: 669) offers the harsh assessment of the treatise *On the Faith*:

> '[W]e gain the unavoidable impression that Ambrose has not, like Athanasius and Hilary and Marius Victorinus, struggled with the problem of Arianism and thought it through for himself, but rather has learnt the conventional arguments because these are the stuff which the official, successful church hands out. Almost all his ratiocination proceeds upon the method ... of assuming as true what he is supposed to be proving, and too often his arguments are, as rational discussion, beneath contempt.'

WORKS

1 The order generally follows that conveniently given in William G. Rusch (1977: 50–65)

TRANSLATIONS

1 An ancient treatise or homily often begins with an expression of self-deprecation on the part of the writer or preacher. The self-deprecation with which *On Virgins* begins, however, is unusually long and elaborate and seems to go beyond what was expected in this formal exercise in humility. Perhaps Ambrose is making an oblique reference to the lack of success that he experienced in preaching about virginity in Milan, which he mentions in 1.11.57–58.

2 The early Christians often referred to death days as birthdays (i.e., into eternal life). From relatively ancient times Agnes' 'birthday' was celebrated on 21 January.

3 Ambrose is probably alluding to the fact that the name Agnes is derived from the Greek word *hagnē*, meaning 'chasté

4 Ambrose calls attention here to the resemblance between the name Agnes and the Latin word *agnus*, meaning 'lamb.' The lamb was a sacrificial animal, and Agnes was to be sacrificed in martyrdom.

5 Where Ambrose read this we do not know.

6 The Vestal Virgins and the priestesses of the Palladium are one and the

same. The Palladium was a statue of the goddess Pallas, better known as Minerva, which was preserved in the temple of the goddess Vesta, who was the daughter of Saturn. The Vestal Virgins, who maintained the cult of Vesta, were obliged to abstain from sexual relations for thirty years, after which they could marry.

7 The Phrygian rites are so called because they were dedicated to the goddess Cybele, whose cult seems to have originated in Phrygia (present-day southwest Turkey in Asia). Her worship included orgiastic behavior.

8 The god Liber is more familiarly known as Bacchus. He was the patron of wine, and his rites were characterized by drunkenness and associated activity.

9 The sixth-century BC Greek courtesan Leena is being referred to here. She was frequently mentioned in antiquity, even by Christian authors such as Tertullian and Athanasius. Ambrose, however, has mixed two stories from separate sources.

10 This section is remarkable for its characterization of Christ as a virgin with feminine attributes, namely, with a womb and breasts. But such a way of representing Christ was not unknown in antiquity: cf. Origen, *Commentary on the Song of Songs* 1 (on S. of S. 1:2). On the feminine Christ in early Christian art in particular cf. Mathews (1993: 121–41).

11 The water spoken of here may be intended to call to mind the water of baptism, sealed by the anointing of the Spirit (i.e., confirmation), or in its purity it may be an image of virginity itself, sealed and hence inaccessible to the wild beasts of the passions. Cf. St Ambrose (1989: 145, nn. 150–51).

12 This and the following few sentences were probably composed with the Arians in mind, since they denied the divinity of Christ. Cf. also 1.8.48.

13 The sacraments of Christ's body are clearly the different aspects of his incarnation. In Christian antiquity the term 'sacrament' did not have the restricted application that it currently does. Rather, virtually anything that could be seen as a vehicle of grace might be considered a sacrament; Christ's incarnation certainly qualified in this regard.

14 The Mauretanian virgins were evidently members of families that had been taken in captivity and used as slaves. Such women might well have embraced consecrated virginity if it meant some mitigation of their condition. Mauretania, on the northwest coast of Africa, would have been a source of slaves for the Empire. Cf. McLynn (1994: 67–68).

15 This phrase seems to leave little doubt that the eucharist was celebrated every day in Milan, although daily celebration was not a universal practice, as we read in Augustine, *Letter* 54.2.2. Cf. also Ambrose's own remarks in his *Letter* 20.15. Ambrose appears to have been the first person to use the term 'consecrate' (*consecrare*) in reference to the eucharist. Cf. St Ambrose (1989: 163, n. 211).

16 Gori (St. Ambrose 1989: 167 n. 4) gives reasons for thinking that the martyr in question may be St Cyprian, the only martyr to have written in Latin on virginity before Ambrose's time. But Ambrose could as well be referring to St Agnes, whom he offers as a model toward the beginning of this treatise.

17 The extended description of Mary that follows owes more to St Athanasius' work, *An Epistle to the Virgins* (in *Corpus Scriptorum Christianorum Orientalium* 151.55–80), than it does to the gospels. It is certainly one of the longest passages on Mary to be found in Latin literature up to this point, and it helped to gain Ambrose the distinction of being among the earliest promoters of the cult of Mary. In 2.2.7 Ambrose refers to her as 'the mother of God,' and Gori (St Ambrose 1989: 169, n. 8) says that he is the first Latin writer to call her such.

18 Ambrose has made Mary a Christian before the fact in order to make her example more relevant to Christian virgins.

19 St Thecla is known exclusively from a late second-century work entitled *The Acts of Paul and Thecla*. Her fame derived in part from the fact that she was supposed to have been a convert of St Paul's, but there is considerable reason to doubt her existence.

20 The story of the Antiochene virgin which Ambrose narrates here has numerous parallels with that of Theodora of Alexandria who, according to the report of her martyrdom, was rescued from a bordello by a Christian soldier named Didymus. They were then both put to death. Theodora's martyrdom, which has some claim to authenticity, is dated to the persecution of Diocletian at the beginning of the fourth century.

21 The 'famous story' in question pertains to the myth of Iphigenia, the daughter of Agamemnon and Clytemnestra. As she was about to be slain at her father's behest in order to appease the goddess Diana for his having killed the goddess' favorite stag, Iphigenia herself disappeared and a goat miraculously took her place.

22 The 'pledge' (*vadimonium*) refers to the fact that, as the following paragraph explains, the soldier is a bondsman or guarantee for the virgin. The man in whose mouth these words have been placed has inexplicably grasped the situation.

23 The legend of Damon and Phintias (better known as Pythias), which Ambrose repeats here, is a famous one. As philosophers they would have been above any fear of death. The tyrant was Dionysius the Younger of Syracuse.

24 Although 'that king' is Dionysius the Younger in the case of Damon and Phintias, it is Dionysius the Elder in what follows. The two were often confused. This entire section, up to the end of §38, is a digression.

25 Liberius was Bishop of Rome from 352 to 366.

26 Ambrose's sister Marcellina's profession of virginity is referred to in Paulinus, *Life* 4. She made it when she and her mother and Ambrose were living in Rome, probably early in the reign of Liberius. Christmas at that time was being celebrated in Rome on 25 December, although that date was not observed universally. The tomb of Peter, in the great basilica dedicated to St Peter that had been erected by Constantine a little earlier in the century, would have been an appropriate place to solemnize a vow.

27 The allusion here is probably to the virginal fecundity mentioned in 1.6.31.

28 Note that the term 'sacrament' is applied here to virginity.

29 The youth who Ambrose says fell in love is Hippolytus, but Ambrose has misrepresented the original myth. Hippolytus was in fact accused of falling in love with his stepmother Phaedra and was punished by Neptune at the request of his father Theseus. The punishment brought with it death but, according to some accounts, the goddess Diana raised Hippolytus from the dead.

30 Pluto, the god of the underworld, is said to have asked Jupiter to kill Aesculapius for having raised so many persons from the dead, thus depriving Pluto of subjects. Jupiter then slew Aesculapius with the thunderbolts that are associated with him.

31 'The divine readings' (*divinarum . . . lectionum*) are the Scriptures.

32 The 'sacraments' are the eucharist.

33 This remarkable passage about behavior in church paints a different picture of church manners in fourth-century Christianity than one might have imagined.

34 The 'well-known example' is found in Valerius Maximus, *Factorum et dictorum memorabilium libri* 3.3.

35 The story is recounted in Terence's comedy *Heauton Timorumenos* 370–80. The young man's name is Clitipho.

36 Cf. ibid. 373. Ambrose, certainly intending to be humorous, applies to virgins words that were originally directed to the scapegrace Clitipho.

37 'The mystery' is the eucharist.

38 The meaning of this sentence seems to be: Marcellina accomplishes easily, and moreover offers as examples to others, deeds that most persons accomplish with difficulty.

39 The book in question is almost certainly some part of the Bible.

40 At the end of this long passage full of rustic imagery, a considerable portion of which is inspired by Virgil, comes a reference to 'the sacred blood', namely, the eucharistic blood of Christ.

41 The reference is to the psalmist David, who was both a prophet and a king.

42 This brief passage seems to mix two traditional 'hours' for prayer (on rising from sleep and at the evening hour of incense) with other times when prayer was also customary (on going out and in conjunction with meals). The practice of prayer at all such times may be traced back to at least the end of the second century: cf. Clement of Alexandria, *Stromata* 7.7.49; 7.12.80.

43 Pythagoras is being spoken of here. The story about his need to be soothed by music is found in Cicero, *Tusculanae disputationes* 4.2.3.

44 These four elements were believed, according to ancient philosophy, to constitute not only the human body but also the universe itself.

45 It is not clear at this point of which verse Ambrose is speaking. It is unlikely that he is referring to Rom. 7:24. The subsequent lines suggest that he means Ps. 41:3.

46 'The sacrament' is undoubtedly the eucharist.

47 The quotation is from Cicero, *Oratio pro L. Murena* 6.13.

48 What Ambrose might have intended by this sentence is obscure indeed.

49 The following long narrative concerning St Pelagia, her mother and sisters, is a defense of the practice of suicide in the case of threatened

virginity. As such it is a powerful demonstration of the esteem in which bodily integrity was held by many in Christian antiquity. Augustine, however, considered this esteem to be overweening. In *The City of God* 1. 16–28 he asserts that the violation of a virgin's body does not imply the violation of her spirit, which is the more important part of her; that suicide is never allowed, for one may not attempt to prevent another's sin by committing a sin of one's own; and that, although some saints may have killed themselves to avoid being ravished (here Augustine alludes to Ambrose's story without mentioning its author), their example ought not to be imitated.

St Pelagia is said to have died in the persecution of Diocletian at the beginning of the fourth century. Ambrose has joined, whether consciously or not, her story to that of a mother and her daughters – Domnina, Berenice and Prosdocia – who supposedly drowned themselves during the same persecution for a similar reason.

50 The scriptural passage that Ambrose has in mind is unknown.

51 The meaning of 'mother's breast' is unclear. Perhaps Pelagia is referring to the earth, upon which she had been planning to hurl herself.

52 The martyr in question is St Soteris, who is named in the next paragraph. Claimed by Ambrose as a relative, she apparently died in the Diocletian persecution. As a virgin she could not of course have been 'the begetter of your line' except in a spiritual sense.

53 Ambrose is quite dependent on Basil the Great for what follows, but the negative description of women's behavior and motivations is in any event a commonplace of antiquity (both pagan and Christian) and reflective of its prejudices.

54 The following sentences play on the similarity of Dis (the god of the underworld) and *dives* (the Latin word for 'rich person'). The two words are related anyway. The comparison is the more effective in that Dis' more familiar name is Pluto, and Pluto was often confused with Plutus, who was the god of wealth.

55 Ambrose carefully refrains from calling wealth evil; it is, rather, capable of being misused by evil persons.

56 'Mercy' (*misericordia* in Latin) was a common way of referring to almsgiving in early Christianity, and Ambrose intends it to be understood thus here.

57 A stater was a small silver coin of Jewish origin.

58 Hence 'He has cursed God and the king' actually reads: 'He has blessed (*benedixit*) God and the king.' Such a use of the verb 'to bless' (*benedicere*) was not unknown in the Latin translation of the Bible.

59 It is meretricious wickedness (*meretricia*) because it anticipated the prostitutes' (*meretrices*) bathing in the king's blood. The play on words is untranslatable.

60 'The Tishbite' is Elijah: cf. 1 Kgs. 17:1, 21:17.

61 This sentence is hard to understand in its context. One would have expected Ambrose to say that there were *more*, rather than fewer, who did not use what was theirs – if he is speaking of the poor, who are always more numerous than the rich, and of their access to the goods of the earth that are rightfully theirs.

62 This passage is reminiscent of and probably inspired by the famous image developed by Plato in *Phaedrus* 246 AB, 253 C – 257 A.

63 Ambrose here offers an alternative interpretation of Ps. 76, which he had begun to interpret in one way in 14.61 (where the bishop refers to it as Ps. 75, in accordance with the Greek enumeration of the Psalms with which he was familiar).

64 The levite, the priest and the high priest are respectively the deacon, the priest and the bishop, each of whom performed certain functions at a baptism.

65 The east, where the sun rose and light originated, was a symbol of Christ, and hence turning to the east symbolized turning to Christ. The west, on the other hand, where the sun went down and which was associated with darkness, symbolized the devil, and turning away from it represented turning away from the devil.

66 The theme of the high antiquity of the Church, and therefore of its sacraments, its 'mysteries,' is often repeated by the Fathers. The mid-second-century document known as the *Second Epistle of Clement* (14.1) goes so far as to claim that 'the spiritual Church' pre-existed the creation of the sun and the moon. It was a common notion among Christians, Jews and pagans that, the older a thing was, the greater validity it had. Cf. also 8.44–46, where Ambrose seeks to demonstrate that 'the sacraments of the Church are ... more ancient than those of the Synagogue.'

67 The word *spiritus*, contained in the Latin text of the passage that Ambrose used, can mean either breath or (Holy) Spirit. Here and in a number of subsequent passages Ambrose clearly understands it to be the latter, and so it is translated.

68 'This element of the world' refers to water, which was considered by the ancients to be one of the four constitutive elements (along with air, fire and earth) of the universe.

69 In warning his listeners and readers to focus not on the merits, or holiness, of the ministers but rather on their functions, Ambrose may have in mind the Donatists of North Africa. They were a schismatic group which insisted that the efficacy of the sacraments depended upon the holiness of those who administered them.

70 The admonition not to believe in 'a greater, a lesser and a least' is stated with the Arians in mind. The mention of 'the cross of Jesus' refers to the fact that Christ has not only a divine but also a human nature, the latter of which made him capable of enduring the cross.

71 'Had to wash his foot ... when the serpent tripped him up:' *Plantam lavare debebat .. quando eum subplantavit serpens.* The play on words is untranslatable.

72 There is an allusion here to the washing of the feet at baptism, which is explicitly mentioned in the treatise *On the Sacraments* 3.1.4. The term 'hereditary sins' appears to mean the inclination to sin that remains after baptism; if that is the correct explanation, then Ambrose is exaggerating the power of the footwashing to remit it.

73 The exact meaning of this sentence, which seems to contain a *non sequitur*, is unclear.

74 Ambrose is certainly aiming at the Arians when he emphasizes that the Son is of one substance with the Father, for this was precisely the point that they denied.

75 Although Scripture is primarily about spiritual truths, Ambrose, like other Church Fathers, is eager to find in it other kinds of truths as well. Augustine expresses this attitude when he says in his treatise *On Christian Doctrine* 2.42.63 that Scripture contains everything that a person needs to know, and that it is better presented there than in worldly literature.

76 Origen mentions a similar division in the prologue to his *Commentary on the Song of Songs*. Augustine attributes this threefold division of wisdom or philosophy to Plato in *The City of God* 8.4, but in fact it is only hinted at in his works.

77 Reason seems to be understood here as the Word of God, whom the Fathers declared to be the source of human reason.

78 In the prologue to his *Commentary on the Song of Songs* Origen makes a similar comparison, using these three books of Scripture.

79 Although Ambrose alludes to the Lukan beatitudes here, he goes on to cite not from the beatitudes themselves but from the section that follows them.

80 This passage was clearly written with the Arians in mind, who 'divided' the persons of the Trinity.

81 This complicated sentence proposes an image which was exceedingly popular in Christian antiquity – that of the Christian as athlete or, more specifically, as wrestler. What precisely 'these contests of sacred disputations' (*haec sacratarum disputationum certamina*) may mean is unclear.

82 The four living beings of Rev. 4:6–7 were already being used as images of both the evangelists and Christ by the end of the second century: cf. Irenaeus, *Against Heresies* 3.11.8.

83 'Julian's recent law' dated from 363 and forbade Christian teachers to teach classical literature unless they also acknowledged and taught what the Emperor Julian ('the Apostate,' who ruled from 361 to 363) insisted was the truth of the pagan religion that was contained in that literature. In other words, they were not permitted to approach such literature in a neutral and certainly not in an adversarial way. Since classical literature was the basis for almost all education, pagan and Christian, at the time, the effect of the law was to force Christian teachers to stop teaching if they wished to be faithful to their own religion.

84 Ambrose alludes to the fact that, even since the time of the Christianizing emperor Constantine in the first third of the fourth century, paganism continued not merely to survive but also to enjoy privileges and to hold an attraction for Christians.

85 'That pagan' is Symmachus.

86 Damasus was Bishop of Rome from 366 to 384.

87 The brother in question was the Emperor Gratian.

88 Ambrose refers to the information that he had been sent by the Christian senators.

89 Theodosius was in fact not related by blood to Valentinian, but Ambrose calls him Valentinian's 'parent' (*parens*) because Valentinian

was only 8 or 9 years old at the time and Theodosius was his senior by nearly thirty years and served as the protector of his interests. Valentinian's great youth is referred to in §15.

90 These were the famous Vestal Virgins, dedicated to the goddess Vesta.

91 The brother is the dead Gratian.

92 Reference is made here to Magnus Maximus, who usurped the imperial title in 383 and led an army against Gratian. He was a Christian and usually acted on behalf of orthodox Christianity.

93 Valentinian's father, Valentinian I, had been tolerant of all religious beliefs. Ambrose attempts to excuse his tolerance in this instance by suggesting that it was based upon ignorance, although it seems unlikely that the elder Valentinian would have been unaware of the existence of the Altar of Victory in the Senate house.

94 Although addressed to all three (legitimate) emperors, Symmachus in fact directs his appeal to Valentinian, the oldest in terms of actual rule and the only one living in the West.

95 In other words, victory should be honored at least as a concept if not as a divine being.

96 Constantius, co-emperor from 337 to 350 and sole emperor until 361, removed the Altar of Victory in 356, but Symmachus lays the blame for what he calls this 'impropriety' on the novelty of the situation that he faced and on the bad example of his father Constantine, whom he diplomatically refrains from naming. Constantine (died 337) had been the one, of course, who initiated the state's more tolerant attitude toward Christianity and first behaved negatively toward paganism. Although Symmachus refers to Constantius as Valentinian's 'ancestor' (*parens*), the two were not related by blood.

97 Symmachus is speaking here of Constantius' visit to Rome in 356.

98 §§8–10 of this appeal are the most famous part of the documentation pertaining to the Altar of Victory. Symmachus' plea for toleration is all the more attractive – or at least poignant – by reason of our awareness that he represented a lost cause.

99 Hannibal, a celebrated Carthaginian general, threatened Rome between 218 and 203 BC. The Senones were a Celtic people who may have accompanied the Gauls when they captured Rome in 390 BC.

100 Dodona was a town in ancient Greece that was famous for its temple and oracle of Zeus. The trees of Dodona were oaks, since there was an oak forest nearby, and Symmachus is saying that those whom famine touched ate acorns.

101 Valentinian's 'divine brother' is Gratian, who had previously removed the Altar of Victory. Symmachus alludes to the fact that a delegation of pagan senators desired to see Gratian on this account, but was kept from him by the emperor's aides, who did not want him to know that – as Symmachus claims, although it seems improbable – public opinion was on the side of the pagans.

102 Marcus Furius Camillus (died 365 BC) defended the Capitol at Rome against the Senones. The Tarpeian Rock is a cliff at the southwestern corner of the Capitoline Hill. Marcus Atilius Regulus was a heroic

figure in the First Punic War between Rome and Carthage (264–241 BC), who was defeated and seized by the Carthaginians in 255; according to tradition he was sent to Rome on a peace mission by the Carthaginians, returned to Carthage after having advised the Romans not to accept the terms of peace, and was tortured to death in Carthage. Scipio Africanus (236–184/183 BC) defeated Hannibal in 202, thus bringing the Second Punic War to a victorious conclusion for the Romans.

103   The captive emperor in question is Valerian, who was defeated and taken prisoner by the Persians in 260. The emperor under whom the world was held captive was his weak son Gallienus.

104   In the initiation rite of the cult devoted to the pagan god Mithra, the one being initiated was spattered by the blood of a bull that was slain for the occasion.

105   Reference is being made here to a law of Valentinian I, dating to 370, that forbade clerics and those who professed celibacy from inheriting the property of widows and orphans. The reason for the law was that clerics and celibates (i.e., monks) were particularly skilled at inveigling property out of such people. Jerome, in Letter 52.6, laments the fact that an enactment of this sort was necessary.

106   A number of laws creating financial hardships for the clergy are spoken of here. Ambrose declares in the final sentence that the clergy actually welcome them as providing them with an opportunity to promote the public welfare.

107   Decurions were citizens of the upper middle class who were legally obligated to take upon themselves the administration of the towns in which they lived. This often involved crushing expenses, from which the decurions wished to escape.

108   Chaonia was an area in Greece whose first inhabitants supposedly ate acorns; hence 'Chaonian fruit' is a poetic name for acorns

109   On Dodona cf. note 100. The oak trees of the temple associated with Zeus were said to be endowed with the gift of prophecy.

110   The Gauls correspond roughly to northern France, Belgium and Germany west of the Rhine. The two Pannonias included parts of present-day Hungary and the former Yugoslavia. Raetia Secunda is somewhat equivalent to Bavaria. Liguria and Venetia (here referred to in the plural) covered northern Italy.

111   Early Christian theologians frequently understood the moon, when it appears in the Old Testament, to be a symbol of the Church, just as the sun was taken to be a symbol of Christ.

112   'So that all might realize . . . for without an adversary . . .': *ut adverterent omnes . . . nulla enim sine adversario. . . .* This seems to be a rather weak pun on Ambrose's part.

113   Ambrose is probably alluding here to the so-called House of Romulus on the Palatine Hill.

114   Cybele was a goddess of fertility, whose priests annually washed her shrine (carried on chariots) in the Almo River, a small stream that flowed into the Tiber.

115   Ambrose touches on the fact that the Romans customarily adopted the

gods of those whom they conquered, who would presumably have been hostile to them. Cybele was originally a Phrygian goddess.

116 Venus was known under many different names, far more than Ambrose enumerates here, which is an indication of the popularity and widespread character of her cult.

117 The Emperor Constantius, who removed the Altar of Victory in 356, did so before he was baptized, or 'initiated into the sacred mysteries.' His baptism occurred in 361, the year of his death.

118 The 'most faithful prince' seems to be Gratian.

119 Gnaeus Pompeius, or Pompey the Great, lived from 106 to 48 BC. A distinguished Roman statesman and general, he was assassinated in Egypt. Canopus, a town on the Mediterranean coast in Egypt, is given here as the place of his assassination, but the most ancient sources mention neither it nor whether any of the persons who killed him was a eunuch.

120 Cyrus the Great lived from 590/580 to c. 529 BC. The story of his ignominious treatment at the hands of Tomyris, queen of the Massagetae, after his death in battle, is recounted in Herodotus 1.214.

121 Hamilcar (died 229 or 228 BC) was a Carthaginian general and the father of Hannibal.

122 Ambrose is referring here to Julian the Apostate. In his invasion of Persia in 363, as recounted in Ammianus Marcellinus, he improvidently burned his ships on the Tigris River because he did not have sufficient troops to guard them.

123 The meaning of this sentence is obscure.

PAULINUS OF MILAN,
THE LIFE OF SAINT AMBROSE

1 Athanasius was Bishop of Alexandria from 328 to 373. He wrote *The Life of Saint Anthony c.* 356. This extremely influential work purported to record the life of Anthony in all its miraculous detail. Anthony himself probably died *c.* 356 at a great old age. He is considered by many to be the Father of Monasticism. Jerome lived from 331(?) to 420 and, while most famous for his scriptural and polemical writings, also produced several brief monastic *Lives*, of which that of the hermit Paul (died *c.* 340) is the best known. Sulpicius Severus was a Gallic historian who lived from *c.* 363 to *c.* 420 and who propagated the cult of Martin of Tours (335[?]–397) in a number of works, especially his *Life*.

2 The prefecture of the Gauls included present-day France, Spain, Portugal, much of Great Britain, part of Germany and part of northern Africa. Since Trier was the seat of the prefect, it is assumed that Ambrose was born there.

3 The praetorium was the residence of the prefect.

4 Of this Candida nothing else is known.

5 Dionysius preceded Auxentius as Bishop of Milan from 346 until 355, when he was sent into exile by the Arian Emperor Constantius.

6 There exists an earlier account of the famous scene of Ambrose's election as bishop than that written by Paulinus. It is to be found in

Rufinus, *Ecclesiastical History* 2.11, produced shortly after 395, and it has a greater sense of urgency:

> Meantime, when Auxentius, the bishop of the heretics, had died at Milan, the members of both factions were being carried away by their different attachments. Serious dissension and dangerous unrest were threatening their own city with speedy destruction if either faction did not obtain what it wanted and had proposed. Ambrose, who was then the consularis of the province in question, was exercising the magistracy. When he saw the city on the verge of ruin, for the sake of the place and of his office he immediately entered the church in order to calm the people's unrest. And when he had pleaded there at length for peace and calm in accordance with the laws and with public order, there was a sudden outcry from the people as they were struggling and fighting among themselves, and a single voice rose up. Demanding Ambrose as their bishop, they cried out that he be baptized at once (for he was a catechumen) and given to them as their bishop. Unless Ambrose were given to them as their bishop there was no other chance for a unified people and a unified faith. Despite his opposition and great resistance, the people's desire was reported to the emperor, who ordered it to be implemented as quickly as possible. For he said that it was God's will that a sudden reversal should bring the discordant faith of the people and their dissenting hearts to a single consensus and a single judgement. And soon thereafter he acquired the grace of God, was initiated into the sacred rites and became a bishop.

7 Of this Leontius nothing more is known, although the title 'clarissimus' indicates that he belonged to the senatorial order.

8 The vicar, who is unnamed, was the head of the diocese of Italy, which included the provinces of Liguria and Aemilia; as such he was Ambrose's immediate superior.

9 'The sacrifice' is the eucharist.

10 Anemius was strongly anti-Arian and became one of Ambrose's staunchest supporters.

11 Augustine, *Confessions* 9.7.15, also credits Ambrose with instituting the custom of antiphonal singing in Milan, whence it spread throughout the West. Augustine adds, however, that the practice was Eastern in origin.

12 Nabor and Felix are believed to have died in the Diocletian persecution in 304.

13 Ambrose, in other words, was being portrayed as placing himself on the same level as the martyrs, who were able to disquiet evil spirits.

14 The work in question has come down to us as *On the Sacrament of the Lord's Incarnation*.

15 Letter 24.

16 The diocese (as it was called) of the Orient ('the East') was a vast administrative unit covering Syria, Palestine, parts of Armenia and

other territory. The Count of the Orient, who is mentioned a few lines later without being named, governed the diocese.

17 The town in question was Callinicum, situated on the Euphrates River.

18 The Valentinians were followers of the teaching of Valentinus, a gnostic who flourished in the mid-second century. They did not, as Paulinus says later parenthetically, worship thirty gods, but rather a divine entity (*pleroma*) consisting of thirty aspects or aeons. By the late fourth century, when these events occurred, the Valentinians were long past their heyday. Ambrose, Letter 40.16, speaks of a temple (*fanum*) having been destroyed, not a grove (*lucus*).

19 Letter 40.

20 Letter 41.

21 In other words, until about 9.00 a.m.

22 In other words, from about 7.00 a.m. until about 9.00 p.m.

23 Letter 17, translated on pp. 174–79.

24 Paulinus quotes here from Letter 57.7, 11.

25 Neither Decens nor his son Pansophius are otherwise known. The boy's mother Pansophia is mentioned in §50.

26 Vitalis, a slave, and Agricola, his master, suffered in the persecution of Diocletian at the beginning of the fourth century.

27 Letter 61.

28 This John was the Emperor Theodosius' tribune and secretary (*notarius*). He was praetorian prefect from 412 to 413, and again in 422.

29 Of Nazarius (and Celsus, who is mentioned in §33) we know little more than what is said here.

30 Stilicho, half-Roman and half-Vandal, was a great military commander who, with the death of Theodosius in 395, ruled the Western Empire on behalf of the late emperor's son Honorius. He was executed in 408. Eusebius was praetorian prefect of Italy from 395 to 396. Of Cresconius nothing more is known.

31 Of this Theodore nothing else is known.

32 Rather little is known with certitude of this Macedonius; a few lines later Paulinus alludes to a fall from grace after the death of Gratian. The master of offices was responsible for the civil service of the Empire, and particularly for the palace bureaucracy, among other things. His power was far-reaching.

33 Paulinus uses the word 'birthday' as it had been used in this context since at least the middle of the second century – namely, as a term for a Christian's death-day.

34 'Levite' was a much-used term for a deacon in Christian antiquity.

35 This reference to the end of the world is something of a commonplace in patristic literature, although it naturally became less common with the passage of time and the Church's continuing immersion in the affairs of the world. It suggests the strong eschatological perspective of the early Christians.

36 The deacon Castus is mentioned again in §46 as still alive when Paulinus was writing. He evidently had some responsibility for Paulinus, who was himself not a deacon at the time, but the exact nature of this responsibility can only be guessed at. It is interesting that Paulinus would not

have made the connection between the vision of a flame over Ambrose's head and the Pentecost event, and would need to have been shown it by Castus. One wonders how biblically literate Paulinus may have been.

37 The story that follows indicates that Stilicho's servant was using the basilica as a sanctuary or place of refuge, a practice that was not unusual at this period.

38 Nicentius is also mentioned by Ambrose in Letter 5.8 in relation to an accusation leveled against a virgin, which Nicentius proved false.

39 Venerius was the most distinguished of this group, whose later activities Paulinus records at the end of the paragraph. He was held in high esteem and is venerated as a saint.

40 Bassianus died in 413 and is the patron saint of Lodi.

41 In other words, about 5.00 pm.

42 Honoratus' exact dates are unknown. He is venerated as a saint.

43 The major church was the cathedral, also known as the New Basilica.

44 The coincidence of a letter written on the day of the addressee's death would only have been striking in an age when far fewer letters were written and sent over a long distance.

45 Zenobius, venerated as a saint, is said to have died in 424.

46 Radagaisus was a Germanic adventurer who twice invaded Italy. Paulinus refers here to the second invasion, which occurred in 405–406, when Radagaisus led a host of Ostrogoths and other Germans. The barbarians were stopped and defeated outside Florence, and Radagaisus was executed in August 406.

47 Pansophius and his father Decens are mentioned in §28.

48 The Moors Mascezel and Gildo were brothers. When in 397–398 Gildo led a revolt in North Africa against Roman rule, Stilicho appointed Mascezel to quell it. The rebellion was put down with very little resistance and Gildo was executed in July 398. Mascezel himself, however, did not long survive his brother: he died violently, perhaps at Stilicho's order, shortly afterwards.

49 Namely, the province of Africa.

50 Sisinnius and Alexander, along with Martyrius, died in the Val di Non (Anaunia), near Trent, in May 397. They were murdered by a pagan mob whose anger they seem to have provoked.

51 Of this Donatus nothing else is known.

52 Aurelius, who occupied the chief see of North Africa from 388 to 423 was one of the imposing ecclesiastical figures of his time and a close collaborator of Augustine. Of his brother, the deacon Fortunatus, we know nothing more. Vincent of Colossitanum was one of the organizers of the Council of Carthage in 411, and he seems to have died after 419. Muranus of Bolita is otherwise unknown. Both Colossitanum and Bolita were in North Africa.

53 Augustine is being referred to here.

BIBLIOGRAPHY

For a fuller bibliography on Ambrose see publications by N. McLynn or D. Williams

Amati, Amato (1897) 'Sant'Ambrogio. Genealogia, cronologia, carattere e genesei delle idee,' *Rendiconti, Reale Istituto Lombardo di scienze e lettere*, Milan, ser. 2, vol. 30.

Buck, M.J.A. (trans.) (1929) *S. Ambrosii de Helia et ieiunio*, Washington, DC, The Catholic University of America.

Cazzaniga, Egnatius (1948) *Sancti Ambrosii De Virginibus*, Turin, G. B. Paravia.

Connolly, R.H. (1952) *The Explanatio symboli ad initiandos. A Work of St Ambrose*, Cambridge, Cambridge University Press.

Courcelle, Pierre (1973) *Recherches sur Saint Ambroise: 'Vie' anciennes, culture, iconographie*, Paris, *Etudes Augustiniennes*.

Dudden, F. Homes (1935) *The Life and Times of St. Ambrose*, 2 vols., Oxford, Oxford University Press.

Fischer, Balthasar (1970) 'Hat Ambrosius von Mailand in der Woche zwischen seiner Taufe und seiner Bischofskonzekration andere Weihen empfangen?' *Kyriakon: Festschrift Johannes Quasten*, Münster, Aschendorff, vol. 2, pp. 527–31.

Fontaine, Jacques *et al.* (1992) *Ambroise de Milan: Hymnes*, Paris, Cerf.

Greenslade, S. L. (trans. and ed.) (1956) *Early Latin Theology*, Philadelphia, Westminster.

Grillmeier, Aloys (1975) *Christ in Christian Tradition*, vol. 1, 2nd revised edn, trans. John Bowden, Atlanta, John Knox Press.

Hanson, R.P.C. (1988) *The Search for the Christian Doctrine of God: The Arian Controversy, 318–381*, Edinburgh, T. and T. Clark.

Kaniecka, Mary S. (1928) *Vita Sancti Ambrosii . . . a Paulino eius notario*, Washington, DC, The Catholic University of America.

Krautheimer, Richard (1983) *Three Christian Capitals: Topography and Politics*, Berkeley, University of California Press.

Lamirande, Emilien (1983) *Paulin de Milan et la 'Vita Ambrosii'*, Paris/ Montreal, Desclée/Bellarmin.

McGuire, Martin R.P. (ed.) (1927) *S. Ambrosii de Nabuthae*, Washington, DC, The Catholic University of America.

McLynn, Neil B. (1994) *Ambrose of Milan: Church and Court in a Christian Capital*, Berkeley, University of California Press.

Mathews, Thomas F. (1993) *The Clash of Gods: A Reinterpretation of Early Christian Art*, Princeton, Princeton University Press.

Paphnutius (1993) 'Histories of the Monks of Upper Egypt,' in Tim Vivian (trans.) *Histories of the Monks of Upper Egypt and the Life of Onnophrius by Paphnutius*, Kalamazoo, Cistercian Publications.

Paredi, Angelo (1964) *Saint Ambrose: His Life and Times*, trans. M. Joseph Costelloe, Notre Dame, University of Notre Dame Press.

Pellegrino, Michele (1961) *Paolino di Milan: Vita di S. Ambrogio*, Rome, Editrice Studium.

Rusch, William G. (1977) *The Later Latin Fathers*, London, Duckworth.

St Ambrose (1963) *Given to Love*, trans. James Shiel, Chicago, Scepter.

St Ambrose (1989) *De virginibus, De viduis*, ed. Franco Gori, Sancti Ambrosii Episcopi Mediolensis Opera 14/1, Milan, Biblioteca Ambrosiana.

Steier, August (1903) 'Untersuchungen über die Echtheit der Hymnen des Ambrosius,' *Jahrbücher für klassische Philologie*, Supplementband 28.

Von Campenhausen, Hans (1929) *Ambrosius von Mailand als Kirchenpolitiker*, Berlin/Leipzig, Walter de Gruyter.

Weisheipl, James A. (1974) *Friar Thomas D'Aquino: His Life, Thought and Works*. Garden City, NY, Doubleday.

Williams, Daniel H. (1995) *Ambrose of Milan and the End of the Arian–Nicene Conflicts*, Oxford, Clarendon Press.

Zucker, L.M. (trans.) (1933) *S. Ambrosii de Tobia*, Washington, DC, The Catholic University of America.

INDEX